Laura
Maytown
Thornborough
Mt Mulligan
Mungana
Chillagoe
Lappa
Irvinebank

Cooktown
Dimbulah
Mareeba
CAIRNS

Georgetown
Forsayth
Einasleigh
Kidston
Gilberton

TOWNSVILLE

Charters Towers
Ravenswood

Winnecke
Aritunga

ROCKHAMPTON
Mount Morgan

Theodore
Cracow

Gympie

BRISBANE

Farina
dnamutana
Sliding Rock
n Creek
Beltana
Nuccaleena
Blinman
Simmonston
mond / Bruce

Marree
Tibooburra

Milparinka
Mt Browne
Tarrawingee
Euriowie
Purnamoota
Silverton

Mt Drysdale

Hawker
Wilcannia
Cobar

BROKEN HILL
Thackaringa

Canbelego
Nymagee
Shuttleton
Gilgunnia
Mount Hope

Waukaringa
Johnburg
Cradock
Dawson
Black Rock

Harden
Temora
Stockinbingal
Cootamundra
Galong

Airly / Glen Davis
Newnes
Hartley Vale
Lithgow
Joadja

SYDNEY
Mittagong

ADELAIDE

CANBERRA

Moliagul
Tarnagulla / Llanelly / Waanyarra
Fryerstown / Vaughan
Steiglitz

BENDIGO
Castlemaine / Chewton

Casterton
Merino
Coleraine
Hamilton
Portland
Meredith

MELBOURNE

GEELONG

Zeehan
Strahan
Gormanston & Linda
Sarah Is.
Pillinger
Crotty

Queenstown
Maria Is.

HOBART

Port Arthur

Clive Hilliker • THE AUSTRALIAN NATIONAL UNIVERSITY

AUSTRALIAN
GHOST

TOWNS

To BARRY
WISHING YOU good HEALTH
AND HAPPINESS
FROM YOUR LITTLE BRO
MICK

AUSTRALIAN
GHOST
TOWNS

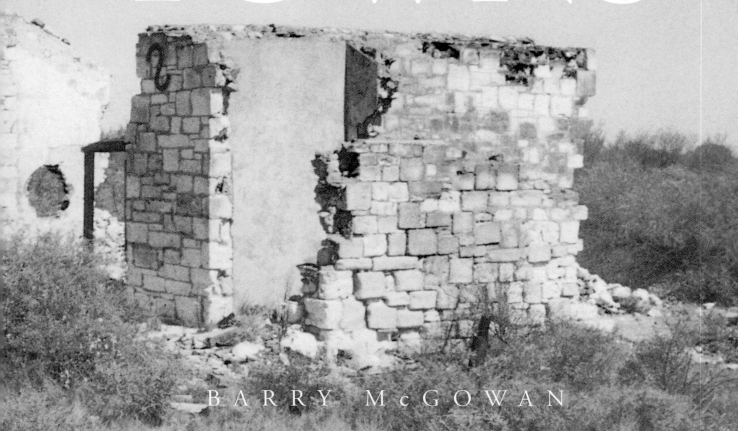

BARRY McGOWAN

Lothian
BOOKS

Thomas C. Lothian Pty Ltd
132 Albert Road, South Melbourne, 3205
www.lothian.com.au

National Library of Australia
Cataloguing-in-Publication data:

McGowan, Barry.
  Australian ghost towns.
  ISBN 0 7344 0354 2.

  1. Ghost towns - Australia. 2. Australia - History.
  I. Title.
994

Cover and text design by David Constable
Typeset by David Constable in 14/11 pt Sabon
Printed in Australia by The Australian Book Connection

Half-title page: Day Dawn, WA
Title page: Hospital ruins, Cue, WA

ACKNOWLEDGEMENTS

Western Australia and Northern Territory

Battye Library (Perth), Josef Bollmann, Judy Carter, Cue Tourist Information Centre, Gwalia Historical
Society, Tim Hewson, Stan and Mary Haeusler, Sue Harlow, Simon Hawkins, Andy and Jane Hayes, Ellen
De Hayr, Derek Keene, Warren and Dorothy Kimble, Peter Lalor, Laverton Visitors Centre, Ian McKay,
Ron Miller, Northern Land Council (Katherine), Northern Territory Police (Maranboy and Katherine),
Eric Omodei, Onslow Goods Shed Museum, Onslow Tourist Centre, Shyama Peebles, Kevin and Margaret
Pusey, Roebourne Visitor's Centre, Warren and Gail Roos, Kevin Seivright, Laura Shannon, Rosemary and
Clinton Steele, Shire of Cue, Shire of Menzies

Queensland

Fred and Sandra Brophy, Cairns and District Historical Society, Phillip Charlier, Chillagoe Heritage
Museum, Etheridge Shire, Warren Develin and Mary Dhu, Stan Dunwoody, Jo Evans, John and Sharon
Fitzgerald, Lyn and Rob French, Cate Hartley and Andy Bell, Jeff Holmes, 'Lappa' Liz, Loudon House
Museum, Tommy Mulhall, John Nethery, Oxley Library (Brisbane), Parks and Wildlife Service (Chillagoe),
Des Persal, 'Woody' Pigram, Dianne and Gina Schluter, Geoff Tolcher, Cassandra van Nooten, Alan and
Natashia Zabel

New South Wales and South Australia

Arkaroola Visitors Centre, Peter Bevan, Broken Hill Railway Museum, Broken Hill Visitors Bureau, Muriel
Chapman, Barbara Clarke, Cobar Museum, John Collins, Kevin Dawes, Denis Degrussa, Pat Dunn,
Lorraine Edmunds, Brian Eves, Flinders Ranges Visitor Information Centre (Quorn), David Frost, Doug
Grose, Annie Hamilton, Jenny and John Hills, Leonie and Greg Knapman, Cynthia and David Langford,
Mark Longobardi, Greg and Athol Luke, Bernadette and Norm McMillan, Shirley and Michael Mitchell,
Joy Prisk, Pat Shiels, Gwen Smith, Margaret and Doug Sprigg, John Teague, Gwen Telfor, Rae Webber,
Beth, Kevin and Jeremy White, Phillip Young

Victoria and Tasmania

Noelene Bradshaw, Castlemaine Historical Society, Castlemaine Visitor Information Centre, Greg Dickens
(Department of Mineral Resources, Hobart), Phil and Gillian Dickson, Lynne Douthat, Galley Museum
(Queenstown), Alleyne Hockley, Joan Hunt, John Kehrer, Jeannie Lister, Bob Luehman, Maryborough
Visitors Centre, Merino Public Hall Commitee, Midlands Historical Society (Maryborough), Parks and
Wildlife Office (Maria Island), Port Arthur Visitors Centre, Bruce and Betty Osborne, Les and Madge
Simmons, Strahan Visitors Centre, John Tully, West Coast Pioneers' Memorial Museum (Zeehan)

Contents

Foreword   vi

Preface   vii

WESTERN AUSTRALIA AND NORTHERN TERRITORY
Ghosts of the Murchison   3
An American Dream   12
Tombstones and Tumbleweed   21
The Winds of Change   30
Under Northern Skies   39
East of Alice   48

QUEENSLAND
Archibald Wilson's Lament   59
From the Etheridge to Irvinebank   68
A Brooding Mountain   78
The Road to the Palmer   87
A Stockbroker's Paradise   97

NEW SOUTH WALES
Valleys of Oil   107
Along the Kidman Way   117
Boom and Bust on the Barrier   126
Corner Country   136

SOUTH AUSTRALIA
From Waukaringa to Yudnamutana   149
Leaving the Land   159

TASMANIA
A Place of Punishment   171
Perdition and Paradise   180
When Copper was King   190

VICTORIA
From Steiglitz to Fryerstown   201
Tarnagulla and Beyond   211

EPILOGUE
A Tale Too Often Told   221

Glossary   230
Notes   232
Index   244

Foreword

AUSTRALIA'S BURST OF MATERIAL PROGRESS HAS BEEN SO SWIFT AND recent that at first sight a ghost town seems to be out of place. But in every region travellers using even the main roads come across the remains of these dead or fast-asleep towns. Some ghost towns, once they come into view, are distinctive because their larger buildings still stand, grand but empty. Several of these abandoned banks, post offices and town halls would attract the eye even if they stood, amongst the architecture of the centuries, in the bustling main street of a European provincial town.

There are hundreds of ghost mining towns, stretching all the way from the Northern Territory to the west of Tasmania. In the wheat country are silent crossroads where once stood school, blacksmith's shop, general store, baker, bank, sports ground, and perhaps three churches and the Railway and Wheatsheaf hotels, nearly all of which have long since disappeared. In the forests are the hidden remains of timber-milling townships, all grown over. Here and there, from the Snowy Mountains to the tropics, are the remains of big construction camps that were towns in themselves — until the big dam or long railway bridge was completed.

Many of these inland towns, when young and vigorous, had called for their own port. There must be close to 100 ghost ports around the long Australian coast — pearling, whaling, mining, wheat and convict ports that once flourished but now are tiny or not even on the map. At several of them a post or two of the long piers still stand, either in the water or in the encroaching sand or mud. There are even dead river ports far inland, but no steamship whistle has been heard at their tumble-down wharves within living memory. Most of these towns have vanished for two reasons: their natural resources dwindled, and new machines and gadgets arrived to replace human hands and feet and the hooves of horses.

Barry McGowan had the bold idea of writing a comprehensive book on ghost towns. He set out to see as many as possible; he investigated their history and caught their flavour. He is especially interesting on the mining towns, a field of history that he knows so well. His book, indirectly, is almost a history of remote and rural Australia — its triumphs and failures and its persistent spirit of 'give-it-a-go'.

Geoffrey Blainey
August 2002

Preface

MY IDEA FOR A BOOK ON GHOST TOWNS WAS BORN MANY YEARS AGO when I was a much younger man. In my youth I was captivated by George Farwell's imaginative and enchanting book, *Australia's Ghost Towns*, first published in 1965. The small paperback edition was my constant companion for many years in my wanderings around the Australian outback. For a South Australian the topic held a particular interest, as there were many examples of such towns in the State's mid and far north. These towns can be encountered quite unexpectedly — a few ruined chimneys and walls standing as solitary sentinels in an otherwise barren landscape.

But of course, not all ghost towns are in such arid surrounds, and not all towns that I would classify as ghost towns are abandoned, for there are often a few — or in some cases more than a few — residents about. And the ghost towns of today are not necessarily those of tomorrow. Things change. Remarkably, and perhaps as the best illustration of this process, George Farwell included both Cooktown and Port Douglas in his book. At the time he was correct, but now Cooktown is experiencing something of a revival, and Port Douglas is a booming tourist resort. May some of the towns I have visited share a similar fortune.

While researching this book I was constantly tantalised, perhaps even tormented, by the question of definition. My companions and many of the people I met on my travels often asked me the question, how do you define a ghost town? Clearly a town with no people and only ruins immediately qualifies. But what of the towns where only rubble remains, and in some instances barely that? And how abandoned is abandoned? Is there a magic cut-off point in terms of the remaining inhabitants? Is it 10, 20 or 100? Merely to put the question in these terms suggests that the answer is more complex than that. A town that once had 3000 persons and now has empty shops, deserted streets and only about a hundred residents, invariably has the appearance of a ghost town, and the very real prospect of becoming one.

And then there are the regional differences. In Western Australia and, to a lesser degree, the Top End of the Northern Territory, a significant proportion of the abandoned towns are localities, with no buildings or only a few piles of rubble, and a railway siding or cemetery, if even that. This barren aspect is a reflection on the proclivity of the former inhabitants to take everything with them when they migrated from one mining field to another. It is also a reflection of the portability of many of the buildings, a large proportion of which were simple wood or iron structures, which could be easily dismantled or destroyed.

The process of 'recycling' or demolishing buildings in old mining towns has occurred across Australia, but in South Australia and New South Wales there appears to have been a higher proportion of stone-built, and therefore, more durable dwellings. The tendency to demolish buildings for their bricks and stone appears to have been less prevalent, partly because some of the towns are located in very remote areas, and partly because they are on private property. Another important factor has been the impact of heritage legislation. The importance of these provisions cannot be overstated. They are all that lies between a continuing visual appreciation of Australia's human heritage in rural and outback Australia and oblivion.

In more settled environs such as Victoria, the question of definition and regional difference is particularly important. The evidence of Victoria's turbulent and immensely prosperous goldmining years can be seen in the grand churches, courthouses, mechanics' institutes and hotels. But there are very few gold towns that have been abandoned entirely or reduced to the small struggling hamlets that are so prevalent elsewhere in Australia. This can be attributed largely to the fertility of much of rural Victoria, and the ease with which such towns have become a haven for refugees from Melbourne. The vista of grand buildings standing incongruously in empty paddocks or near-deserted streets, with their shuttered shopfronts and houses, does not readily present itself.

Much of what I have written about has its basis in my perambulations across Australia over the last 20 years, often in the company of sometimes excited, but also occasionally bewildered family members. My two boys, Andrew and Douglas, were brought up on a diet of outback camping, rough dirt roads, deserts and dust, which included two long trips to Central Australia and to Queensland, as well as two desert treks and countless other trips.

For this exercise, however, I could not rely solely on my memories and faded photographs. I had to start anew, taking a snapshot in time, at the beginning of a new millenium. The most extensive and taxing of my journeys was the first segment through Western Australia, the Northern Territory and Queensland. I flew out of Canberra on the not particularly auspicious date of 11 September 2001, driving from Perth around the Eastern Goldfields, and then journeying by bus to Darwin, with stop-offs at Karratha and Halls Creek in the Kimberley.

In Alice Springs I was met by my brother, Christopher, who flew up from Mount Gambier in South Australia and accompanied me around the Alice and through North Queensland. I will say an unequivocal thank you to Chris for his companionship. By the time I reached Alice I was already showing signs of travel fatigue, and it was great to have him with me. I managed the final Queensland leg to Cracow on my own before heading back to Canberra for a very hectic period of research and writing. During this time I undertook several side trips with my younger son, Douglas, to the oil-shale towns east and south of Sydney.

The next leg was through western New South Wales, South Australia and Victoria in the month of January. On this occasion I took my long-suffering Pajero. It was the middle of summer, and not the best time for travelling, for some days were well above 40 degrees. But it was then or never. I was very fortunate to be accompanied by my old friend Bob Comley. We drove huge distances and visited some extremely remote locations, such as Nuccaleena and Yudnamutana in South Australia, often travelling over roads that were little more than rugged goat tracks. But we had a good time and met some great people.

The final leg of my trip, this time on my own, was to Tasmania. Aided by some beautiful autumn weather, it was possibly the only time in my wanderings that I almost felt like a tourist. On my return to the mainland I made another visit to the Victorian goldfields, this time, to Steiglitz.

The book follows the pattern of these travels, although I should stress that it is not written as a *Guide Bleu* to the outback. It is not a travel book, although hopefully it will encourage visitors, for I have written about places that have interested or, in some instances, fascinated me, and hopefully they will have the same impact on others. Neither is the book a catalogue of ghost towns, for there were a number of 'favourites' that, with much regret, I had to preclude. The towns selected were the ones that I regarded as the most interesting and demonstrative of their type, and, within the time constraints, the most accessible.

The final chapter ends where the book begins — with the question of definition and with a glance to the future. Towards the end of my travels I became increasingly fascinated with the question of process, for I wasn't just writing about the past, but the present. The decline and fall of a town can be very rapid, as with many mining towns, or extremely slow, as with many agricultural and farming towns. It is, however, a process, and one that continues today. Rural Australia is in a continuing state of crisis, one that has not been helped by the actions of large corporations or governments and the relentless march of technological change. Whether these processes result in ghost towns is another matter. Organisations such as RAPlink (Regional Action Partnership Link), and a myriad of other local community organisations are working to ensure that they don't.

My thanks go to many people, for the book is not just about the towns but those that lived or live in them. I met some extraordinary people and received some extraordinary assistance. Some of these people are mentioned in the text or in the footnotes, but that has not always been possible. To partly redress this I have included all who have helped in the acknowledgements. Of the institutions, a special mention should be made of the National Library in Canberra, whose magnificent collections and extremely helpful staff in the Petherick, Newspaper and Pictorial rooms, in particular, were central to my efforts. In a similar vein I should also mention the assistance I received from the library staff of the Australian Geological Survey Organisation in Canberra and the Mitchell Library in Sydney. There were, in addition, a large number of regional historical associations and local communities that also helped. Special thanks also go to Rod Quinn from the ABC, Canberra, and Ian Warden from the *Canberra Times*.

I received enormous help and encouragement from my colleagues in the heritage and academic communities, in particular Drs Michael Pearson, Peter Bell and John Merritt. Peter has recorded and written about a number of the towns and areas that I visited, and very kindly offered to peruse several of the chapters for me. John has continually impressed upon me the need to write history that is not only informative, but also interesting and lively. I am also very grateful for the interest and assistance received from Peter Lalor of Sons of Gwalia Ltd.

Special mention should go to Sharon Mullins of Lothian Books, who offered me constant encouragement, and to her company for having the foresight and vision to embrace the project so readily. A special thanks also to Margaret Barca for her helpful editing.

Finally to family and friends. There were so many who, through their interest in my work, gave me the added encouragement to go 'the extra mile'. Family always takes the brunt of such endeavours, for it is they who endure the absences, the inevitable panics when things cannot be found, or when things break down. Perhaps the most taxing of all, they have to tolerate living with someone who is too preoccupied to notice the time of the day, let alone be sociable or communicative. To my partner Chong Choe, to Sean and Genie, also to my two boys Andrew and Douglas and my parents and family back in Mount Gambier, thanks for your patience and love. I look forward to a period of increased fraternisation and familiarity.

WESTERN AUSTRALIA
AND
NORTHERN TERRITORY

Previous page: **Remains of hospital**
kitchen chimney, Cue, WA

Ghosts of the Murchison

ARRIVING IN THE MIDDLE OF NIGHT, I FOUND CUE LOOKING LIKE ANY other outback Australian town. Its well-proportioned main street was lined with shops, a hotel and other buildings. But with daylight the appearance of activity was rather more qualified, for very few of the business premises were occupied. Cue still has a population of several hundred residents, and to that extent does not share the ghostly shroud of many other towns on the Murchison goldfields such as Day Dawn, Big Bell and Nannine. Still, its population is only a fraction of what it once was, and its quiet streets and shuttered shops certainly convey an image of abandonment.

Many of the buildings along the main street of Cue hark back to the early goldrush days in the 1890s. Foremost amongst them are the sandstone government offices and, across the road in the caravan park, the commodious prison cells. Other important historical buildings are the old shire office, now the tourist visitor centre, the somewhat eerily disposed and abandoned two-storeyed Masonic Hall, and the present shire office, which is located in the restored Gentleman's Club building. The club was visited frequently by the youthful Herbert Hoover, who later became the President of the USA. Hoover was a representative of Bewick, Moreing and Company, which owned and managed several important West Australian goldmining properties.

The old hospital is located on the outskirts of town. Its impressive ruins include the main building and kitchen; the baker's oven is still visible. Local lore has it that the hospital was haunted and that a former matron had spoken of mysteriously turning door handles, unexplained footsteps and knocking on doors.[1] Across the gully from the hospital the old recreation ground, with its weathered concrete cricket pitches, is a testament to busier times.

Further out of town is the cemetery, the scale of which would do justice to a town much larger than Cue. The size of the cemetery reflects the incredibly difficult conditions under which most miners and their families lived on almost all the early West Australian goldfields. Typhoid was evident at Cue as early as 1892, but initially there was no hospital and no doctor and very little appreciation by the government as to how serious this disease would become. Cue was described by one writer as a 'hot-bed for enteric fever'. The tent hospital was run by an unqualified man, and the death toll was so great that the government was urged to send a doctor.[2]

Dr Monteith duly arrived and was assisted by his wife, but it was impossible for them to attend to all the sick in town, let alone the whole goldfield, and throughout the region men lay unattended except for the help of their mates. According to historian Vera Whittington, the summer of 1893 brought on such a typhoid onslaught that the 'death toll was of terrible length'.[3] A contemporary visitor, Julius Price, remarked that the disregard of a number of sanitary measures had caused fever to be more prevalent at Cue than any other town he had visited. He considered it a bad place to be unless in the 'soundest of health'.[4]

In such circumstances it is not surprising that the provision of an adequate number of sanitary pans and arrangements for their disposal were major items on the council's agenda. However, by the summer of 1894 the much-awaited new hospital had not been built; there was a rapid rise in new typhoid cases and further overcrowding at both Cue and Day Dawn's tent hospitals. There was considerable anger at the death of Sydney Grace, the schoolteacher's 24-year-old wife; the schoolteacher and his son also developed typhoid. By June 1895 the town cemetery was 'filling fast' and a new one was needed. In spite of all this, by the following year the council was being complimented on the healthy and sanitary condition of the town.[5]

The first gold discoveries in the Cue area were made at Nannine and Bayley's Island, which was located in the middle of Lake Annean.[6] Two of the miners, Michael Fitzgerald and Tom Cue, became friendly with several Aboriginal stockmen on Coodardy Station, who pointed out the whereabouts of gold at a location to be later known as Cuddingwarra. On another occasion an Aboriginal man picked up a 10-ounce nugget and, pointing in the general direction of present day Cue, remarked 'plenty big fellow slug over there'. As Tom Cue was in Geraldton seeking supplies, Fitzgerald set out with two Aboriginal men on New Year's Day in 1892. They found gold, but were soon forced to retreat through lack of water.

Fitzgerald was subsequently joined by Ted Heffernan, who has been credited with discovering gold at nearby Day Dawn. Not long after, in just one day, the two men found almost 300 ounces of alluvial gold where the main street of Cue is now located. On his return Tom Cue was added to the party. He later rode into Nannine and registered the claim in his partners' names. Although Tom Cue did not find the first payable gold, he earned immortality, for the district's principal town was named in his honour, and he was the one credited with the discovery.[7]

Unlike most West Australian goldmining towns there were never any

The tent hospital was run by an unqualified man, and the death toll was so great that the government was urged to send a doctor

sensational individual finds at Cue, though there was a greater amount of alluvial ground than at many other fields. There was an uninterrupted line of workings about three kilometres long and one kilometre wide as if a 'thousand gigantic hogs had pig-rooted and grubbed it up'.[8] The proliferation of smaller mines appears to have given rise to a greater degree of individuality and enterprise on the field than was evident on the more heavily capitalised ones. George Hope, a local newspaper correspondent, described the early days thus:

> There is a freedom of restraint, an absence from conventionality, a go-as-you-please style of life at once noticed by a stranger from town on arrival on the fields. The further out you go the more pronounced is the freedom. In Cue itself there were once no women, no goats, and no clergy. For dress, a loose flannel jumper, with short sleeves, a hat, moleskins and hob-nailed bluchers constituted the daily garb on nine-tenths of the inhabitants as they came to the well to fill their canvass water bags or to replenish their empty tucker-bags at the store after work ...[9]

The rough and ready phase of Cue's development soon passed. In 1893 a progress committee was established, which lobbied successfully for more adequate hospital accommodation, bank branches, a miners' institute and a recreation ground. Eventually a council, roads board and a stock exchange were established. By 1897 the government buildings had been erected to house a large post office, the registrar, a warden's court and police quarters. A public hospital featured broad shady verandahs, male and female wards, a temporary ward, staff and nursing quarters, and dining rooms.[10] Cue was described as a:

> well built busy little township with its business blocks, churches, stores and private residences compared to the frontier mining camp of a few years ago, constructed for the most part of canvas and brush, with corrugated iron architectural monstrosities defining the course of the main street at intervals ... Four years ago all there was of Cue could have been loaded on half a dozen wagons and carted away without leaving a vestige behind.[11]

The handsome, two-storeyed stone-built Murchison Chambers included 18 offices and two shops, and there were three banks: the Union, Western Australian and Bank of Australasia. A brewery and two aerated water manufacturers, an ice factory, an ironmonger and timber merchant and a canvas manufacturer (specialising in tents, water bags and ventilation sails for the mines) served the burgeoning population. Gascard's livery stables occupied around half a hectare of ground and provided accommodation for 60 horses, a blacksmith and repair shops.

And there were always the hotels. These were not necessarily the rough and ready affairs so popularly portrayed, for they did not survive only by dispensing alcohol, but also by providing accommodation. George Hope

A horse team outside Cue
with a 7 ton load, 1902
(Courtesy Mrs D Kimble, Perth)

described the dining room of the Metropole Hotel, with its 'snowy drapery and polished glassware', which invited 'an appetite'. All the hotels had billiard tables, for it was a most popular pastime and the tournaments attracted 'much interest and attention from all classes'. Concerts were also held. Not surprisingly, given the hot dusty climate, there was also a very great demand for shower baths, which were by then an adjunct to all the hotels and private houses. This demand saw the establishment of an iron and tinware factory, with a bicycle shop attached. One of the best-loved drinking establishments was Tweedie's Shypoo shop, which resembled a continental beer hall.

On the other side of the coin there were Wesleyan, Roman Catholic and Anglican churches, a Salvation Army barracks, a branch of the Australian Natives' Association and the Loyal Pride of Cue Lodge. One particularly important institution was the philanthropic 'Sisters of the People', which was founded in Perth in 1895 under the auspices of the Wesleyan Methodist Church. Its role was to provide skilled nursing for the sick poor in their own home, and it was strongly supported by the miners, businesses and residents, who purchased a home and furnished it for the Sisters. At the height of one of the periodic typhoid epidemics Sister May attended to 16 out-of-door fever cases, bathing patients every few hours, cooking beef tea and walking from one miner's camp to another. For 10 weeks she ministered from 5.30 am to 12.30 pm and often sat all night at a sick bedside.[12]

Another visitor to the Murchison field was Vivienne May (no relation to Sister May), who travelled through Western Australia in 1897. Sundays, she observed, were characterised by picnics and drives and the people 'seemed to be very happy'. The source of this contentment was not difficult to find.

> There were many families in Victoria and elsewhere who bless the day when the goldfields of Western Australia were discovered, and a great many miners in these districts have brought over their wives and families and have made humble but comfortable homes for them. They all seem happy, and I have talked with many of the women, who tell me that, though the life is rather rough, yet they have money always regularly coming in, while, on the other side, they had nothing to keep themselves with the failure of the banks and general crash in Melbourne having ruined so many people.[13]

Cue was on occasion challenged for pre-eminence by Day Dawn. Gold was found at Day Dawn by Ted Heffernan in a huge blow of quartz described as akin to the ruins of an 'old frontier baron's castle' rising from the plains. In early 1893 residential and business areas were pegged out on the main street. Some of the early businesses were Marshall's Commercial Hotel, Frenchie Dubois' restaurant, Russell's bakery and restaurant and, next door, ex-circus clown Tommy Dodd's well-patronised hop-beer factory.

Day Dawn was the home of the Great Fingall mine, which was the mainstay of the Cue district from the late 1890s on. The town is now, however, totally abandoned, and almost all the buildings have been destroyed in more recent mining operations. Nevertheless, the astute observer can find some walls and other structures along the main track, which was once Heffernan Street. The most impressive building is the substantially intact Great Fingall mine office, perched above a cavernous open cut.

Day Dawn was built in a more orderly pattern than Cue, and on the main street were the municipal chambers, miners' institute, the Golconda, Commercial and Day Dawn hotels and most of the stores. Outside of the mines the largest enterprise was the timber and hardware business of Crooks and Brooker, which included a steam sawmilling plant.

Of the miners' institute, George Hope recalled nostalgically that

> the youth and beauty of the place love to trip the light fantastic toe, and … to whirl their partners in the mazes of the delightful dance on the occasion of a ball, when musical talent abounds, and gay dresses are in evidence freely, till it becomes an easy task amidst the bright surroundings to imagine oneself back in those regions of civilisation and comfort …

Armstrong's store, Cue. Bicycles and cars were important modes of transport on the goldfields. (Courtesy Shire of Cue)

Other enterprises and institutions were the Grand Hotel, the warden's court and registrar's office, the post office, the Union and Western Australian banks and a hospital. To provide for the spiritual needs of the community, the Wesleyan, Church of England and Roman Catholic Churches had all established premises. Day Dawn also had an Oddfellows Lodge and a myriad of sporting associations. A bicycle track, football ground, cricket pitch and tennis court were located at the recreation ground.

A particularly important organisation was the Public Water Supply Department, which had jurisdiction over a vast area of country. In addition to the large offices, the premises included a storeroom, feed store, carpenter's shop, employees' living rooms, stables and shed. The department's main task was the construction and maintenance of the wells, some of which were revenue-producing and required caretakers. The department employed about 30 men and kept 20 horses with the necessary drays and a herd of 17 camels.[14]

Both Cue and Day Dawn had a mix of nationalities. At Day Dawn this was due partly to the employment policy of Bewick, Moreing, the owners of the Great Fingall. Herbert Hoover preferred Italians to Australians, and authorised their employment soon after commencing work at Bewick, Moreing. There were also a large number of Afghans working with the camel teams, and a number of Japanese. At Cue and Day Dawn, and indeed on all the West Australian goldfields, there was anxious anticipation of the referendum on Federation. Regular meetings of the Day Dawn and Cue Federal League were held, the last of which was at Day Dawn in July 1900 just before the referendum. Great rejoicing greeted the result, as Western Australia was to join the new Federation.[15]

Nannine lies about 80 kilometres north of Cue in the middle of a desolate gibber and mulga plain. Originally it consisted of many tents and one or two pretentious buildings of mud bats and corrugated iron. By 1898 it possessed a post office in a solid stone building, a registrar's office, warden's court, police barracks, miners' institute, a roads board, one church, two cricket clubs, a bakery and other stores. Of the four hotels, those kept by Dan Downey and the Bond brothers were regarded 'as the equal of any on the Murchison, and superior to most of them'.[16]

The Bond brothers also had a garden about eight kilometres out of town near a natural lagoon, where the water was raised by a windmill and piped over the garden, producing fresh fruit and vegetables in abundance. They also owned a bakery. In November of that year their garden was described as 'blossoming like a rose amidst the surrounding waste of mulga', with crops of apricots, grapes, peaches and lemons. The Jose family had a vegetable garden nearby, and the Parker family had planted a garden near their Star of the East mine.[17]

Despite these portents of prosperity, at Christmas 1898 it was lamented that there was a great depression in both business and mining. Many people had left on holiday and, judging from the appearance of the town, had taken much of the surplus cash with them, for no sports or amusements whatever were advertised. By early 1900 mining news was subdued, but just a few months later the townsfolk were preparing for a boat regatta, presumably on Lake Annean. The correspondent appropriately remarked that the forthcoming event was 'unique in the annals of the Murchison'. He described the 'deep blue waters of the lake' contrasting with the 'emerald islands, and the white winged yachts skimming over its surface'.[18] Today the visitor is hard-pressed to even find where Nannine once stood, for all that is left are the remains of the post office walls. The only bodies in the town lie in the cemetery, which is set atop a brightly hued sandhill overlooking Lake Annean.

During the early 1900s the Great Fingall at Day Dawn prospered, and by 1908 a railway line had been laid into the bush for carting firewood. The train was also used for picnic outings. A year later, however, the Great Fingall appeared to be in decline. This gloom ended towards the end of the year when gold was discovered at the 625-metre level, but by the end of 1910 the outlook was again gloomy. As a reflection of these changed conditions one of the main items of local debate was the proposed amalgamation of the Cue and Day Dawn councils and roads boards. Another indication of decline was the reduced attendance at the Day Dawn Empire Day celebrations in May compared with the previous year.[19]

A letter to the editor of the *Murchison Times and Day Dawn Gazette* some months later stated that although the administrative costs were identical to those in 1908, the population had since halved and about one-fifth of the buildings had been removed, resulting in higher rates. Another letter, from a migrant worker living at 'Ski town', complained about residents having to clear the roads at their own expense, despite paying rates. The roads boards and councils were amalgamated in November 1912.[20]

At Nannine matters were even more parlous. A public meeting was held in June 1912 to protest against the removal of the warden's and registrar's offices to Meekatharra. Nannine's social life had not entirely evaporated, for a charity social and dance and a dance in aid of the race club were proposed for later in the month, and the annual hospital ball was held in July. By November, however, there had been a decided downturn in activity. In mining matters there was little to report and some of the old identities were 'leaving quietly'. It was remarked that sickness was less prevalent than the previous summer, but that may have been due to the smaller population. The correspondent also lamented that the hospital was not getting the support of the residents. Contributions were not as large as they should be, while 'donations are as scarce as teeth in a Shanghai rooster'.[21]

The end came in October 1921 when the mine collapsed beneath the sand dump ...

Increasing costs and acute labour shortages were a continual problem during World War I, affecting both development and production at the Great Fingall, and in April 1918 the mine was closed. It was worked thereafter by tributers, but this did not prevent a constant exodus of people from the town. Homes were dismantled and sold for what the iron was worth, and the electricity formerly supplied by the mine ceased. In October of the following year the Day Dawn railway station was closed. The end came in October 1921 when the mine collapsed beneath the sand dump, with several hundred thousand tons of sand falling into the mine and raising dangerously the level of water. With the sand dump slowly fretting away, and dust blowing across the plains and creeping back into the mine, the few remaining mine buildings and the remnants of the town must have presented a most dispiriting aspect. It had been one of Western Australia's most profitable mines, and in its relatively short existence 1 182 000 ounces of gold had been extracted.[22]

Fortunately for the district, gold had been found north of Cue at Coodardy (renamed Big Bell in 1913) in the early 1900s. The early yields were promising enough to warrant the installation of a processing plant several years later, but the mine could not be worked economically and in 1924 all mining ceased. In 1932 the mine was acquired by the American-owned Premier Gold Mining Company, and several years later work commenced on the construction of a modern mining and processing plant. Cue was the main point of supply for the mine and a railway line was built for that purpose. The company announced in 1936 that it was to proceed with mining. A large community had been established at the mine site for several years, but now it was to grow substantially.[23]

One important focus of the community was the raising of funds for a local hospital, and for this purpose various social functions were held. For instance, in September 1937 there was a boxing contest and an athletic sports meeting, followed by a dance. As the hall was not available, the latter was held at the school. So crowded was the function that the dancers had to take to the floor in relays or otherwise stay outside and look in from the windows. The official opening of the mine in October of that year was an amazing affair, for the long list of dignitaries included the Premier, the Leader of the Opposition and the Minister for Railways. Over 200 guests were invited to the opening and the 'sumptuous luncheon', at which there were two representatives selected from the ranks of the 400 men employed by the company.[24]

A grand ball was held on the evening of the opening of the mine, in aid of the hospital. Everyone was there, including the Lieutenant-Governor, Sir James Mitchell, and his wife. The civic-minded company built single and married men's quarters, an Olympic-size swimming pool and several tennis courts, well lit for night matches. Not long after the opening ceremony the company declared that it would play an active role in assisting in the erection of the hospital. Big Bell's active Progress Association prided itself on developments, noting the construction of roads, erection of a railway station and other buildings, clearing of the sports ground and formation of a football ground and cycle track, introduction of electric lighting, a picture theatre and garden, and a large hotel. Meanwhile, the Big Bell Wheeler's Club was busy organising cycling races for local enthusiasts.[25]

The Big Bell mine, like most other goldmines, closed during World War II, and kangaroos, rabbits and stock roamed the streets. The mine re-opened at the end of the war. 1951 was Big Bell's peak year, with 470 mine employees and a town of well over 1000 residents. There were 160 houses, 120 two-man huts on the mining leases, a hotel, picture theatre and a dozen shops. The mine closed in 1955, with the town's few remaining shops being sold for as little as £60 each. The correspondent for the *Countryman* remarked that 'the silence of the closed-down mine, deserted streets and gaps where houses used to be are stark proof that the town is dead'.[26]

On approaching Big Bell the traveller is immediately struck by the enormity of the two-storeyed hotel, truly a castle in the bush, its resplendent stonework reminiscent of a Coogee Beach hostelry. Only on closer inspection does the ubiquitous wire fence become obvious. Two other abandoned buildings remain in the town, a house and the Catholic church. Elsewhere, the house and shop sites can be discerned by the concrete slabs, discarded household items, bricks and the occasional derelict car. Big Bell is again the scene of large-scale mining activity and several hundred men are employed and live on site, but the old town remains as it was when the mine closed.

This area also has other, older treasures. North-west of Cue is the Wilga Mia ochre mine, which is believed to have been worked by Aboriginal people as long as 30 000 years ago. West of Cue is majestic Walga Rock, the repository of a number of Aboriginal paintings. One of these depicts a large sailing boat, even though the rock is several hundred kilometres from the sea. There has been speculation as to who the original artists might have been. Some have suggested that it was a group of shipwrecked Europeans. More likely the paintings were done by Aboriginal people who had been on the coast, not an inconceivable notion given the vast distances travelled by tribes along the early trading routes. While gold may have given birth to Cue, the town's future may well lie in its more ancient Aboriginal heritage.[27]

An American Dream

B EFORE BREASTING THE FABLED GOLDMINING TOWN OF GWALIA, IN THE dry red plains of the Eastern Goldfields, I took the opportunity of visiting Lawlers and Agnew, to the north. There is a hotel at Agnew, a few shacks of unknown vintage, and a relocated 20-head stamper and head frame from the old mines, which are now the scene of a massive nickel-mining project. At Lawlers there is much less. The police station is located in a mining company compound, while the rest of the town is no more than bricks and rubble. Yet, this was once a town of some importance.

An observer in April 1898 commented that Lawlers was a 'fresh clean little town', although much smaller than Cue. A month later another observer described Lawlers as a 'clean, bright goldfields town'. There was a post and telegraph office, a miners' institute, a 'capitally constructed hospital' with a resident doctor, four hotels with a couple of billiard tables and a piano, an aerated water manufacturer, a butcher and a branch of the Camel Stores. He was particularly taken with the Rose Hotel, which he described as the best on the Murchison. The principal mine was the East Murchison United, owned by the firm of Bewick, Moreing.[1]

Gwalia is located well south of Lawlers, near the still busy town of Leonora. Unlike Lawlers, there are many abandoned buildings in the town. One of them had been a shop, one a boarding house and the other a hotel, and almost all the others were homes or huts. Some were timber, but the larger number were built from the ubiquitous galvanised iron. So authentically have they been preserved, that it looks as if the miners walked out only yesterday. The town was abandoned when mining operations ceased in 1963, and is now the scene of renewed goldmining operations by Sons of Gwalia. Prior to those operations commencing, the company allowed the huts located on the site of the proposed open cut to be auctioned off by the Leonora Tourist Committee for the right to restore.

The huts fetched between $20 and $1000, and volunteers who 'bought' the huts were given title, allowing them to restore them under guidelines, using as many of the original materials and colour schemes as possible at their own cost. Hessian and information sheets were provided by the company. Over 100 people were involved. The local support was astounding. Some people collected building materials, others painted. Some obtained access to farm stations for artefacts, including window frames, others gardened or provided newspapers for the walls and perspex for the windows.[2]

Many of the buildings did not need to be removed and are located on their original sites. These included Mazza's store, Patroni's boarding house, and the old state-owned hotel, which has now been fully restored by the company. Also on their original site are the assay room, mine manager's house and mine office, now the museum, all of which are located in the company's large museum complex. This complex also houses the giant head frame and other related machinery and the locomotive, 'Ken', which was used on the extensive narrow gauge 'woodlines'. These were established to collect mulga timber for the steam boilers, which powered the mine and battery equipment.

Gwalia is inexorably linked to the USA — the first mining manager was Herbert Hoover, who became US President in 1929. Nowadays he is most remembered as the president who presided over America's decline into economic chaos during the Great Depression, and who was defeated soundly at the 1933 elections by Franklin Roosevelt. But his presence in Australia resulted in an engineering triumph, if not an industrial one. Not only was the Gwalia mine one of the richest and most enduring goldmines on the Eastern Goldfields, but as Bewick, Moreing's representative in Australia, Hoover also presided over the development of many other mines, one of which was the Great Fingall near Cue.

Hoover was only 23 at the time of his appointment to Bewick, Moreing, and at great pains to hide his age. He did not suffer fools gladly and was ruthlessly efficient in his judgement on both mines and men. According to his biographer, George Nash, his mining policy was to 'mend the lame ducks' by 'killing the dead ones', a position which was not all that indistinguishable from his views on industrial relations. Closer to home, staff problems obliged him to sack a number of men. He was already forming unfavourable convictions about Australian mining expertise and mining practices, declaring them to be well behind California in both regards, and he certainly had a poor opinion of Australian attitudes toward work and productivity.[3]

These views were to have far-reaching consequences, not only for mining towns such as Gwalia, but also for the Eastern Goldfields as a whole. Early in 1898, after only two months on the job, Hoover reported a dramatic decline in working costs at a number of mines. The company's success at the East Murchison mine at Lawlers was, however, hard won. Reforms included an increase in the hours of work from 44 to 48, the introduction of single-hand drilling, the changing of shifts underground and the importation of more skilled miners. These reforms were not greeted with enthusiasm by the workers, who refused to use the tools, threw them into the stamp mill or buried them. When the miners went on strike, however, management filled key positions with Italian labourers.[4]

There is some controversy over Hoover's initial role at Gwalia. The mine was originally found and financed by three Welsh-born storekeepers from Coolgardie, who sold it to the London and Westralian Mines and Finance Agency for a paltry £5000. By 1897 a 10-head battery had been put in place and mining had commenced with very favourable returns. Some historians have stated that Hoover was next on the scene, recommending that Bewick, Moreing buy the property.[5] However, Geoffrey Blainey has argued that the first recommendation came instead from Edward Hooper, a resident partner in Bewick, Moreing. It was only then that Hoover inspected the mine.[6]

Nevertheless, Hoover's meticulous report was critical in persuading the company to buy the mine, which he described as a most valuable one with enormous potential. His conclusions were published with the original prospectus, and on the first day of public trading on the London Stock Exchange, Sons of Gwalia shares more than doubled their price. Hoover was soon promoted to a junior partner in Bewick, Moreing, which entitled him to a share of the annual profits. At the 'ripe old age' of 24 he was appointed as manager of the Gwalia mine.[7]

Within only a few days of his appointment he implemented a cost-cutting program to address the challenges of high material, labour and transport costs. He moved swiftly to introduce changes to work practices on similar lines to those at the East Murchison United, and was soon at loggerheads with the work force, most of whom had only joined the union a short time before. Hoover increased the hours of work from 44 to 48, introduced single-handed drills and recruited several Italians. These changes were accepted, although further ones were not, and a threat to strike was met by a counter-threat by management to import more Italians. He contacted labour agent Pietro Ceruti of Bardoc, who provided a growing work force of Italians for the mine.[8]

By using migrant labour, Hoover laid the foundations for Gwalia's unique multicultural community. A large proportion of the underground miners was Italian or Slavic and of a total work force of 462 in 1903, 124 were 'foreigners'. Leonora was always the British town, and a visitor to Gwalia in 1917 observed that the trade at the hotel was confined to Italians. A police report stated that the only British who lived at Gwalia were men who had occupations that meant that they had to be near the mine. The 1903 figures suggest, however, that at that time the majority of miners were Australians.[9]

With his industrial problems seemingly resolved, there were no further difficulties and Hoover could concentrate on reorganising the mine. Construction of the new plant took most of 1899, but when it was completed production soared to over 90 000 ounces, and the directors paid 10 per cent dividends in that year and the following year. Hoover also turned his mind to the question of housing, but he was only concerned with office buildings and cottages for the staff, not the miners. The mine was too far from Leonora to

The Nannine cemetery lies atop brightly hued sandhills overlooking Lake Annean.

There has been much speculation about who painted this boat, which is located in a gallery of Aboriginal paintings at Walga Rock, near Cue.

Aboriginal paintings at Walga Rock, near Cue

The Big Bell Hotel is a veritable 'castle in the bush'.

The 'Pink House', a derelict miner's cottage at Gwalia

Patroni's boarding house is a testament to the time when Gwalia was home to a large migrant population.

With the exception of the police station and cemetery, the once thriving town of Lawlers is now little more than bricks and rubble.

The steam tram service to Gwalia was established in an effort to attract business to Leonora.
(Courtesy Gwalia Historical Museum)

commute, and many miners continued to camp near the mine in corrugated-iron huts and tents made from bags. Water had to be carried from the mine condensers, and many of the huts had no sanitary facilities and no kitchens. Many of the miners, however, obtained meals at the boarding houses.[10]

Later that year Hoover received an offer of a position in China. He accepted with enthusiasm, for it meant an increase in pay, respite from the oppressiveness of the outback and a chance to marry and settle down in a more amenable environment.[11] Hoover returned to Australia in 1901, now a partner in Bewick, Moreing and responsible for supervising the company's properties. One of his most lasting achievements was the translation in 1913, in collaboration with his wife Lou, of Georgius Agricola's *De Re Metallica*, a 1556 German treatise on mining technology that even now is spoken of with reverence by engineers and mining historians over the world.

Gwalia continued to grow. Timber-framed iron cottages appeared, and a town was surveyed. However, the lots were offered on a leasehold basis, providing little incentive for the establishment of businesses. In addition, the Leonora Road Board put up considerable opposition. The dilemma over the siting of the school was symptomatic of the tension between the two towns. The Education Department was unable to choose between five possible sites in the two towns, with the result that the Gwalia schoolteacher first taught in a tent, then in a rented church hall in which the children fainted during the summer. When the school did open in November 1901, in a compromise location midway between the two towns, it suited no one. The teacher refused to live there and the children refused to walk there, preferring to attend the two convent schools.[12]

Despite these tensions there were many instances of cooperation, such as the Gwalia–Leonora brass band and the weekly moonlight concerts. There was also a joint operatic society and a joint scouts troop. To attract custom to the Leonora businesses the council established a steam tram service linking the towns in 1903. The opening was celebrated with the Gwalia–Leonora band leading a colourful parade down Leonora's main street.[13]

Despite the efforts of Leonora's businessmen to thwart Gwalia's commercial development, by 1902 the town had a chemist, bookshop, two billiard rooms, two tobacconists and hairdressers, a bakery, tailors, bootmaker, butcher, soft drink shop, tea rooms and, impressively, a cigar lounge. There was also a Masonic Lodge, which held meetings in the Wesleyan church, a football club and a union hall in which many functions were held. That same year the State Hotel was opened at Gwalia. Concerns at the sly-grog trade in Gwalia led the government to build Western Australia's first state-owned hotel. Up until then there had been twenty or more sly-grog shops in or around the town. In January 1900 two women, who were owners of rival sly-grog shops, were embroiled in a fight in which one of them was maliciously wounded, and the other gaoled for four months as a consequence. The two-storey brick building was, and still is, the most imposing building in the town.

The Sons of Gwalia mine continued to prosper during the early 1900s, and by 1906 it had paid dividends worth more than its entire issued capital. Material costs were also lower following the extension of the railway from Menzies to Leonora in 1902. However, as at so many Western Australian mines, there was a continuing and growing need for mulga firewood for the boiler, fireboxes and water condensers. The need for firewood led to the construction of a light railway (the woodline) into the bush for timber gathering purposes. The train was a local institution and every year it was used for a company picnic. At the annual picnic in 1906 about 250 people travelled by the train to a spot in the bush some 17 kilometres away.[14]

Socially the twin towns were well catered for. Railway picnics were common, particularly in spring when the wildflowers were at their best. For instance, in August 1912 the Leonora and Gwalia football clubs combined to run a picnic excursion and 'flower train' to Kookynie, and in September a railway picnic for the district was held on the Malcolm racecourse, as was the annual woodline picnic. There were several picture theatres, one of which was in Gwalia, which at one stage also boasted a glee club and a Caledonian Society. Entertainments such as concerts were held regularly by the scout troop and the churches, and Christmas was a special time, with children's picnics in abundance. A notable special function was the opening of the Gwalia mine's new gas-producer plant in 1914 by the State Governor, Sir Harry Barron, when a holiday was declared for the town.

Frustration at the lack of businesses in Gwalia led eventually to the formation of a co-operative society, which was opened in 1913. The main building was transported from Malcolm in a jinker pulled by 48 donkeys and located near the state-owned hotel. Although the Leonora businessmen were not happy with this development there was little they could do about it, as it was a co-operative. The society was funded by shareholders, with small subsidies from the company and the union, and its profits were distributed as

Frustration at the lack of businesses in Gwalia led to the formation of a co-operative society.
(Courtesy Gwalia Historical Museum)

welfare payments within the local community. By 1920 the co-op had acquired the theatre business, which was run by a People's Picture Show Committee, and had built a children's playground.[15]

Employment and good wages notwithstanding, there was much hardship and tragedy at Gwalia, not only due to periodic epidemics of influenza or other illnesses, but because of the mine. Miners' phthisis, or 'dust on the lungs', was as prevalent at Gwalia as it was on other goldfields because it took an uncommonly long time for the authorities to recognise and act on the problem. Sons of Gwalia's safety record was not good, and in the early 1900s there were a number of deaths from earth collapses and explosions. The worst accident occurred in May 1911 when the winding-engine broke down, and a skip hauling 12 miners up the incline shaft hurtled 600 metres to the bottom, killing three men and seriously injuring eight others. Later that year the plant was converted to electrical power, using a wood-fuelled gas-producer plant, and a new steam-winder was installed.[16]

One of the most significant accidents was a fire in the gas-producer plant in 1921. In a few hours the engine room, 50-head battery and ore bin and buildings were a mass of twisted steel, burnt-out machinery and debris. The fire-fighting equipment was not up to the task, and the winding room and boilers were only saved by workers using buckets. According to the authors of the *Gwalia Conservation Study*, the area of the plant that was destroyed was uneconomic and much of it, including the gas-producer plant, needed replacement. Essential and profitable areas, such as the haulage system and the slimes treatment works, survived. The scale of the disaster forced the company to dismiss almost all its work force, allowing it to save money on labour costs and rebuild the outdated section using the insurance payout.[17]

For the dismissed miners the effect was devastating. The State Government assisted with the rebuilding of the mine, and sustenance payments were paid to men with dependents who lived locally and were prepared to prospect, but this only benefited about 20 per cent of the miners. Houses were sold at give-away prices, as many thought that the mine was now finished. With the mine closed down from about mid-December for several weeks, many women and children were joined by their husbands on their annual pilgrimage to the coast. By 1923, however, the Gwalia mill had been rebuilt, and the opening was attended by a very large contingent of parliamentarians. But the work force was now only 300, a substantial decrease from before. The community did survive, however, and indeed went through a period of expansion. By 1924 the co-operative had extended its activities, and a butcher's shop with its own piggery, abattoir and refrigeration plant was opened.[18]

By 1928 dwindling ore reserves and rising costs of production had led the company into negotiations with the State Government for financial assistance, which they duly received. Further development revealed new reserves and in 1930 the company made a small profit, the first since 1921. In 1931 the price of gold rose, the Australian pound devalued and the government paid a bounty on increased gold production. So swiftly did the company's fortunes turn around that by the following year the government loan was repaid and enough profit was left over to pay a dividend. The 1930s were, therefore, a time of prosperity for Gwalia and a number of other Western Australian goldfields. Symptomatic of these changed circumstances was the advent of the Gwalia Motorcycle Club. The main attraction was the district's smooth clay-pans, where members could try their skills without injuring others.[19]

Notwithstanding the mix of nationalities in the Gwalia–Leonora area, there is little evidence of conflict between the different groups. Despite the arrival of the motor vehicle, camel teams were still used extensively and there were Afghan camps in Leonora and Gwalia. Aboriginal people lived in the town, and some of them were employed on the surface works at the mine. A contributing factor to this harmony was the joint policy of the police and the company to run the worst troublemakers out of town. If miners were found guilty of a serious offence, or they were persistent offenders, they were reported to the company, who sacked them and put them on the next train for Kalgoorlie. The Kalgoorlie race riots on Australia Day in 1934 were the worst in Australia's history, but they did not spread to Gwalia. Indeed, after the riots a number of migrant families from Kalgoorlie resettled in Gwalia and Leonora. Eric Omodei, one of the last Gwalia residents still living in the town, confirmed that local race relations were excellent.[20]

With the outbreak of World War II, labour shortages were exacerbated by the internment in 1940 of Italian nationals who were in the work force, and production fell sharply. Many houses in Gwalia and Leonora were vacant and, despite years of ore reserves still remaining, an air of gloom hung over the district. Social functions continued to be held but were more directed towards the war effort; for example, the Red Cross, Salvation Army and Patriotic Fund donated funds raised by the woodline railway picnic.

One of the main business areas in Gwalia was known as 'the Block'.
(Courtesy Gwalia Historical Museum)

In 1948 working hours were reduced and there were several wage increases. Labour shortages were still very serious and only 10 men were employed on the woodline. In 1949 the company shipped 67 miners directly from Italy, but a year later less than half were still at the mine. 1950 was the last year in which a dividend was paid. The following year the company's position was made worse by a machinery failure that put all underground and some surface workers out of work for a fortnight. This was followed a few weeks later by an accident in which a skip broke away, plunging to the bottom of the inclined shaft and crushing three men who were working there.[21]

Eventually mechanical scrapers and loaders replaced men, electric locomotives replaced underground horses, and plant equipment was replaced. However, the state government had to intervene with further loans, and the prospects for repayment this time were poor. Belatedly, it was recognised that the living conditions in Gwalia were totally unsatisfactory and a major reason for the difficulty in attracting labour. A state loan was used to build a kitchen and dining hall seating 100 and a central bathroom for 42 men. In 1957, however, the co-operative closed down, leaving Mazza's store as the town's only shop. The theatre closed down the following year and in 1960 the State Hotel was sold to a local syndicate.[22]

By 1963 the ore in reserve was below the economic threshold and there was no alternative but to close the mine. The news was treated with great gloom in Leonora, for more than 70 per cent of all business in the district was connected with the mine, miners and their families. There were at that time three general stores, four hotels and several other businesses, a number of which would now have to close. But for the miners the news was not as bad. Employees transferring from Gwalia to other goldmining centres would

Moving the co-op building from
Malcolm to Gwalia
(Courtesy Gwalia Historical Museum)

receive a rail freight reduction on all belongings and all Leonora–Gwalia residents affected by the closure were invited to settle in an area in south Boulder, near Kalgoorlie. It was considered that the majority of displaced miners could be absorbed into the mining industry at Kalgoorlie, though it was later conceded that this applied mainly to underground, not surface or plant workers, or the more elderly.[23]

Nevertheless, the exodus took place immediately, for there seemed to be ample employment opportunities along the Golden Mile. The weekend before New Year's Day almost everyone in town was packing all personal and household items they intended to take, but many were only taking essential belongings, leaving the rest to the wind and dust. Some would possibly return and salvage some of their abandoned possessions. The departing train for Leonora and Gwalia left on New Year's Day. Seventeen carriages were loaded with household effects and people. A few days later all was quiet and empty, with little, if any sign of life at the mine, in houses, shops, school or the churches.[24]

Gwalia joined the ranks of abandoned mining towns. Today, it is easy to forget just how significant the mine was. By the end of 1963 it was the sixth-largest gold-producing mine in Australia, and only one of two mines outside the Golden Mile which could measure its output at over two million ounces.[25] Leonora has obviously shrunk, for there is now only one hotel and two general stores, and although mining has recommenced at Gwalia, the miners are employed on a fly-in, fly-out basis, and live in the mine compound with all meals provided. Gwalia is still a ghost town, and likely to remain so. However, it is also a memorial to the past, and hopefully that aspect will continue to be nurtured.

Tombstones and Tumbleweed

ABANDONED GOLDMINING TOWNS ARE SCATTERED ACROSS THE LENGTH and breadth of the Eastern Goldfields of Western Australia. The greatest cluster lies in an arc, north of the Kalgoorlie–Boulder Golden Mile to Leonora and east to Laverton. Many of them once boasted populations of several thousand, but now there is little left except a few piles of broken glass and bricks and the inevitable graveyard, if even that. Some towns, however, have hung on, a shadow of what they once were, but with just enough to hint at their former glory.

Menzies, located on the main highway between Kalgoorlie and Leonora, looks from a distance like any other small country town. The attractive sandstone shire council building is reminiscent of the government buildings at Cue on the Murchison Goldfields, and there is a hotel, caravan park, service station and police station. But all other town businesses are abandoned, and some, such as the Lady Shenton and Maori hotels, have been that way for many years. Menzies, like Cue, was a boom town in the 1890s and the centre of a once prosperous goldmining district. At one time it had a population of many thousands, but now there are only a few hundred residents.[1]

The similarities with Cue do not rest there, for in early 1896 a typhoid fever epidemic swept through the town. Temperatures were extreme, food was short, and there were cesspits and rubbish festering in the hot sun. The town was cleaned up, but even that could not check the outbreak. Both public and private hospitals were overwhelmed, and many young people were amongst the dead. A prime suspect was the post and telegraph office, for one after another the staff fell ill with fever and several died.[2] Typhoid was still prevalent in the early part of 1897.[3]

In her travels through the goldfields, Vivienne May described Menzies as the nicest small mining town that she had seen, which suggests that the sanitary conditions must have been substantially improved by then.

There was a myriad of other small mining settlements nearby, such as Kensington, which had two breweries, and the Twelve Mile.[4] The warden, W. Lambden Owen, painted a slightly different picture of Menzies, and commented on the lack of fresh water and the reliance of the town on camels. Water was obtained by condensing salt water from the mine shafts and ephemeral lakes, and was brought into town by camels. All stores were transported by horses, bullocks, or camels driven by Afghans, and camel races and picnics were the main form of recreation. Camels were borrowed for the latter occasion. Bicycles were another common mode of transport, and were usually ridden along the narrow pads made by the camels.[5]

By 1898 Menzies had the warden's office and principal government offices for the whole of the North Coolgardie Goldfields. Wood and iron structures were being replaced by stone and brick, the Banks of Australasia and Western Australia had built 'very commodious and ornamental stone premises', and the two-storeyed brick Grand Hotel all gave the town an air of permanency. The principal streets had been macadamised and in the outlying towns more permanent buildings were being constructed, and footpaths and streets had been formed. Schools, a government hospital, a club, recreation centre, miners' institute, the Union Bank and numerous businesses had been established. There were over 6000 residents within a three-kilometre zone, and the principal mines, the Lady Shenton and Queensland Menzies, had produced a combined total of over 40 000 ounces of gold, at an incredible yield of about four ounces a ton. Yields of that magnitude would today have mining speculators delirious with excitement.[6]

In 1901 the *Western Mail* correspondent spoke eloquently of several of the business proprietors in the Menzies district, in particular the Montgomery Brothers, who were drapers, clothiers and house furnishers. Praise was heaped upon the Maori Hotel, described as the 'favourite abiding place of miners, of prospectors from outside centres, and ... all who wanted to secure accommodation at this homelike hotel'. The hotel had 16 bedrooms, three parlours, two bars, a commodious dining room and extensive stables. Its hall was over 30 metres long and had seating accommodation for 500 persons, whilst the 'scenery and stage fittings were amply sufficient to meet the requirements of all travelling theatrical companies'.[7]

By the following year, the newly constructed town hall was described as the 'finest out of Perth, putting the municipal buildings of Kalgoorlie, Boulder and Coolgardie completely in the shade'. It featured a 'handsome tower' and a large and imposing entrance. One side was devoted to the town council offices and the other to a reading room. Behind the facade was a spacious hall constructed of corrugated iron, which was much larger than the Maori's hall. There were also numerous plain and roomy church buildings, including a spacious and well-built Salvation Army barracks. Less impressive were the post and telegraph office, which continued to be housed in an iron shed, and the absence of proper street lighting, for the streets were in semi-darkness, interrupted only occasionally by 'a dim kerosene lamp post'. By this time there were also two newspapers, a courthouse and hospital.[8]

Numerous goldfields towns sprang up in the area west of Menzies. At Niagara, mine shafts lie scattered along the roadside, and near them small indications of former life: a pile of broken glass, a few pots and pans, tin cans, occasional bicycle seats and frames, and bricks and stones where once a chimney stood. Apart from the occasional water tank and brick foundation, the only real indication that there was ever a township is provided by the cemetery and the dam. The dam was built in 1897 to provide water for the steam locomotives, at a locality known as Niagara Falls, in honour of its more famous namesake in America. Building the dam was a much more expensive undertaking than originally envisaged, for the government grossly miscalculated the depth of rock to be excavated and the cost of transporting the concrete, which was conveyed by a team of camels owned by an Afghan, Abdul Waid. Ironically, not long after its construction, a good supply of underground water was found at Kookynie.[9]

Yet Niagara was once destined for greater things. In 1897 it was described as a promising town, with four hotels (two had fair accommodation), three stores, a wine saloon, chemist, baker, two butchers and other businesses. The majority of the houses were built of sun-dried bricks and in the case of one hotel it was commented that 'it would be hard to find a stone house of equal comfort in such a remote part'.[10] But, only five years later, the *Western Mail* lamented that the once 'flourishing town, with seven hotels doing a roaring trade and several hundred men on gold, had now become a deserted village'. A few small mines were being worked and the gold won paid for the running of a hotel or two and the stores. Adobe walls, stripped of their woodwork, gave the town a dismal appearance. The train between Menzies and Kookynie stopped at the Niagara Falls Hotel, 'where a good cup of tea and a scone' were supplied to the travellers while the train was filled from a large tank built on piers, which was in turn filled by water from Niagara dam.[11]

It was while wandering around the mine sites near Niagara that I had a curious encounter. There was no one around, no birds graced the hot noon-day sky, and there was not a kangaroo or emu in sight. I was startled by a noise from behind: not a rustle as one would expect from a snake or lizard, but more of a shuffle of human dimensions. A glance behind me could find no answer, until wandering a little further away I stood staring at a goat that was shyly glancing up at me from the mouth of a mine tunnel sunk into the side of a shallow pit. I admired the commonsense of this subterranean goat, for he was probably in the coolest spot for many miles around.

The goldfield goat was an important animal. Ivan Elliot, in his book *From Kookynie to Keysbrook*, has described the role they played in the daily life of the Kookynie miners and their families. Everyone had a few goats, sometimes up to eighty. The goats on the south end of town got together every morning and went out south of the town, feeding along the creek all day and returning into town in the evening. On their return they arranged themselves into their own small groups before proceeding to their respective properties, where they were locked up for the night. Those on the north side did likewise, although

… wandering a little further away I stood staring at a goat that was shyly glancing up at me from the mouth of a mine tunnel …

Main street, Menzies. The building on the right is the Town Hall. (*Western Mail*, Christmas Edition, 1901; by permission of National Library of Australia)

heading in a different direction. The goats were invaluable, for they provided both milk and meat, and their hides could also be sold.[12]

Kookynie was established a little later than Menzies. Most of the houses were timber framed with a galvanised-iron roof, outside walls of house canvas, and inside walls lined with hessian. The walls were treated with whitewash and waterproof. Most houses had a bough shed in the yard; they were the only place the night-shift men could sleep in the daytime. In the business district there were several brothels occupied by Japanese women.[13]

In 1901 the *Western Mail* correspondent remarked that in less than three years it had 'materialised from a patch of scrub into a busy bustling mining centre', and was about to be declared a municipality. The main street was lined with 'substantial buildings of pretentious design', proof of the residents' faith in the permanence of the district's gold resources. The correspondent lauded the comforts and appointments of the Kookynie Hotel, the proprietor of which, a Mr Campbell, was one of the best-known men on the goldfields, and chairman of the Kookynie Progress Committee.[14]

The Progress Committee was responsible for the clearing and formation of the road from Niagara to Kookynie, connecting the main tracks to the north, obtaining funds for a school and miners' institute, and establishing postal and telegraphic facilities and sanitary depots. Officialdom was very tardy in providing a school and miners' institute, and was only persuaded on the former when a photograph of the children was published in the *Western Mail* and sent to the Minister for Education. The miners' institute was established only after an approach from the committee to the Premier, Sir John Forrest.[15]

By 1902 the population within an eight-kilometre radius of Kookynie exceeded 3000, and the town probably eclipsed Menzies, which had the grander buildings and town improvements. Kookynie, however, had electricity in part of the town, supplied from the power station at the Cosmopolitan mine. By the following year it was apparently the busiest and most prosperous town in the northern goldfields. Its population was 2000, of whom 1200 resided within the municipality, and towards the end of the year electricity had been installed throughout the town. The council erected its own poles and cables, selling the electricity to consumers at a profit and using the proceeds for the street lighting. An efficient fire service with fire hydrants was also introduced, footpaths laid out, trees planted and parklands fenced. A hospital and brewery were built in 1904, the latter by Ivan Elliott's father, and a swimming pool was constructed using water pumped from the Cosmopolitan mine. The water was always fresh and ran from the baths to Champion Creek, making it a haven for all types of wildlife.[16]

Kookynie was not, however, to remain a haven for the miners, for the main mines closed in 1912, and by the following year the seven remaining hotels had only 77 adult males on whom they could depend for custom.[17] The mining registrar's office was closed in 1917.[18] Yet unlike some other towns, Kookynie did not die completely, and there is still one hotel left, the Grand. Paddy's and the National hotels have been largely demolished, but a few walls stand amidst a sea of brick rubble. Some distance away are the rather more substantial remains of the Cosmopolitan Hotel. Elsewhere, there are several older but occupied houses, and an occasional lone chimney. Remains of the mining and processing plant for the Cumberland and Cosmopolitan mines are located within the town boundaries. The remnants of the Altona mine can be seen on the outskirts of the town. The present owners of the Grand Hotel, Kevin and Margaret Pusey, have spent an enormous amount of time, effort and money restoring the hotel and an abandoned block of shops.

About 30 kilometres south of Laverton, on the fringe of the desert country, is the former mining town of Burtville. Unlike Kookynie and Menzies it was not a large mining centre, but by 1904 it had about 400 residents, of whom only 30 were females, and 16 children. It had two hotels, three stores, a progress committee, fire brigade and football team, and fresh vegetables and cows' milk were available.[19] There are no huts left, but the sites can be discerned easily by the piles of bottle fragments, cans, cooking implements and the like. Curiously, the huts were located some distance from the main hotel, but prophetically, within a stone's throw of the cemetery. As at Niagara, many of the mines have been left intact with their timber collars and stone embankments. The galvanized-iron huts have, unfortunately, been bulldozed.

Burtville's main claim to fame is the manner in which its inhabitants died, for it is claimed that only one of the cemetery's occupants died peacefully, if that is possible. That the others may have met untimely, and in some cases violent deaths, was not surprising, for neither before nor since have I seen such a comprehensive scatter of broken bottles. Shyeema Peebles, from Laverton, has described Burtville as 'at the end of the line', for beyond there was nothing. Of the fifteen death records that Shyeema provided, five died from suicide, three from accidents, two fell down mine shafts, one was struck by lightning, one was shot and murdered and one died from natural causes. In the other two cases the cause of death was unknown.[20]

Between Laverton and Leonora lie the former mining towns of Mount Morgans and Malcolm. The story of their rise and fall fits a familiar pattern. Vivienne May was at Mount Morgans at its infancy, for the first hotel had just been opened and she had great difficulty in getting accommodation and had to share the room of the landlady's daughter. The owner was doing a roaring trade and the large dining room served as a dormitory at night. A workmen's club and library had been built of mud bricks, but the post office was still primitive and was merely a canvas tent with a bough shed over it.[21]

Ironically, the permission to peg out town sites was given by the warden at Mount Margaret, which was soon deserted by the miners, who moved all the houses to Mount Morgans. Many of the miners made their way to Mount Morgans by bicycle, a popular mode of transport in such a featureless terrain. By December 1899 the town had some 'very good buildings', notably the National Bank, Allanson's shop and two hotels, and there were 400 residents, a quarter of whom were females. Two police officers were stationed in the town and a lock-up was under construction, with a hospital to be built the following year.[22]

By 1901 the town was well laid out, with some good substantial buildings, notably stores and hotels. It was lit with electricity supplied from the Westralian Mount Morgans mine, with electricity to be installed in all the leading business premises. The town also had local self-government, a mayor and high land values. First amongst the hotels was Paddy Byrne's Tattersall's, the exterior of which was impressive and the interior first class. The turnover was more than double that of any other hotel, and it was described as the meeting place for all classes.[23]

The mining property was purchased recently by Homestake Gold, which has restored the old shire office building, the town's only remaining edifice, and incorporated it into the mining compound. Stone foundations and part of a wall of one other building are located near the shire office, but apart from the remains of the railway platform and the cemetery, there is little else left. The cemetery has the usual array of headstones erected by sorrowing wives, workmates and occasionally husbands and parents. One particularly moving headstone was dedicated to Jack Laurie, a New Zealander who died in 1903. It reads, 'Oh for the touch of a vanished hand or the sound of a voice that is still.' His wife, Alice, returned to New Zealand soon after with her four children, and the grave has since been restored by her grandchildren.

An expectant crowd awaiting news
of the 'Golden Sickle' nugget,
Kanowa
(*Western Mail*, 5 August 1898; by
permission of National Library of
Australia)

Malcolm is located between Leonora and Mount Morgans. The site is now
bare waste ground. At the time of Vivienne May's arrival in 1897 she was
struck by the number of windmills and wells in the town. The post office was
one of the few permanent buildings, and the warden's offices or courthouse
comprised two hessian tents with bough sheds built over them.[24] However, a
year later Malcolm enjoyed its first fancy dress ball at the Southern Exchange
Hotel, and within a few months, another hotel and a mechanics' institute
were built, a minstrel banjo band formed, and several stores erected, including butchers and bakers. Progress was rapid and by 1901 there were five
hotels, a newspaper, photographer, hospital, school and numerous businesses
such as a cycle shop, a plumber, tinsmith and galvanised-iron works, brewery,
tailor, bootmaker, blacksmiths, general stores, butchers and bakers. But only
a few years later the hospital was closed due to the decreasing population, and
in 1905 the newspaper followed.[25]

Another gold town in the middle of nowhere is Mount Ida, about 150 kilometres west of Leonora on a dusty dirt road. Its population never rose much
above 500, and mining ceased in the 1950s. Like so many other towns, almost
every miner's hut has been carted away, fallen down or bulldozed. However,
one large fibro house, possibly the mine manager's, and an abandoned truck,
the wall of a brick building, and the fibro men's change rooms, with possibly

a small store attached, remain. The galvanised-iron mine office, battery foundations, some older shafts and a powder magazine are located away from the main track, and behind the massive cyanide tailings heap are two architectural marvels, a hut with a bough shed and another which incorporates a bus. In Mount Ida's early years there was a difference of opinion on whether the town should have a telegraph line or bike pad into Menzies. The single miners were in favour of the latter and won their way.[26]

There are many other old gold towns scattered throughout the north-east, such as Euro, Bardoc, Kurnalpi, Mulline, Mulwaree, Davyhurst, Goongarie, Broad Arrow, Ora Banda, Siberia, Kunanulling, Bulong and Kanowna. The most notable remains are the hotel and several miners' cottages at Broad Arrow, the remains of the hotel and the state battery at Ora Banda, and the remnants of a large stone hotel at Kunanulling.

Perhaps the most renowned of these towns is Kanowna, or White Feather, as it was originally called, about 20 kilometres east of Kalgoorlie. Gold was found on this field only a few months after Paddy Hannan's famous find at Kalgoorlie. The town grew rapidly and by the end of 1894 there were half a dozen stores, all of which were tents covered by bough sheds, several hotels, a billiard saloon and a hospital, which was also in a tent covered by a bough shed. Not long after, it was decided to move the town to its present site and a town planning committee was formed. It was agreed that there would be no hessian humpies, tin shanties or bough sheds, and that all buildings were to be of good quality. There were about 700 men and 80 females, and the overall population within a six-kilometre radius was about 3000.[27]

In 1897 there was a second rush when the famous deep leads were discovered. By the following year Kanowna was regarded as the premier town of the Eastern Goldfields, even surpassing Kalgoorlie.[28] The town was supplied with electricity, and had two hospitals, a courthouse, police quarters, mechanics' institute, churches, the Salvation Army, the Union and Western Australian banks, a pharmacy, bicycle shop, brewery, Caledonian Society, Masonic Lodge and fire brigade. Sporting groups, bands, musical and dramatic societies, churches and a race club catered for the miners' many social needs. Prosperity was short-lived, however, for by 1900 the population had already decreased considerably.[29] In 1907 the population had begun to move away and buildings were dismantled and shifted to other centres. By 1959 the town had ceased to exist. Today the only remains are the railway platform and the cemetery.

There were a number of intriguing, almost legendary, events at Kanowna. One of the more remarkable was the cemetery rush. In 1897 Tassie O'Connor was working a claim near the cemetery, when he noticed that the lead had changed direction and was likely to run across the cemetery precincts and beyond. He pegged a claim out on the opposite cemetery fence and made a fortune. When word of the find became known there was a demand that the cemetery be opened up for mining. Although the graves could be protected it was felt that this proposal would create a bad precedent. Nevertheless, under pressure the government relented.

By the time that the cemetery was to be opened, about 3000 people had assembled along the boundary fence. At 2 pm on 3 December the local police-man dropped a white handkerchief to signal the start of the pegging. Ironically, the cemetery lead was only moderately successful, but the damage was enough to ensure that a new cemetery would be built.[30] The results of this feverish incident can still be seen today, as the mine shafts and mullock heaps sit cheek by jowl with the grave headstones and other markers.

One other incident of notoriety was Father Long's nugget. Father Long arrived in Kanowna from Ireland early in 1896. He was well-liked and trav-elled extensively through his parish by camel and bicycle. Although he was very familiar with mining processes he had never seen a large nugget until the day he was shown one shaped like a sickle. He was sworn to secrecy not to divulge the location, but this did not deter hundreds of men from looking for the site. Recognising the fevered state of mind of many of the men, he agreed to make an announcement from the balcony of Donnellan's Hotel.

By 2 pm on that fateful day between 5000 and 6000 men were assembled, in all manner of vehicles and all very well equipped. As soon as Father Long mentioned the location, the crowd broke up and a mad race began. The claims were pegged out and the next day the men returned to work on them. However, it didn't take long for them to realise they were not in gold country and the diggings were soon deserted. They did not blame Father Long, for it was felt correctly that he had been cruelly deceived. Sadly, the popular young priest died the following year of typhoid, at the age of 27, his sudden and pre-mature demise perhaps in some way mirroring the fate of Kanowna and many other towns like it.[31]

The Winds of Change

I N THE FAR NORTH OF WESTERN AUSTRALIA LIE THE FORMER PORTS OF Onslow and Cossack. They have much in common, including their susceptibility to cyclones. Onslow is not, however, located near the sea.[1] The curious traveller could spend a considerable time wandering around the old town precincts without so much as sniffing a sea breeze, let alone glimpsing the sea. Most of the old town is located on sand dunes, and is surrounded on the landward side by clay pans, with further clay pans and sea marshes stretching away on the seaward side. With the exception of a palm tree near the police buildings and the occasional low shrub, the vegetation is almost entirely spinifex and dune grasses.

The most impressive remains are the stone government buildings, which include the police station, court, gaol, police quarters and a concrete underground water tank. The cell floors still have the iron manacles used for chaining prisoners. Other building remains are scattered among the dunes and require perseverance to find. In a number of instances part of the walls are still standing. The remains of the two hotels, the Ashburton and the Rob Roy, with the usual scatter of broken bottles, the telegraph office, resident magistrate's home and hospital are still visible. The abandoned relics of cart and bullock drays and the bogies from a tramcar stand weathering in the sun.

Onslow was chosen as a port for the pastoral industry in 1885 because of its proximity to a boat landing built by pastoralists on the nearby Ashburton River. The landing had deep water and gave both access and safety for the lighters carting goods between ships and shore. However, the site was far from perfect. During and after a cyclone the Ashburton could run with enough force to tear luggers and lighters from their moorings. Improvements made to the river landing in 1892 included a lengthening of the landing, which would be well above flood level, the construction of a tramway and erection of a bond store and goods shed on the river bank. Unfortunately,

Once a town of several thousand people, Kookynie now has only a handful of residents.

The only building remains at Burtville are the walls of one of the hotels.

A large pile of broken bottles, lying undisturbed for decades, marks the site of a hut at Burtville.

At Kanowa the mine shafts and mullock heaps sit cheek-by-jowl with the graveyard headstones.

The most impressive remains at Onslow are the stone-built government buildings, including the gaol. You can still see the manacles anchored in the cement floor.

At Onslow the rusty relics of carts and bullock drays stand weathering in the sun.

The abandoned port of Cossack was once the centre of a thriving pearling industry.

these improvements were of questionable value. The lighters had to sail over the bar at the river mouth, and with increasing siltation this task became more hazardous.[2]

At first the town grew slowly. In 1888 there were 17 teamsters, a hotel-keeper, several storekeepers, and several employed in lighterage, post and tele-graph work. By 1895 the character of the town had changed. Civilisation had arrived with a magistrate, medical officer, policeman, teacher, tutor, black-smith, saddler and wheelwright, as well as 13 teamsters. The impressive brick and stone police station and police quarters had been opened a few years ear-lier, and the house originally built by James Clark as his retirement home, became the magistrate's house sometime after 1897. A hospital, built some-time before 1900, accommodated European patients inside and Aboriginal patients on the verandah.[3]

The position of schoolmaster was held by various persons in the town, including at one time the telegraphist and at another time, the custom officer's wife. Lessons were held in different private homes, the churches or the hospital, depending upon circumstances. The roads board had a similarly peripatetic existence, with meetings usually held in a home conveniently located opposite one of the hotels. Other buildings were a goods shed and bonded store. Water was always a problem and most residents relied on rain tanks, while some, like the hotels and police station, relied on wells. Otherwise water could be purchased from James Clark, or from distant Ten Mile Pool on the Ashburton River.[4]

Despite this growth, Onslow continued to be handicapped by its inade-quate port facilities. In 1897 work began on a sea jetty, but before it was completed it was destroyed in a cyclone, which not only wrecked the public works department's boring equipment, but also the whole of the jetty decking, as well as lifting the piling and demolishing the workers' quarters. It also damaged the police buildings, the residency and all private buildings. In 1899 a new start was made on the jetty, but to save costs it was only half the length of the first, and as it was built close to the estuary, it was also subject to siltation. In addition, because the new jetty was about nine kilometres from the town, a horse-drawn tramway had to be built. The shallowness of the water at the jetty meant that lighters were still needed. This largely defeated the purpose of the jetty, which was to export livestock and speed up and cheapen the cost of wool exports by dispensing with the lighters.[5]

For a time Onslow benefited from other developments, such as the open-ing up of the Ashburton goldfields and the development of the Uaroo mines. By 1908 a mule team, two donkey teams, six camel wagons and 12 horse teams were carting goods between Uaroo and Onslow. The main stimulus was, however, the development of the pearling industry, which was already well established at Cossack and Broome. In 1904 the Westward Pearling Company was based in Onslow, most of the divers coming from Japan, the Philippines, Malaya and Indonesia. At Onslow, unlike Cossack, the pearling crews, who were predominantly Malay and Japanese, did not live in the town, but near the jetty, where they had their own communities and stores.[6]

This growth came to an abrupt end in January and April 1909, when cyclones ravaged the town and the pearling fleet. On the latter occasion the hall used as a church was swept away, the Rob Roy Hotel had much of its roof removed, and the Temperance Hotel was severely damaged. Two lighters, a lugger and a cutter were washed ashore, stores on the jetty were ruined or blown into the sea, the tramline was washed away in many places, and the passenger car was turned over by the wind and blown away.

Passengers and crew on the ship *Gorgon* had a particularly difficult time. During the height of the storm it was impossible to stay on the deck for more than a few seconds and the anchors began dragging and threatened to pull the boat under. When the anchors were let go the boat was washed ashore and lifted by a large wave over a sand bank and into a creek amongst the mangroves, where it was swept about in circles for several hours. More seriously, some days later it was reported that four pearling luggers with their Malay crews, 24 in all, had been lost at sea.[7]

The cyclones were the catalyst for discussions that eventually led to the abandonment of the town. There were calls for port improvements and the local MLA suggested that there were two alternatives: either extend the jetty into deep water or build a new one on the opposite side of the Ashburton River. This latter proposal was later rejected because of the cost of building a bridge across the river. One improvement that was made, however, was the construction of a lookout on the town goods shed so that the ships could be seen some nine kilometres away. Prior to this, James Clark would send one of his children up onto the roof of the Rob Roy Hotel as a lookout.[8]

Not long after, the ground in the debate shifted between choosing a new site altogether, with Point Beadon the most popular choice, or constructing a new jetty near Onslow. One point in favour of the former was the increasingly dilapidated condition of the town. It had no made streets and there were few buildings that could not be moved, and all were in a state of disrepair. Eventually, the government decided on the construction of a new jetty at Point Beadon, which meant that the existing town of Onslow would be abandoned, and the buildings removed to the new town site.[9] The wheels turned slowly, however, and the new jetty at Point Beadon was not constructed until 1925. From that point on the town was quickly deserted, with many residents leaving to resettle in the new town, which was renamed Onslow not long after.

Cossack, located about 400 kilometres north of Onslow, was established in 1863 as a port for the town of Roebourne and surrounding farm properties. One of the ships on the original party looking for a suitable site, the *Tien Tsin*, gave its name to the new port, which was renamed Cossack in 1872. Like Onslow the port site had many disadvantages. It was shallow and goods could only be landed at certain times, there was no permanent water, and at spring tides the adjacent marshes, which lay between the port and Roebourne, were impassable. Over the next few years several expeditions searched for a more suitable port, but none could be found.

The post and telegraph station, Onslow
(Courtesy Onslow Goods Shed Museum)

One of the biggest drawbacks was the marsh between Cossack and Roebourne. To avoid it many settlers unloaded their goods at Cossack into a flat-bottomed boat or barge and landed them at a spot where the marsh was firm. But other travellers had no alternative but to ride through the marsh or, if they were on foot, wade through the mud and water. It was only when a causeway was eventually constructed that Cossack began to grow. Settlement was also thwarted by the lack of a reliable water supply, eventually rectified by the construction of concrete underground water tanks in 1877.[10]

The commencement of pearling gave Cossack a real boost, as it was the only port in the north-west and an obvious choice for the pearling fleet's headquarters. In the 1860s the majority of pearling vessels were less than 50 tons and usually employed a team of Aboriginal or Malay divers. Many of the boats were owned by pastoralists, who supplemented their farm income in the slack seasons by pearling, using local Aboriginal people as divers. With the use of larger and more numerous boats, the demand for divers soon outstripped the supply of labour, probably due to an understandable reluctance by the divers to engage in what was essentially a difficult and hazardous industry for little more than food and some clothing.[11]

This reluctance was also more than likely linked with the increasingly questionable recruiting practices of some pearlers, who resorted to tactics little short of kidnapping. Although after 1873 kidnapping and the employment of

A camel train with wool bales outside the Onslow goods store (Courtesy Onslow Goods Shed Museum)

Aboriginal women on the boats became illegal, the legislation was inadequately policed and the 'recruiting' gangs responded by travelling further afield. The 'blackbird' gangs resorted to extreme cruelty and even murder to get their way. Some, such as Robert Shea, were murdered by Aborigines in retaliation, and others, like Thomas Mountain, were prosecuted and gaoled. However, pursuing and prosecuting the culprits was dangerous. As historian Kay Forrest has commented, it more than likely claimed the lives of the Inspector of Pearl Shell Fisheries, Pemberton Walcott, and perhaps several other men, and ruined the health and careers of others.[12]

Once on the boats the Aboriginal divers were at the mercy of the pearling masters, some of whom overworked or underfed them. Others beat them, hung them from the rigging, or made them swim around the boats for several hours at a time as punishment for not getting enough shell. In addition, some pearlers used the offshore islands as prisons or dumping grounds to hold the men until they were further required.[13] Even at its best the life of a diver was dangerous and uncomfortable, for the men were separated from family and friends for six months or more on crowded boats with the added risks of sharks and cyclones. It was an existence little short of slavery, and if at the end of it all they managed to survive there was no guarantee that they would be landed on shore even remotely close from whence they had come.

A candid account of these practices was offered by Arthur Bligh, a visitor to Cossack at this time. He considered that the Aboriginal workers were well treated. However, in the next breath, he recounted that if they attempted to run away they were tracked, brought back and thrashed. Even if they dodged the trackers, they had little chance of escaping as they would have to risk their lives by passing through hostile tribal land. During a vessel refit it was common practice to place the Aboriginal divers on offshore islands, and he recounted that on some occasions they escaped by swimming ashore, even though they were many kilometres away.[14]

Before long it was obvious that Aboriginal labour needed to be supplemented, and three years later there were twice the number of Malays as Aboriginal people at Cossack. Treatment of the Asian divers, particularly the Malays, was however, also poor. Some divers were ill-treated and ill-fed, and at the end of the season abandoned in Australia and not paid their wages. Their mortality rate was also high as they were not accustomed to the diet, the poor rations and the prolonged diving. Official concerns at these malpractices led to the introduction of legislation and regulations in 1875, and the Dutch authorities, in what is now Indonesia, forced the pearlers to pay a bond for each diver recruited from the islands.[15]

These restrictions led to a sharp drop in the number of Malays used on the boats. But with the increased use of diving gear the services of the Aboriginal divers were also dispensed with, and other Asian, particularly Japanese, divers were more frequently employed. This mixture of people gave Cossack a distinctly multiracial character. Historian Kathy De La Rue quotes one observer, Charles Flinders, who referred to the dockside crowd as:

> A few white-clothed Europeans and hundreds of coloured people, with Malays and Koepangers predominating … The creek was full of schooners and luggers, and the foreshore camps were swarming with coloured people … some of whom were clad only in brightly coloured 'sarongs', their brown bodies glistening in the sun, the Malays' jet black hair well plastered with coconut oil, making a striking contrast with the dull-looking Koepangers clad in trousers and shirt …[16]

It was difficult to estimate Cossack's population. For much of the year many residents were out with the fleet, and many were not included in the Census figures because they were not classed as 'Europeans'. Estimates range from 300 to 1000, the latter figure exceeding Roebourne's population. The pearling industry also affected the composition of the population, which by the mid-1890s was two-thirds Asian. Generally they lived apart from the Europeans in what was known as 'Chinatown' or 'Japtown', where they had homes, stores, grog shops and gambling dens. A few, however, became market gardeners, some owned pearling ships, and one Japanese family, the Muramatsu, became important citizens with commerce and pearling interests.[17]

Kathy De La Rue has commented that the Europeans saw the hard-working Chinese and Japanese storekeepers amass money and at the same time manage to keep their prices below those in the European stores and still live well. There was, however, little racial conflict, for the Asians were essential to the pearling industry. They also were of benefit to Europeans in other ways, primarily by running the market gardens and thus providing fresh vegetables in adequate quantities for the first time since the European settlement of the north-west.[18] Another flourishing industry with a largely European clientele was prostitution. Susan Hunt has noted that the victims and proprietors of at least three Cossack establishments were Japanese women.[19]

William Lambden Owen arrived in Cossack in 1887 and his reminiscences provide an early glimpse of life in the port. The public buildings included the stone post office and customs house, the Nor' West Mercantile Company's store and a small wooden church. Most buildings were chained to the ground to keep them from being blown away during the cyclone season. The chains were 'passed over the roof and bolted to boulders sunk in the ground around the foundations. Some preferred anchor chains, others steel cables'. Despite the chains, the houses were sometimes unroofed, seriously damaged or flattened, and small vessels were blown three or more kilometres inland. One of Owen's first tasks was the connection between Roebourne and Cossack by tramway, a task that would reduce freight charges and provide some relief to those who had to walk through the marshes.[20]

Cyclones wrought considerable damage at Cossack and elsewhere along the coast. The cyclone of January 1881 blew the customs house away and only the bar remained at the White Horse Hotel. But it was nothing compared to the cyclone of 2 April 1898, which lasted for 10 long hours and almost totally wrecked the town. Telegraphic communication between Cossack and Roebourne was quickly lost, and the tramway embankment across the marsh, and its approaches, bridges and railway lines, were washed away. Many of the residents had amazing escapes. Following the collapse of their houses, Messrs Hemingway and Thompson spent the night in a 1600-litre water tank. The Wilsons had a particularly harrowing time. They left their collapsing dwelling and proceeded to Paterson's residence a few hundred metres away.

A grave marker in the Japanese cemetery at Cossack

They were for four hours hanging on to the spinifex in the middle of the storm before they reached their destination. Wilson lost sight of his wife for an hour, and then only found her by chance.[21]

Enormous damage was done to the shipping. The *Beagle* was piled up on the rocks in front of the Weld Hotel, with the stern resting on the fallen jetty wall. After staying with the *Beagle* through the worst of the storm, Captain Lyons was washed overboard and received a 'severe knocking about by the floating wreckage as he struggled to land'. Of the other boats, the *Maggie Mollan* was a total wreck, the *Harriett* was high and dry on the beach, the *Croydon*, which was moored on the opposite side of the creek, was also carried onto high land, and the cutter *Rose* was washed up onshore. Smaller craft such as passenger boats were carried greater distances inland. The only boat to remain at her moorings was the police boat.

Almost all the town's buildings were destroyed or substantially damaged. The goods shed was 'now simply a frame with twisted portions of corrugated iron attached', the concrete floors had sunk and were lying in small sections, and the centre of the jetty had been washed away. The sea had burst in the doors of the goods shed and strewn cargo about, and the stores on the jetty destined for Condon were strewn from one end of the beach front to the other. Tee and Company's office, the Weld and White House hotels and Paxton's boarding house were scattered in all directions. The new custom's house and the residence of J Meagher had been unroofed and the buildings of the Nor' West Mercantile Company were flooded and considerable damage done to the stock. 'Japtown', recounted the *West Australian*, 'was one heap of ruins', and the flimsy iron and wood houses 'were felled like skittles'.

The lighthouse keeper on Jarman Island had an 'extremely trying time'. Seawater washed over the lighthouse and, aided by the wind, broke one of the glass lanterns. Water then poured in, putting out the light, and at one stage there was over one metre of water over the lighthouse floor. The roof of the quarters was stripped, the chimneys blown down, portions of the masonry shifted, the windows and doors blown in and the quarters swamped by the water that rushed downhill. Elsewhere on the island the storeroom and boat-shed disappeared, all stores were destroyed, and the lifeboat was carried out to sea.[22]

By the early 1900s Cossack was in definite decline. The pearling fleet had moved to Broome, the Kimberley and Pilbara gold rushes had diminished as prospectors moved on to other fields, and the inlet was too small to accommodate large shipping. In 1913 a leprosarium was established near the town and it operated there until 1931. The following year some of the buildings were sold off, but the main hospital buildings were not removed until 1947. A turtle-soup factory was established in the 1930s in the bond store and included a can-making facility. Several families and squatters stayed on until World War II. One lived at the schoolhouse and another in the police barracks; the courthouse was occupied by a Greek fishing family for many years. The Muramatsu, who owned the old bonds store, ran it as a general store until their internment in Darwin during World War II. After the war Mrs Muramatsu returned to live in the corner room at the back of the customs house, where she sold haberdashery and clothes.[23]

At the end of World War II many of the buildings, including the Weld Hotel, were pulled down for building supplies elsewhere in the district. The decline continued until the mid-1970s when the Cossack Project Committee was formed to begin restoration. This was followed by the Cossack Restoration and Development Committee, and then in 1988 the Westrek Foundation continued the work. A supervising committee was formed, which included members from government, the Roebourne Shire, Woodside Petroleum, Hamersley Iron and Robe River Iron Associates. At the time the Cossack project manager was Gerry MacGill and the caretaker/supervisor of Westrek was Brian Hoey. Brian recalled that in those early years Cossack was not very pleasant to live in. Sandflies were in plague proportions, and there were no trees or bushes, and many of those that were planted were attacked by large white ants. But he stayed, the trees eventually thrived and the sandfly problem lessened.[24]

With the exception of the old bonds store and the remains of Knight and Shenton's store, all other buildings in the main part of town have been restored. These include the stone courthouse, the customs house and bonds store, the stone post and telegraph office, Galbraith's store and the police barracks, cookhouse and lock-up. The barracks are now used for budget accommodation. Some distance from the town is the modest stone schoolhouse.

There are other historic sites along Perseverance Street, but in most cases there are few remains. Part of a verandah and crumbling garden walls are all that is left of a pearler's house, and the remnants of a wall, stone floor and stone path are the last vestiges of Mrs Pead's boarding house. In the Asian quarter the concrete pads of the laundry and concrete underground water tanks of the Muramatsu remain, but other house sites are more difficult to discern, being no more than a thin scatter of broken bottles and tins amongst the sand dunes. At the market garden a stone worker's hut, the stone walls surrounding the garden and the concrete underground storage tanks are still very much in evidence.[25]

The courthouse is the grandest building in Cossack, and perhaps the whole of the north-west. Built in 1895, it now houses the Shakespeare Hall Social History Museum. While wandering around the museum I chanced to meet Ellen DeHayr who, with her husband, was on a working holiday managing the budget accommodation at the old police barracks. She told me of several ghostly apparitions. On their arrival the main bedroom at the barracks had been very cold and she had a sensation of a definite presence and of someone watching her. At other times she had heard the piano playing at the court-house at night, despite the fact that the doors were locked and the DeHayrs were the only residents in the town.[26]

That there may be ghostly presences at Cossack does not entirely surprise, for death, and violent death at that, was commonplace. If caught out at sea in a cyclone, the small pearling vessels had almost no hope of surviving. The Cossack cemetery bears witness to some of these hardships, though many more perished at sea.[27] Cossack has been transformed by the efforts of Brian, Gerry and many other volunteers. The town has been saved from its slide into oblivion, and one day Onslow may have a similar experience.

Under Northern Skies

HALLS CREEK WAS THE SITE OF THE FIRST GOLD RUSH IN WESTERN Australia in 1885. At that time the nearest town was Derby, more than 500 kilometres to the north-west, and prospective miners were warned of the need to be well provisioned and of the dangers of both the dry and wet seasons. Early reports of gold finds were exaggerated and those who dashed to the area were often poorly equipped and ill prepared.[1] Harriet Day, the daughter of the then Government Resident in Darwin, commented that nearly all the old miners who could raise enough money to buy stores had rushed to the diggings either overland or by steamer. Many also travelled across the Northern Territory from Queensland.[2]

One of the most interesting accounts was by a Tasmanian who returned from the diggings late in 1886. He arrived at the 'canvas town' of Wyndham, where the horses had to be swum onshore from the boats for about 600 metres. At the time it had a population of about 2000 and was 'raising itself to the dignity of a swamp with a whisky shop floating in the middle'. On the track to the diggings nearly every man had one or more horses and there was a variety of conveyances such as wagons, carts, hand-carts and wheelbarrows. Most men turned back before they reached the diggings, and past the Eighty Mile Camp they came across at least sixty drays that had been smashed or abandoned because the horses had died. On arrival they found 300 men at Halls Creek, another 200 at McPhee's camp, 200 at Brockmans Gully and between 500 and 600 at Black Elvire. Despite the tough conditions, it seems that good order prevailed. In his three months there the Tasmanian observer never saw a quarrel or dispute that was not amicably settled.[3]

Some of the men were soon destitute, and in August 1886 a fund-raising concert was held at Wyndham. The following day two ships steamed out of port with 60 or more penniless men among the passengers. Some men were forced to break stones for the public works agent while they waited to hear if

The remains of the public offices at Halls Creek look like a collection of elongated anthills.

passages on boats were available. There were no reliable means of estimating how many were on the field; some were arriving as others were leaving and some were still on the track. The numbers were somewhere between 1000 and 4000, probably closer to the former.[4]

It did not take long before the first clashes occurred between the local Aboriginal people and the Europeans, allegedly over the abduction of an Aboriginal woman. One of the earliest arrivals on the field, Barney Lamond, described a spearing incident at the appropriately named Spear Creek, in which one European was killed. A party of miners rode out after the alleged culprits, and afterwards Lamond wrote that four Aboriginal people were killed and several wounded.[5] However, these numbers are likely to be a gross understatement. One other witness, Fred Burdett, described in detail the massacre of all adult males at the main Aboriginal camp, including any others whose path the miners chanced to cross.[6]

The Kimberley field had its share of legendary characters, but perhaps the most famous was Russian Jack, who in later years achieved notoriety on the Murchison goldfield. Many of the miners pushed wooden wheelbarrows laden with their possessions to the diggings. According to one account, within about 30 kilometres of the field, Russian Jack came upon another man lying completely exhausted by the side of his barrow. He picked up the man's load and placed it on the top of his own, exclaiming that if the stranger was too tired to walk, he could jump on too — an offer the man declined![7]

The good order commented upon by the Tasmanian digger was confirmed by the warden, who proclaimed Halls Creek the most orderly field he had known. He attributed this to the predominance of older, more stable miners and the poverty of the field. If Fred Burdett's account can be believed this assessment must have been made prior to Christmas of that year, which erupted into an orgy of drunkenness and fighting. By this time a number of reef mines had been opened up and small settlements established nearby. At Ruby Creek the population was larger than at Halls Creek and there were substantial buildings, a police camp and a progress committee.[8]

David Carnegie, an explorer and later a government minister, visited Halls Creek in the late 1890s. By then the town consisted of the post and telegraph office, warden's office, courthouse, a hospital, gaol, police station, sergeant's house, butcher's shop and house, a store and a hotel. All the buildings were constructed from mud bricks and galvanised iron. As well, there were several 'nomadic dwellings', such as tents, humpies and drays. Carnegie described Christmas and New Year's Day as great days of revel, with athletic sports and horseraces. His comments on Aboriginal people were, however, very unsympathetic, even by nineteenth-century standards.[9]

By 1908 the last of the mines had closed, although a few prospectors lingered on. In her book, *Old Halls Creek*, Cathie Clement retells one visitor's comments about the amount of drinking in the town and the sight of the publican shooting fowls in the main street in preparation for Christmas dinner. By this time the town's fortunes were more closely linked to the pastoral industry than mining, and concerns with cattle killing and a wish to rationalise existing welfare services led the government to purchase Moola Bulla Station and relocate many Aboriginal people there. These people included children of mixed descent (who had been taken from their Aboriginal mothers), those living a more nomadic lifestyle, and those who were being punished for relatively trivial offences.[10]

Perhaps the only real improvement in the early part of the twentieth century was the establishment of an Australian Inland Mission (AIM) nursing home. Two staff members arrived in 1918, and the new hospital was constructed not long thereafter, partly from local and government contributions. The previous year the unfortunate postmaster was forced to operate on a seriously injured stockman following instructions received over the wire from a doctor in Fremantle.[11] In the 1930s the writer Ion Idriess described Halls Creek as a 'tiny group of houses … squeezed to the very creek edge by the small steep hills'. He also commented on the number of Aboriginal people working in the town as labourers, wood-cutting, drawing water for a private house, gardening, or herding goats and donkeys.[12]

World War II awoke Halls Creek from its slumber. The base station for the Flying Doctor Service was shifted from Wyndham to Halls Creek to put it out of reach of Japanese air raids, and signallers from the North Australia

Observer Unit were located in the town. However, little maintenance was undertaken on the buildings, and a number of them fell into disrepair. Following the war a site was proposed near the airport about 14 kilometres away, and by the early 1950s most businesses and services had relocated to the new town. A few residents, including the publican, stayed a little longer, but by 1960 they too had left.[13]

A number of people tried to conserve what was left of the old town, but once stripped of their iron and timber the mud-brick buildings deteriorated rapidly.[14] Today only the walls and fireplaces of the public offices are still standing. From some angles the building looks like a collection of elongated anthills. With each successive wet season more of the mud bricks disappear, and without roofing the remains will very soon wash away into the dust from whence they came.

From Halls Creek my journey continued to the Top End of the Northern Territory, to an area north of Pine Creek known as the Northern Goldfields Loop. There are a number of abandoned or nearly abandoned towns in this area, all of which were associated with the goldfield's boom in the Territory from the 1870s on. Several were also associated with the construction of the railway to Pine Creek during the 1880s, and the construction of large military camps during World War II.

Perhaps the most important of these settlements was at Brocks Creek.[15] Brocks Creek was a goldfield centre from early 1873 on, and in the late 1890s it was the main service centre for several nearby mines, such as the Zapopan and the Howley, each of which had its own mining camps. Zapopan was lauded as one of the most promising mines in the Territory, but was thwarted by high water levels and refractory ore, and the loss of much of the gold in the tailings. It closed in 1907.[16]

Brocks Creek boasted one of the largest Chinatowns on the goldfield, and included the largest and most elaborate temple outside of Darwin. Timothy Jones, in his book *The Chinese in the Northern Territory*, has recounted the reminiscences of a visitor in 1931, who recalled that the walls were covered in Chinese characters painted in gold representing those who had passed away, and who had paid £25 for this memorial. In 1897 a township was formally surveyed about half a kilometre east of the Chinatown site. It had a police station, railway station and station master's residence, several stores, a racecourse, hotel and a Social and Mutual Improvement Society, which aimed to provide concerts, readings, chess, draughts and other entertainments and activities for the residents.[17]

The hotel was established by Fannie Hays and Thomas Crush, two of the Territory's more colourful and enterprising pioneers. Tom was secretary of the local racing and cricket club and the local branch of the North Australian League, and represented the Territory in the South Australian Parliament from 1908 to 1910. He passed away in 1913, and Fannie married her third husband, Harry Haynes, in 1916, and stayed on at Brocks Creek for another 30 years. In addition to backing many struggling prospectors, she also ran the post and telephone service for many years.[18]

In the nineteenth century the Territory goldfields were almost completely dominated by Chinese miners and entrepreneurs. An acute shortage of labour in the mining industry had led the administration to import Chinese labourers from Singapore. Their employment was to be under strict contract conditions. However, some of the men were obviously unsuited to the work, others became ill and some deserted and went fossicking on their own account. It was later revealed that some men had been forced to board the ship by Chinese agents and storekeepers to whom they were indebted. Worse still, by the time the men arrived most of the mining companies had collapsed or were about to do so, and little work was available. In addition, some of the companies did not pay the men.[19]

As a result of these depressed conditions, many Chinese went mining for themselves, and most of them opted to stay on in the Territory as gold prospectors rather than return home at the completion of their contracts. One of these was Ping Que, who had arrived in the Territory as either a headman or merchant. He commenced mining at the Union Reefs in 1875 and subsequently entered into a partnership with a European miner before mining again on his own account, using imported Chinese labourers. Before long he was the leading merchant and one of the leading miners in the Territory. He also owned stores and butcher's shops, and was involved in transport and in the adjudication of disputes between Chinese factions. Other Chinese were also engaged in a similar range of activities, including market gardening.[20]

The main increase in the number of Chinese on the goldfields was, however, due to a rich alluvial find in 1877, which became known as the Twelve Mile or Chinaman's Rush. A number of the men made enough money to

Remains of the Pine Creek railway, near Grove Hill

Chinese hut at Twelve Mile
village

return wealthy to either Hong Kong or Macau or to set up businesses elsewhere in the Territory. Subsequently, a large number of Chinese were also employed to work on the construction of the Darwin to Pine Creek railway, and by 1888 there were 6000 Chinese in the Territory. By that time the Chinese were reported to be in almost complete possession of the known goldfields, with every kind of labour and a large number of businesses entirely in their hands.[21]

Timothy Jones has commented upon the degree of mutual acceptance between the Chinese and Europeans on the goldfields. The main social event was the annual races and sports meeting, which was attended by the majority of European, Chinese and Aboriginal locals. At least one horserace was reserved for Chinese horsemen. In addition, it was also not unusual for Europeans and Chinese to join forces in mining ventures. At Brocks Creek in 1899 the Chinese opened a new racecourse and organised the meeting. The program included races for horses owned and ridden by Europeans.[22]

At Brocks Creek, European and Chinese communities existed until World War II, when the localities were evacuated and occupied by the military, who destroyed most of the buildings, including the Kwong Sing Di Temple. Today, all that remains is the concrete floor of the temple, two concrete blocks for the front of the building and part of the stone plinths on which two large stone lions stood. At the main town site the concrete floors for the military establishments, the police station and Fannie Hay's hotel are still visible. Several large water tanks and some barbed wire fencing are all that remain of a large military prison for recalcitrant soldiers, which was built near the town.

Grove Hill is the only inhabited settlement on the Goldfields Loop, and the hotel, now run by Stan and Mary Haeusler, is the only place of replenishment for the thirsty traveller. The original town of Grove Hill was located about four kilometres south of the current hotel site, and in 1887, in addition to the mining plant, it boasted a hotel, various stores, a blacksmith's shop and an assayer. However, when the Pine Creek railway was built the site was bypassed, and a new settlement of the same name was constructed at the railway siding. In the 1930s Bill and Margaret Lucy used galvanised iron and material from the old tramway to build the hotel, which incorporated their original cottage.[23] The unique architecture of the hotel makes it one of the gems of the north.

Further south is Burrundie, which by the end of 1884 had been surveyed as a suitable site for the main township on the goldfields. It was centrally placed, as it was only one or two hours travel by horse from Yam Creek, the Union Reefs and Pine Creek, and close to the Mount Wells mines. The town was laid out with 24 streets. In 1885 a police station and post office were constructed, and a store was opened the following year. In 1888 a hospital was built. The doctor's wife described the town as consisting of a store, police station, an inn, a small bank and a warden's house. There were not more than six or seven women within 80 kilometres of the town. Burrundie was also the main base camp for the railway gangs, and a large Chinese camp was located nearby.[24]

The demand for explosives during the building of the railway led to the construction of two of the Territory's more remarkable pieces of architecture. One powder magazine was built like a large burial vault, with the storage room located underground and thus susceptible to flooding during the wet season. In keeping with this style of architecture the other was built above ground like a large church building, albeit one without any windows. By 1900 Burrundie's population had all but vanished, and by 1912 most of the buildings had either fallen down or been removed to Pine Creek.[25]

Further south is the majestic 10-head battery site at Spring Creek, and further south again is the Chinese village site at the Twelve Mile, which was the location of a gold rush by Chinese miners. There are ten or more hut sites, one of which has substantial chimney remains, and a pig oven, which suggests that a small temple would have been located nearby. Twelve Mile would have been typical of many of the Chinese villages on the goldfields, except that in this instance there was an abundance of stone with which to construct the buildings. Close to the village is a dam and water race.

South of the Goldfields Loop is the abandoned mining town of Maranboy. Although the town is easy to access, it is on Aboriginal land and permission must be obtained from the Northern Land Council. Tin was found at Maranboy in 1913, but the new mines were 180 kilometres from the railhead at Pine Creek, and there were no formed tracks. By March of the following year there were about 50 to 60 miners working the field, but mining was confined to bagging the richest and most easily obtained surface stone and carting it to a dilapidated crushing machine some 110 kilometres away. Otherwise the miners had to stockpile the ore. However, many of them were unable to wait for long periods without funds and were forced to leave.[26]

To add to the miners' woes there was often a lack of food supplies at the local store. A miner complained in the *Northern Territory Times and Gazette* that it was almost impossible to buy flour, and that there was only canary seed left. Worse still, within months of opening the battery in 1916 a malaria epidemic struck the community, resulting in the death of several inhabitants, including four-year-old Audrey Stutterd, the daughter of the battery manager. Contract labour refused to travel to the field, and with no medical facilities closer than Pine Creek, many miners left town. A temporary hospital was set up quickly to stem the flow of miners, and in the following year an AIM (Australian Inland Mission) hospital was built, staffed by two nurses.[27]

In 1919 there were 37 Europeans at Maranboy and 30 Aboriginal people. However, plunging metal prices almost caused a cessation of mining and by 1922 only nine miners remained. Prices eventually rose, only to fall again, reaching their lowest level during the Depression year of 1931. In that year Christmas was described as the poorest ever known, and to make matters worse the hospital was moved to Katherine. In the early 1940s the price of tin rose and the population again increased. Yet the end was in sight, and for the most part the mines merely lingered on until their closure in 1965.[28]

Unlike the northern goldfields there were no Chinese at Maranboy. Legislation passed in 1886 precluded Asians from mining on any field discovered by a European for a period of two years. Sue Harlow, in her book *Tin Gods*, has commented that this legislation had significant implications as the miners came to rely on Aboriginal labour, which in turn became vital to the field's survival. Large groups of the Jaowyn people would gather at Maranboy at various times for ceremonies and trade, and many Aboriginal people built their camps close to the town, for example, outside Dan Dillon's store, the families working on his mining claim and in his store.[29]

In 1943 the nine European miners left at Maranboy employed 24 Aboriginal men on their claims and maintained their dependants. Aboriginal miners did the bulk of the hard work, with the white miners acting in the capacity of supervisors. A local Aboriginal man, Spider Brennan, recalled that each European miner employed between two or three of his people.[30] Mick O'Reilly, in his book *Bowyangs and Boomerangs*, described the Aboriginal miners as 'very adaptable and proficient in all classes of mining', and in prospecting.[31] Today, apart from the police station and residence, Maranboy is a ghost town, and the land has been returned to the Jaowyn, who live at the nearby settlement of Barunga.

Sue Harlow has also commented on the role of women at Maranboy. Of particular note were the AIM nurses, who had an enormous impact on the

Rugged bushland near Halls Creek in Western Australia's Kimberley Region

The vault-like entrance to one of the powder magazines at Burrundie in the Northern Territory

This defunct ten-head battery at Maranboy presides over the landscape like a resplendent 'monarch of the bush'.

At Arltunga you can still see the remains of the post office (foreground) and the manager's house (background).

Mine openings at the Great Western
Mine, Arltunga

One of the many stone-building
remains at Arltunga

The assayer's house at
Arltunga village

The remains of part of the Mabel
mill are some of the many old
pieces of mining equipment
scattered around Ravenswood.

daily lives of all residents and those of the surrounding district. In 1918 the hospital was overflowing with 30 cases of malaria in one month and a few years later all the miners were suffering from this illness. Even the nurses fell prey. Dysentery and influenza epidemics, mining and other accidents all took their toll. As well as tending the sick, the nurses provided a 'homely atmosphere' where bachelor miners could call in for a cup of tea, cake and a chat. Their well-stocked library was appreciated, but their efforts to hold Sunday evening services were not as well received. Mick O'Reilly recalled visiting the hospital in the evenings for a social visit and to listen to some music.[32]

The European wives on the field also had demanding lives, and without the help of Aboriginal domestic labour it is likely that many would have left. Nonetheless, the boarding house at Maranboy was run by a European woman, and police officers' wives were expected to undertake some of the daily routine police work, particularly while their husbands were away on patrol. They also acted as postmistress. On the smaller mining claims, some women worked with their husbands, and Aboriginal women also occasionally worked in the mines.[33]

Those women married to men working at the battery lived in better homes, and had the use of running water and electricity when the battery was running. Other women were not as well off, and some lived in crudely built bark huts with furniture made from packing cases and empty petrol tins.[34] Vanda Marshall recalled that her parents' kitchen had bark walls lined with hessian and pasted with newspaper or magazine illustrations, and other walls adorned with curtains and bedspreads and the ceilings with calico.[35]

The hazards of family life at Maranboy were brought to my attention by the 'story of the little girl'. On my arrival I was informed by the resident police officer that the AIM building was haunted. The building was used as the police station and police residence after 1931, and several police officers had either seen or heard a little girl talking and playing outside the police office at night, but on looking outside had found no one. Ron Miller, from the Katherine police, recalled that one officer was so traumatised by his experiences that he had taken compassionate leave. Ron commented that many thought that the ghost was that of little Audrey Stutterd, who died in 1917. Audrey's brother had, however, remarked that the ghost was not Audrey, for she had dark hair, but another girl with blonde hair with whom Audrey had played, and who had later died at the hospital.[36]

Rosemary Steele was stationed with her husband at Maranboy several years ago, when the police station was still located on the ground floor of the former AIM building, and the living quarters were upstairs. She recounted how one evening she heard a young girl talking with her small boy, who should have been in bed asleep. On approaching the boy's room she heard a child's footsteps running away down the corridor. The boy was in fact asleep and her two-year-old daughter was also asleep in her cot.[37] Whether or not one believes in ghosts, the story is well and truly part of Maranboy's folklore.

On my arrival I was informed by the resident police officer that the AIM building was haunted

47

East of Alice

AT THE HEART OF THE CONTINENT, ABOUT 100 KILOMETRES EAST OF Alice Springs, the remains of Arltunga and Winnecke are a stark reminder of the incredible lure of gold. These former goldmining towns had at the most only between 500 and 600 residents, and were extremely isolated. Nevertheless, the towns played an important part in opening up Central Australia for European settlement. At one time Arltunga was larger than Alice Springs, which remained little more than a telegraph station, albeit a very important one, for many years. Today, both Arltunga and Winnecke are totally abandoned.

Almost all the buildings were constructed from golden-coloured local stone. The largest cluster of buildings at Arltunga is at the government works site. Here, the first building to be encountered is the assayer's office, with its elaborate kitchen at the rear. Next to it is the manager's residence, which is the largest domestic building on the field. It had two large rooms and a verandah back and front. Next to it is the post office, which originally had three wattle-and-daub walls. Now, only the chimney and one stone wall are standing. The remains of two other buildings are nearby.

The battery site includes the stone housing for the boiler, the boiler and foundations for the 10-head battery and engine. Nearby is the gold room and offices, which are located in the largest building on the field. The assayer worked in one of the rooms, and the other two were offices for the manager and assayer. Other buildings in the area include a second assay office, which was built in 1905. The miners had complained that at the first office the ground shook when the battery was working, making it impossible for the assayer to weigh the gold and pay them correctly. Further away is the blacksmith's building, including a forge, and several other huts.

Some distance from these buildings is the police complex, which includes a substantial stone building, the remains of another building behind it, the

The assay office in Arltunga, part of what was once the largest town in central Australia

single-cell gaol and a building reputed to be the police tracker's quarters. Originally, an old store building served as the police station. However, by 1907 Mounted Constable Dowdy was complaining about its condition, for the pug had fallen out between the slabs and the galvanised iron on the roof was full of holes. There had been heavy rains and the stores, private belongings and station books and papers had been badly damaged. One room at the station was used as both office and bedroom and occasionally the lock-up, with the prisoner chained to the leg of the constable's bed. The present complex, including the gaol, dates from the 1920s.[1]

At the Crossroads only one building is left standing. The well-preserved baker's oven suggests that it was most likely a store. Several other buildings, including the Glencoe Hotel, which was built in 1910, can also be seen. This hotel did not exactly provide five-star accommodation. Linen was an unknown quantity, and there were no sheets, tablecloths or mattresses. One person asking for a bed was given a blanket and free permission to sleep where he liked, with the exception of the bar. Each room was divided by an iron partition, which did not allow for much privacy. The bathhouse, with insufficient room to change, necessitated a 'wild dash' in 'Nature's garb' when the occasion demanded it.[2] There are a number of other buildings at Arltunga and the White Range diggings, for instance, at the Joker Gorge and Great Western mine areas, and two cemeteries.

Store and bakery remains at
the Crossroads, Arltunga

Winnecke is located on a dirt road about 40 kilometres north-west of
Arltunga, on 'The Garden' Station of Andy and Jane Hays. Our journey to
Winnecke was memorable in more ways than one, for we were caught in a
persistent rain squall and on the return trip to Arltunga the clay-based track
was like a sheet of water. The tyre lugs became quickly blocked with mud and
even in four-wheel drive the vehicle had very little traction, sometimes slip-
ping sideways in a crab-like motion across the track. It continued to rain all
that afternoon and night, providing a reminder of the hazards of travel in
such isolated areas — now as well as in earlier days.

The cemetery, located some distance away from Winnecke, is an intriguing
sight, with lone wooden palings tilted at angles, and others lying prostrate. At
the main village, much more so than at Arltunga, there is always the prospect
of discovery, for there are no restorations, no set paths to follow and no sign-
posts. Some huts are substantial, others merely a few mounds of stones and
low walls. Since my last visit some buildings had deteriorated a little; in one
case a fallen tree branch had dislodged part of a wall, and in another, part of
the wall of the building had fallen away. But it still remains a fascinating area.

Arltunga had its origins in an abortive ruby rush in the Harts Range to the
north of Alice Springs, and at nearby Glen Annie Gorge in 1885 and 1886.
At the latter location the sands of the creek bed were strewn with stones that

Lone wooden palings and grave
markers at the Winnecke
cemetery

looked like rubies. After what must have seemed like an eternity the 'rubies' were declared to be garnets and totally worthless. However, some of the miners stayed on and prospected for gold at a spot called Paddy's Rock Hole, and by 1888 several reef mines had been discovered. Two storekeepers/butchers were established at the Rock Hole, but by the end of the year the field was almost deserted because of water shortages.[3]

By 1890 there were three small crushing plants, only one of which was really effective, and only three reef mines of any note. Much of the mining was for alluvial gold, which came from shallow workings in the gullies, the miners paying as much as one-fifth of their gold to obtain water for washing. Some miners were doing well and making about 12 shillings a day, but most were making little more than 'tucker'.[4] Arltunga was a far cry from the rich alluvial fields found elsewhere on the continent, and the returns appear to have been a poor reward for the hardships endured.

Eventually, there were some 'home improvements'. By 1890 a store and butcher were opened by J Harding, and by 1891 a monthly mail run had been established with Alice Springs. Harding was a mail contractor and he also owned a team of horses for carting the ore. By the following year good permanent water was found for the first time, and by the mid-1890s there were at least two publicans on the field and several other butchers. In 1894 mining

51

was encouraged by the provision of a weekly allowance to several men to encourage them to prospect in the Arltunga–Winnecke Depot area. The following year a warden was appointed.[5]

Following representations from the miners, HYL Brown, the South Australian Geologist, visited the field in 1896 to assess the prospects for future development, in particular the clamour for a government battery and cyanide plant. The journey was motivated not so much by the stunning riches to be won, but by the high unemployment of the 1890s and the loss of many men to the Western Australian goldfields. As a consequence, construction of a government battery and cyanide plant, together with an elaborate complex of stone buildings, was approved.

The task of transporting the equipment and men was prodigious, and was only effected by the hire of camels from the railhead at Oodnadatta in South Australia, about 600 kilometres south. A first instalment of men and machinery arrived in January 1897, the next in February 1898 and a third in March, the latter arriving after a journey of about three months. A fire in the Oodnadatta goods shed burnt much of the remaining stores and equipment and it took over a year to replace them. The battery and plant were opened in February 1898. With the news that a government battery was to be erected, alluvial mining was abandoned, although it was resumed periodically when the battery was inoperative for whatever reason.[6]

About this time gold was discovered at nearby White Range, and soon most of the stone crushed at the government battery came from this source. These discoveries heralded a brief period of hope and anticipation, but also induced conflict between the miners and pastoralists. One pastoralist complained about the 'great amount of drunkedness [sic] and unseemly behaviour' at the mining camp and the practice of horse-duffing and cattle stealing. He suggested strongly that a police presence was necessary, and in response the first mounted constable arrived in early 1899. The constable described the men as 'very orderly and quiet', but admitted that this may not have been the case previously. Some months later he had a different view, describing the miners, with only a very few exceptions, as of a 'very low class'.

By 1900 severe drought conditions almost brought all work to a standstill, for the horse teams that were used for carting the ore from the mines needed feed and water, and both were in short supply. Camels were eventually used, but this was resented by the horse-team owners, one of whom was Harding, and the miners, to whom he allowed credit at his store. Warden Mueller also took the miners' side, but these arguments were rejected by the government. Harding also decided to raise the price of fresh beef, and the battery manager retaliated by asking if his employees could run 50 goats on the reserve near the battery to improve their diet. In retaliation, Harding attempted to run his herd of 350 goats, but he was prevented by the police.[7]

Good rains in 1901 revitalised the mines, bringing more men to the fields, but the increased activity soon meant that the battery well needed deepening. When the boiler collapsed later that year, the battery could not be worked and

One pastoralist complained about the 'great amount of drunkedness [sic] and unseemly behaviour' at the mining camp and the practice of horse-duffing and cattle stealing

the miners could not be paid. This event would have brought the field to an end except that the manager advanced monies on the ore raised. By mid-1902 the battery was back at work, by which time gold had been discovered at Winnecke's Depot.

The population at Winnecke rose from about 20 at the end of the year to about 300 in a few months, but supplies were low and the only well was contaminated by stock, which caused a typhoid outbreak. A Winnecke Vigilance Committee approached the government on the lack of sanitary arrangements and the need to protect the water supplies. A doctor was appointed, but this was too late for some of the victims, four of whom died. The doctor referred fulsomely to 'Excrement of Human Excreta being deposited promiscuously ad lib in every direction'. Following the doctor's departure, the policeman at Arltunga was appointed Health Inspector to supervise the maintenance of proper sanitary arrangements. During this period there were mixed reports on the field. One correspondent suggested that if he had a choice between going back for six months in summer and going to gaol he would take the latter, with a 'few lashes into the bargain'.[8]

One of the few accounts of life at Winnecke is from Doris Blackwell in her book *Alice on the Line*.[9] The exact date of her visit is unclear, but as she describes the workings of the battery, it could not have been before 1904, the year it was constructed, and may have been as late as 1905. Her descriptions are not particularly flattering, though they are picturesque. In one breath she describes Winnecke as a 'calico village, a straggling land of tents and bough shelters'. Elsewhere, she describes it as having an air of 'ugly impermanence', as looking very much like a 'shanty town which would well have disappeared in the first dust storm', and as a 'wild west shanty town'.

Her father, who was the postmaster at Alice Springs, recommended that a post office be established at Winnecke. Prior to that telegrams had to be delivered by foot, usually by an Aboriginal local who walked about 160 kilometres there and back in four to five days. On Doris's first visit she went in style by buggy, and stayed several days with the battery manager and his wife, who lived in two large square tents, partly protected from the sun by a brush wall. House furniture was mainly improvised, but also included deck chairs and a small portable organ.

Saturday night was shopping night in the tent stores scattered throughout the village, after which the men repaired to the hotel for refreshments. The miners carried long calico bags slung over their shoulders for their purchases, each of which was tied off and separated from the others by a series of knots. The miners carried hurricane lanterns that bobbed around like glow-worms. On Doris's second visit a few years later the town was completely abandoned, the stores, houses and hotel disappearing as 'if picked up in a whirlwind and scattered across the nearby Simpson Desert'.

The Winnecke rush was the catalyst for Robert Frearson's 1903 *Guide and Handbook to the Arltunga and Winnecke's Depot Goldfields*. It reads rather like a bushman's *Guide Bleu* to Central Australia. He describes part of the

This slowly crumbling ruin is the largest building left at Winnecke.

journey north from Oodnadatta as 'hard pulling through sand', and warns the indigent to stay at home, for without considerable funds they would almost 'undoubtedly have tremendous hardships to encounter'. The cost of provisions was estimated at 50 to 100 per cent dearer than in Adelaide. He nevertheless commented that Winnecke was 'a magnificent asset for the State' [South Australia]. His claim that some finds had yielded 15 ounces to the ton and that others had yielded between two and ten ounces would have encouraged more than a few prospective miners to throw caution to the wind.[10]

There was a rush of miners to both Winnecke and Arltunga, where some new mines were opened. An attempt was made to establish a proper township at the Crossroads, where the White Range, Paddy's Rock Hole, battery and Claraville roads joined. To add to the optimism, some of the larger mining companies had been attracted to the area, in particular the White Range field. At least two storekeepers were established at the Crossroads by 1903. However, by the middle of that year plans for large-scale development of the White Range field were abandoned.

By 1904 there were about 40 men at White Range and there was enough interest in the Winnecke field to encourage the erection of a battery. Despite this, from 1904 on the Arltunga battery rarely worked more than half the time, and the workload of both the battery manager and the warden decreased. While this had little effect on the manager, there were increasing complaints about Warden Mueller's drunkenness and neglect, and in 1906 he was dismissed, and later gaoled in a separate incident for embezzlement. Manager O'Grady took over Mueller's duties as warden.

Drunkenness was not confined to the mining fraternity. In 1905 a complaint was made concerning the behaviour of Corporal Nalty at the Arltunga races that year. He was described as laying at the back of one of the sheds on the course with two Aboriginal men standing guard over him. The observer commented that it was 'something disgusting, one man laying drunk in the sand with his trousers down over his knees. I went twice and covered his nakedness. Others using disgusting language and no police officer to keep order, ladies could not come near the crowd.' As he was about to retire, no official action was taken. Warden O'Grady also had his problems. In 1911, together with one of the storekeepers, he was accused by Constable Dowdy of sly-grog selling. His position worsened when he asked several stockowners, including Dowdy, to remove stock from the common reserve. He left Arltunga a few years later.

An aspect of interest on the Arltunga field was the role of Aboriginal people. In 1896 they were reported to be working for Europeans, and in 1900 Constable Johnstone commented that many of the miners used Aboriginal women to do the washing and cooking. Sub-Inspector Clode from Port Augusta reported in 1905 that a number of Aboriginal locals were employed by the miners at White Range. The Aboriginal people shared their rations with their old and frail. He also commented that there were two or three Europeans living with Aboriginal women. Clode decried this situation, as he considered that the miners would eventually abandon the women and any children, who would then be a burden on the state. The works manager later commented that the Europeans could not get along without Aboriginal help.[11]

One of the few accounts of life on the Arltunga field is RG Kimber's biography of Walter Smith, who was born at Arltunga in 1893. His mother, Topsy, was Aboriginal, and with her mother she had spent time mining for alluvial gold with a dry blower in the north of South Australia. Walter had many Aboriginal friends, and as there was no school they spent much time together. He remembered the arrival of Hong, the Chinese market gardener from Alice Springs, who travelled to Arltunga once a week. Another weekly event was the arrival of the camel train from distant Oodnadatta, with all types of goods.

Walter worked for a year or more for Harding, who, he recalled, had made his start in life by stealing 800 head of cattle from a Kidman property and then riding deep into the Simpson Desert, later selling the cattle in the north. While only a young boy, Walter rode with Billy Coulthard and witnessed to his horror the cold-blooded murder of two Aboriginal elders. On his return he worked with his father at the Great Western and Joker mines. His father died in 1914, probably from overwork and worry as the mines began to fail. The family had no alternative but to leave for Alice Springs, where Walter worked with an Afghan cameleer before embarking on other bush assignments.

Walter also recounted his memories of Sandy McDonald, the owner of the Glencoe Arms Hotel. Originally a stockman, he had been a 'bum-boat runner' (seller of illicit grog), horse-duffer, miner and card sharp. He was a big man, weighing 144 kilograms and standing just 172 centimetres tall. Invariably he was clothed in a battered felt hat, an unbuttoned, sleeveless, dark grey flannel shirt and an enormous pair of pink and white striped pyjama trousers, and a pair of unlaced boots with no socks. He had been a member of the notorious gang of men known as 'the ragged thirteen', who stole what food and equipment they needed and fought their way from the Top End of the Territory to the Halls Creek rush in Western Australia in the 1880s.[12]

RB Plowman also documents Arltunga's declining years. He refers to the owner of the Glencoe Arms Hotel as Sandy Myrtle, but it is definitely the same person described by Walter Smith. He recalls Sandy being 'a most vindictive man, who showed no mercy to his enemies, but was also hospitable and generous when the opportunity presented itself'. He must have been an awesome sight, for apart from his singular mode of dress, he had a permanent limp and an 'almost equally permanent hand-rolled cigarette stuck apparently by adhesion … on his lower lip'.

Plowman described Arltunga as hardly a township at all. Opposite the hotel was the store, and about a kilometre away was a small cottage, and to the south were the police station and a cottage containing a family. Further south again was the post office and mining warden's residence and battery. There was only one European woman on the field. At the time of Plowman's visit a Sunday morning service was held at the bar of the hotel, which all and sundry attended.[13]

By 1913 only seven men were working the alluvial and all the reef claims were deserted. The battery was inoperative by the 1920s and in 1944 the police station was closed. During the Depression years and the early 1940s there was renewed interest in Arltunga and Winnecke, and a small crushing plant was erected at Claraville. At Winnecke a number of mines were opened by Pasquale (Patsy) Ciccone and members of his family in the 1930s and a battery was installed.[14] But from 1950s on the Arltunga goldfield was practically deserted, apart from the occasional fossicker or prospector.

An account in the early 1950s confirms this general picture of decay, describing the shells of stone houses, and ledger pages from mining records lying on the ground. But there was one inhabitant. In the narrow police cell, a 'lean and bony sunburnt man of indefinite age' was propped up on a rough stretcher reading a paperback novel with the aid of a hurricane lamp. Len, as he was called, was a prospector, and made enough from gold to keep him in provisions. Asked why he lived in the lock-up, he replied that he used to live in one of the cottages, but it gave him the creeps at night looking up and down the rows of empty houses, so he moved in to the cell where it was 'more cosy-like'.[15]

In 1977 Arltunga was declared a historic reserve and several buildings were restored by the National Parks and Wildlife Service. Isolation and an arid climate have helped preserve many of the buildings at both Arltunga and Winnecke. Together, the two towns have more well-preserved building remains than many of their once much larger counterparts elsewhere in Australia. In the barren landscape they are a silent, haunting memorial to those whose optimism saw both towns briefly flourish then fade.

QUEENSLAND

Previous page: Part of the
infrastructure from the Havelock
battery, near Forsayth; yet another
lonely sentinel to the past, slowly
crumbling into the bush

Archibald Wilson's Lament

RAVENSWOOD IS LOCATED ABOUT 150 KILOMETRES INLAND FROM Townsville in North Queensland. Old buildings, abandoned mine workings and towering brick chimneystacks are scattered throughout the town. Some buildings, particularly the two hotels, are large and ornate. The splendid Imperial Hotel is blessed with a set of swinging doors at the front in true 'wild west' style, and a great assortment of furniture from the early 1900s, including iron-framed beds. Other impressive buildings and extensive street kerbing all strongly suggest a more prosperous past. Trees and shrubs are largely absent, except for the ubiquitous rubber vine that shrouds everything in a tangle of greenery.

The Railway Hotel, Thorp's buildings, the courthouse, school of arts building, the Catholic church and the ambulance station are further evidence of busier times. Thorp's buildings were erected in 1905 by mining magnate Sydney Thorp and used mainly by Holliman's, who sold machinery, hardware and timber. Across the road from Thorp's were Browne's buildings, and in particular his grand 1880s hotel. It had 50 bedrooms, billiard rooms, writing rooms, sale rooms for travelling salesmen and a surgery for visiting dentists. Now all that remains are the steps.

The school of arts building was erected in 1882 and was the social centre of the town for many years. Local and professional plays were performed, there were talks and concerts, and silent films were shown, accompanied by the piano music of the Delaney sisters from the Imperial Hotel. Next door is the school of arts library, and behind the library are the remains of a large shop, which was originally a cordial shop attached to Watson's Aerated Waters factory. The top storey of this building was known as Malpass' Hall, the scene of many dances during Ravenswood's heyday.[1]

Also spread throughout the town and environs is a number of miners' huts; on the road to the Totley mine are the remnants of either the operating

Main street, Ravenswood, 1905; only a fraction of these buildings remain.
(*Queensland Department of Mines Annual Report*, 1905)

theatre or morgue for the hospital. The extensive mining remains include several brick chimneystacks for the boilers and, at the Mabel mill, part of the 35-head stamper and mills for treating the tailings by cyanide, and later for treating silver ores from Totley. Poppet heads remain at the North London mine and at the Totley, which is located a short distance out of town. The close, almost cheek-by-jowl admixture of domestic, commercial and mining buildings and structures supports the contention by some observers that, despite its prosperity, Ravenswood had an element of the 'rough and ready'.

Gold was first discovered in the Ravenswood area in 1868, when North Queensland was very sparsely settled. The first small finds were by station owners and stockmen, one of whom, Thomas Aitken, interested several prospectors in these finds. The men were subsequently guided to the most likely spots by a station owner, Marmaduke Curr. Following further finds, Marmaduke took some of the gold to Bowen and returned to his property with 15 diggers in tow. A small township called Middle Camp was formed and by March 1869 there were about a hundred people on the field. Before long the miners had shifted their attention to neighbouring creeks and gullies and formed a new town at Top or Upper Camp, to be later known as Ravenswood. Importantly, the new finds led to the discovery of several quartz reefs, some of which outcropped above ground.

The first crushing plant arrived in December 1869. This was owned by W Hodgkinson, a former explorer and newspaper editor who later became Minister for Mines. But due to breakages the plant did not commence operations until April the following year. During this time the miners endured the hardships of a long drawn-out wet season, for the storms wreaked havoc with the flimsy tents and temporary buildings. To make matters worse there was a general shortage of provisions, including alcohol. By May there was another rush to Ravenswood. The first crushings from Hodgkinson's mill were promising, and by 1871 there was a population of 900 and five crushing plants had been installed. The future of the field seemed assured.[2]

Ravenswood soon became North Queensland's first inland town of importance. By the mid-1870s there were two banks, the Bank of New South Wales and the Australian Joint Stock Bank, a newspaper, courthouse, hospital (funded by public subscription), churches, several large stores, some of which were established by Townsville firms, and numerous hotels and shops. Substantial weatherboard homes with iron roofs were replacing the sapling and calico abodes, which were now found only on the outskirts of town. There was plenty to entertain the miners and their families: an amateur dramatic club, school of arts, two cricket teams, a football team and a jockey club. Business was also booming, with hairdressers, cabinet makers, bootmakers, builders, drapers, dressmakers, tinsmiths, photographers, solicitors and brokers.[3]

At least three hotels and two boarding houses had Chinese owners. The Chinese, refugees from the Etheridge field, were tolerated at Ravenswood because the main focus was now on reef gold rather than alluvial. When the Danish traveller Thorval Weitemeyer arrived in Ravenswood around 1872 he described the settlement and the boarding houses:

> There was an ordinary street composed of hotels, boarding houses and stores, on both sides of the road. Behind the street were tents in which the diggers principally lived. Everywhere was earth-mounds where someone was or had been busy rooting the ground about ... Nearly all the people boarded in two boarding-houses kept by Chinamen one on each side of the street. I think there must have been two or three hundred boarders in each. They were both alike, two large bark-houses, no floor, only two immense tables with forms each side. On these tables were at meal-times, every conceivable delicacy in season, and up and down between the tables an army of Chinamen would run round waiting on their guests.

By 1872 it was obvious that there were problems with the ore, for the reef shoots were unpredictable, and the gold was finely distributed in the quartz and associated with a large number of other minerals. This meant that the ore needed very fine crushing, which increased the loss of gold as much of it was carried away with the tailings. At first the only method available for treatment was smelting, which was expensive, for it required firewood and fluxes and transport costs were very high. Over time other methods became available, for example, chlorination and cyaniding, but the former was not available until the 1880s and the latter not until the late 1890s.

These difficulties caused many miners to leave for other goldfields, in particular the new discoveries at nearby Charters Towers, the more distant and perilous Palmer field and, in 1876, the Hodgkinson. Others mined only the rich shoots and left the rest, but some persevered. The latter group were encouraged by the discovery of silver at nearby Totley in the 1880s, at a time when silver prices were very high. Overseas investment in Ravenswood's mines was further encouraged by the establishment of a stock exchange at

Charters Towers, and in 1887 the Ravenswood Gold Mining Company was formed. This company bought several existing mines, such as the 'Grant' and the 'Sunset', and established a chlorination plant.[4]

Despite the departure of many miners to other fields, there were some improvements, such as the extension of the school of arts to include a library, and the building of a larger hall. By 1878 the field had 1300 people and a new newspaper. In 1880 the warden reported that:

> The town has much improved in appearance and the miners seem more inclined to settle permanently, and one sees very few eyesores in the shape of tumbledown humpies and calico domiciles.

By 1883 the population of the field was about 2000 and the town about 1400. These numbers included 300 Chinese, who either worked for alluvial gold or wages in some European-owned mines, or operated market gardens. The Chinese were also later employed as skilled roasters and chlorinators at the Mabel mill.[5]

However, it was the Sandy Creek mines, or more correctly their new owner, an ex-publican mine manager named Archibald Wilson, who proved to be the saviour of Ravenswood. He acquired the mines in 1894 and worked them vigorously and effectively before turning his attention to the mines of the Ravenswood Gold Mining Company. In 1895 the Queensland National Bank refused to extend the owner's overdraft to cover the wages bill, and the mines were closed and later let out to other miners to work. Undeterred, by 1899 Wilson had raised enough capital on the English Stock Exchange for the purchase of the mines by his new company, the New Ravenswood. In addition, he formed two other companies and refurbished the mines and mill.[6]

The future of Ravenswood depended almost entirely on Wilson and his new companies. However, while Wilson's energy and initiative had led to this revival, his management style and the demands of the company shareholders carried with them the seeds of destruction. Historian Diane Menghetti has described his approach to the companies as high-handed, and he was censured by the directors for not keeping them informed of his actions. He was also, however, under considerable pressure to make high dividend payments, a policy which, in the long run, shortened the life of the mines.[7]

Dividends of 50 per cent were paid in 1901 and 1902, and 75 per cent the following year. Within the first two years shareholders had recouped their entire investment. Ravenswood was now attracting worldwide attention, and there was a flood of miners to the town. Many of the miners could not find accommodation and some were forced to spend their first month in Ravenswood camped in a 'huge iron cylinder'. In 1903 the population peaked at 4700, which gave rise to the town's biggest building boom ever. As many as 250 houses were built in that year. Most of them were small two-roomed cottages, but some were large high-set houses with encircling verandahs.[8]

Symbolising this new prosperity were several new brick buildings, among

Erected in 1905, Thorp's buildings are an ornate reminder of Ravenwood's past.

The stairs that lead to nowhere at Browne's Hotel, Ravenswood

The London North poppet head in Ravenswood overlooks a derelict miner's hut surrounded by the ubiquitous rubber vine.

The abandoned cyanide and flotation plant sits amid a sea of rubble at Ravenswood.

All that is left of an old car sits rusting outside the rickety walls of the manager's house at Kidston.

Smoke billowing from a nearby bushfire provides an apt backdrop to the few buildings still standing at Lappa.

The remains of the once busy
Havelock mill, near Forsayth,
are perched on the side of a
hill overlooking a ravine.

them the Imperial and Railway hotels, Browne's and Thorp's buildings and the ambulance station. The boom lasted until 1905. Wilson's house was an imposing building overlooking the central town area, and symbolised his position as shire council chairman, patron of societies and sporting clubs and 'uncrowned King of Ravenswood'.[9]

A *Town and Country Journal* correspondent visiting Ravenswood in 1903 offered a guarded appraisal of the town, commenting that 'wealth and beauty rarely went hand in hand. In the case of Ravenswood the residents were far too engrossed in what transpired below the ground to be too concerned with what occurred above.' Nevertheless, the town contained many good buildings, and it had clearly outgrown its government structures.[10] Historian Peter Bell has remarked that for many people, 'daily town life was far from luxurious'. The houses, shops and churches were interspersed with mines and mills, and industrial noise, smoke and sulphur fumes were constantly present. Industrial accidents and occupational diseases were constant hazards and deaths of children from typhoid and scarlet fever were even more common.[11]

In the ensuing years problems arose with a number of the mines, and by 1906 many were closed. By 1908 the warden was already worrying that the town seemed to have too many businesses for its population. The New Ravenswood had remained profitable due to the efficient management of the company, for machinery and extraction methods were constantly updated. Ominously, however, early in 1912 most workers joined the Amalgamated Workers Association. In his study of the Ravenswood strike, Doug Hunt has commented that union militancy had not been a problem before, but Wilson's understandable preoccupation with cost-cutting was obviously causing concerns with the workers, whose working conditions had fallen behind those enjoyed by other employees in Queensland.

The Roman Catholic church at Ravenswood is reputed to be haunted.

The wage rates had been below those prevailing at Charters Towers for some years. After an approach from the workers in May 1912, Wilson agreed to match the rates, though at the same time terminating a customary bonus. Subsequently, he installed labour-saving machinery, and when approached by workers for extra staff, he chose instead to buy new equipment to ease the workload. These measures coincided with a decline in company profitability and in November he discharged 33 men. The following morning a demand for increased wages was presented to Wilson. This was soon followed by a claim that union members had been discriminated against in the dismissals, a claim that Wilson denied. Several days later the miners' demands were widened to include a reduction in working hours. On rejection of this claim a strike was declared and union picket lines set up.[12] About this time Wilson allegedly made his famous statement, 'I made this town and I'll bugger it before I'll give in to the strikers!'[13]

The dispute soon spread to other Ravenswood companies. But the town was bitterly divided, for not all workers joined in the strike. By December there were 200 men on strike, though a number of them were leaving daily for Cloncurry and other mining districts. There were still 63 men at work, despite constant pressure and intimidation. The engine drivers were officially ordered to cease work by the president of their executive at Charters Towers, but they refused to do so. An effort was made to stop shipments of concentrates from Townsville, but this was thwarted by the men volunteering to travel to Townsville and do the loading themselves.[14]

There were minor street disturbances, and on New Year's Eve one of the shafts was dynamited. But the action had only just started. As soon as the hotels closed a crowd of strikers began hooting and jeering at a small group of non-unionists. As the non-unionists walked along the main street, the crowd grew and there was more hooting and jeering. Stones were thrown. The police arrived, but they could not keep order. A revolver shot rang out, possibly ricocheting off the ground, and hit one of the crowd in the leg. Following a court hearing two weeks later into another incident, a large number of strikers and others left Ravenswood by train, after an exhibition of 'disorderliness and uproar' at the local railway station. When the train arrived the crowd began quarrelling among themselves and bottles were thrown, one smashing a carriage window.[15]

By April the following year Wilson and other mining managers had conceded on the shorter hours issue, but not on the wages claim. As the strike dragged on, Wilson's relations with some of his management staff deteriorated and there were several resignations. Despite his outward show of bravado, Wilson must have been saddened by these events. He had enjoyed almost universal respect and popularity and now presided over a community that was bitterly divided, and in the case of the strikers, facing increased hardships.

In July there was a compulsory conference and all matters were resolved in favour of the union. It was, however, a Pyrrhic victory, for only a small number of the strikers were re-employed; the others joined the general exodus from Ravenswood. Rising costs, increasingly poor ore reserves, skilled labour shortages and, perhaps most significantly, the refusal of the London directors to provide more capital, signalled the inevitable demise of the New Ravenswood. In March 1917 the company ceased operations, and the following year it was lamented that there 'was not one clearly visible ray of hope for the immediate future'.[16]

Mining continued, but the boom was over, and in 1930 the rail link with Mingela was discontinued. Although there were small revivals in the 1930s Depression, the early 1940s and subsequently, the town fell into decline. Most of the buildings were dismantled and taken away, or fell into disuse and were demolished. Carpentaria Gold has recommenced mining but no new buildings have been constructed in the main part of town, for the miners live elsewhere. The company has, however, provided community facilities such as a golf club, swimming pool and school oval, and has made a major contribution to the conservation of Ravenswood's heritage.[17]

May Crow's book, *Ravenswood Remembered*, sheds some light on Ravenswood's declining years. She recalled that Hans Thomsen, who had built most of the houses in Ravenswood, bought land in Townsville after World War I and moved houses there from Ravenswood. Somewhat ironically, he was also the undertaker. There were, however, still quite a few businesses and associations. The Salvation Army, amateur dramatic society, a minstrel troupe, brass band, Caledonian Society with a bagpipes band, a Masonic temple, Hope of the North and Oddfellows Lodge, a Manchester Unity and United Friendly Societies, Australian Natives' Association, and after World War I, a Wounded Soldiers Society reflected the town's civic-minded activities and busy social life.

Despite the barren appearance of Ravenswood today, May recalled that almost everyone, including her father, had vegetable gardens and many people kept poultry, pigs and goats. She recalled that few people owned blankets but opened up sacks, washed them and covered them with patches. They used the feathers from the ducks and hens in their pillows, and made sugarbags into carry bags or raincoats.

Goats were an important part of town life. They did not require feeding, but went off into the bush each day. On occasions they would not go into the yard, but lingered around the hillside and would not let their kids suckle. This usually happened when they had been feeding on a patch of wild marijuana. When May's mother was first married she was not a good cook, and she fed her failures to the goats. This became so frequent that whenever the goat herd in the yard heard her beating something up in the kitchen, they would all flock around the back door waiting to be fed. On a less happy note, she recalled that many miners suffered from miners' phthisis, or dust on the lungs, and although efforts were made to counter it by watering down the workings, men still contracted it. Her own father died from its effects.[18]

Another reminiscence concerns a Catholic priest by the name of Father Weare. May recalled that he was a man of strong views and not backward in

On occasions they would not go into the yard, but lingered around the hillside and would not let their kids suckle. This usually happened when they had been feeding on a patch of wild marijuana.

65

Delany's Imperial Hotel at Ravenswood is brimming with ghosts.

letting his congregation know his opinion of them. The men were kept to one side of the church and the women to the other. In church the men were chastised for improper or predatory business dealings, and he rebuked ladies whom he considered had their necklines too low or were uncharitable. Outside the church he was kept busy patching domestic quarrels, visiting, giving money from the poor box, writing for those who could not read or write, and chasing up those who were not attending mass, or not sending their children to the convent school. While it was a rich parish, he went around in a ragged old cassock, 'green with age'. It was only after he had left the town that it was discovered that he had denied himself so that he could send money away to have priests educated. One of those establishments was a mission in Calcutta.[19]

In a town of such past grandeur it is not surprising that stories of ghosts and apparitions exist. I had been to Ravenswood previously, but had not heard of the haunted church, let alone the haunted hotel. Woody Pigram, who was attending to tourism matters on the day of my visit, shared some of the stories that have become part of local folklore.

One story told some forty years ago concerned a Catholic priest who was talking to a vociferous sceptic in the church sacristy, when they both heard footsteps on the other side of the sacristy door that led out into the yard.

'That's the ghost I was telling you about,' said the priest. 'See you later.' The two men then fled into the open and deserted yard, the visitor tongue-tied for the first time that evening. On an earlier occasion a priest had rushed one night to a neighbour's house and banged on the door, yelling to be let in. He was trembling like a leaf and on the verge of a stroke, but refused to say what had happened.

In another incident a priest was visiting the town with a high-ranking prelate. He was asleep on a stretcher in the sacristy when he thought he heard his companion walking up and down the sanctuary. He found it wasn't his companion. The footsteps came to the sacristy door several times and turned back. Suddenly the steps ceased at the door and he had the sensation that there was someone in the room. While he could not see anything, the old tripod wash basin moved a little and he again felt a strong presence in the room. Woody has a hunch that the ghost could be none other than Father Weare on some unfinished business.[20]

If that series of stories was not enough, the Imperial Hotel appeared to be brimming with ghosts. There are always some people in hotels who are inebriated enough to see anything, but in all the cases cited by the owner, Dianne Schluter, the people were sober. Her daughter, Gina, had seen a man dressed like a miner at the foot of her bed, and both mother and daughter had heard the piano playing downstairs, even though the lid was closed. They had also often heard whispering by a large number of people at the top of the stairs and had opened the door to find no one there. On another occasion a hotel guest had seen half a man dressed in cricket gear and adjusting his tie hovering above his bed. The billiard room had not been used since 1930 and that also was reputedly haunted. Curiously, Jim Delaney, a past owner of the hotel, was a cricket player and Jo, his wife, and one of their daughters were piano players.[21]

The hotel rooms certainly have an eerie feel. They are small, and include two or three antique iron beds with mosquito nets over them. Indeed, the whole town has an antique, almost haunted feel to it. The combination of strong-willed people such as Archibald Wilson and Father Weare, the long-serving Delaneys, and the bitter industrial conflicts of 1913 may be conducive to spiritual visitations. Regardless of whether such phenomena are real, there are plenty of people in town who believe that they are.

Archibald Wilson lived long enough to see much of his town dismantled and carted away and to lament its passing. But, unlike Job of the Old Testament, there was to be no restitution. He never left Ravenswood, apparently finding 'some solace in drink', and finally passing away in 1935, aged 83. He lies in an unmarked grave; all that is left of his once-grand residence, which had overlooked the busy main street, are the steps and a fireplace.[22]

From the Etheridge to Irvinebank

I N THE LATTER PART OF THE NINETEENTH CENTURY AND THE EARLY TWENTIETH century a large number of mining fields developed in the area west of Cairns in northern Queensland. One of the first of these was the Etheridge goldfield — for a while one of the richest fields in the north. Its prosperity was short-lived, however, for every time there was a rush to a new field the eager miners almost deserted the Etheridge. Added to this, mining methods in the early years were primitive, the mines poorly capitalised and the mill owners wasteful.[1] In later years other mining fields were also developed, but they too were mostly ephemeral and the isolated towns they spawned soon settled back into the dust.

In 1868 gold was found on the Robertson River and at the junction of the Percy and Gilbert rivers. By the following year the population on the field was estimated to be 3000. A carter, W Corfield, reported seeing 'droves of people of both sexes, in all sorts of vehicles, on horseback and afoot' passing him on the road. Because of a 'famine-like scarcity of rations', the discomforts of the climate and poor water supplies, however, within a year numbers had dwindled to just 1300. Gilberton, the main town, apparently bore 'the usual primitive appearance peculiar to mining townships in the first stage of their growth'. For three months of the year no grog could be obtained because of the floods. The clergy had yet to put in an appearance, but there were police quarters, a commissioner's camp, courthouse and hospital.[2]

There was a large Chinese presence on the field, despite the hostility and occasional violence of some of the mining population. They did, however, have the protection of the law. More often, as historian RB Brown has observed, it was the Europeans who needed protection, for they were often outnumbered and out-muscled by the Chinese. By 1870 the Chinese formed a substantial proportion of the population at Gilberton. The town was described as 'swarming with celestials', who had two butcher's shops and were preparing extensive market gardens. Unlike the European portion of town, the Chinese settlement appeared 'organised and well planned'.[3]

Increases in mining activity led to conflict between Europeans, Chinese and Aborigines. The miners competed with the Aboriginal people for the scarce resources of water and game, and there was constant provocation caused by the kidnapping of Aboriginal women and children and indiscriminate shooting. These confrontations did not always go in favour of the miners. Because of the isolated locations of many of the mining camps and the broken nature of the terrain, the loss of food, equipment, horses and life itself were ever-present fears. Between 1870 and 1873 at least 13 Chinese and two Europeans were killed on the Gilbert.

The conflict reached its zenith in 1873 when Gilberton achieved immortality as the only town to be abandoned following an attack by a group of Aboriginal people. Janice Wegner describes this incident in her book *The Etheridge*. She regards the abandonment of Gilberton as significant for further developing a climate of fear and repression among Europeans. In October of that year a large party of men left for the Palmer goldfield, and the Etheridge was nearly deserted. Aborigines attacked Gilberton in November, killing one person and injuring others. There was an understandable state of panic; some residents left immediately and others burnt their possessions in the street, for it was difficult to find carriers. The town remained abandoned until 1876, but was gradually resettled when the Palmer goldfield declined.[4]

Wegner has described Gilberton's desertion as 'part of frontier folklore', for it increased the miners' level of apprehension and was used as a justification for taking harsh reprisals against the Aboriginal people. In 1878 there were further attacks on the field and further panic. The only building now left at Gilberton is a small stone 'fortress'. According to Lyn French, whose family has resided on Gilberton Station for several generations, it was erected by the Martel family. By 1884 Gilberton had obviously been resettled, as it was described as a 'Chinese township'. The only Europeans left were the postmaster, two constables and two deaf and dumb men.[5]

Georgetown is today the 'capital' of the Etheridge Shire. Just a few kilometres away is Cumberland, which in the late 1880s was the main mining centre on the field. The mining company began with substantial capital and a complete crushing plant, but the only evidence left of these activities is a huge brick chimneystack, a dam and the remains of cyanide tailings. In only one place is there any brick, glass or stone from the house sites.

Forsayth, south of Georgetown, was the terminus for the Chillagoe Company's railway from Mareeba. The company wished to supplement the supply of copper ore to its smelters at Chillagoe, and a number of mining properties in the Etheridge were purchased for this purpose. Prior to the construction of the railway terminus in 1911 the largest town in the area was Charleston, which in 1894 had five hotels, a school and a court of petty sessions. As the terminus was located several kilometres away on the opposite side of the river, Charleston was eventually abandoned in favour of the new site. At first the town was called New Charleston, but to avoid confusion the name was changed to Forsayth. Construction of the railway led to a mini-boom and within a few years a hospital, new school, hall and a newspaper were established. This boom was short-lived for it was dependent upon the Chillagoe Company's fortunes, which were at the best of times uncertain.[6]

These days the railway is still in operation, but is now used for tourism. Forsayth is probably in better shape now than when it was first established, but the same cannot be said of Charleston. Almost all that can be seen are some stone footings of the houses, although one home has been built more recently from mud, mortar and beer bottles. South of Forsayth the stone footings and cuttings for the once very substantial crushing plant of the Havelock mine can be seen perched on the side of a hill overlooking a ravine. There is virtually nothing left of the nearby town of Castleton.

East of Forsayth is Einasleigh, which owes its existence to copper mining and also to the Chillagoe Company. Within a short time the town had two hotels, a store, billiard room, butcher's and baker's shops, and smelters. Although the early results were promising, low metal prices and raw material shortages caused the closure of the mines and smelters. They were reopened in 1907 when metal prices rose. But the main impetus for the growth of Einasleigh was the Kidston rush to the south, the building of the Chillagoe Company's railway and the purchase of the copper mine and smelters by the Chillagoe Company.[7] In 1908, at the height of the Kidston rush, Einasleigh was flourishing, with four hotels, four stores, two aerated water factories, two hairdressers, two billiard rooms, and three or four newsagents and tobacconists. A 'bumper time' was expected when the 'iron horse' arrived.[8]

The fortunes of Einasleigh and Forsayth were linked largely to the Chillagoe Company, which continued to over-invest in plant and facilities ahead of proving the reserves or economic feasibility of the mines. It was aware that the Etheridge mines were not suited to large-scale exploitation, but continued in the hope that they could be worked as a group or that something better would turn up. More importantly, the mines were not producing enough ore for the smelters, and they were gutted for the richest ore without regard to systematic development. The closure of the Chillagoe smelters in 1914 had disastrous results for the Etheridge towns.[9] Today, Einasleigh, like Forsayth, has only one going business concern: the hotel. The remains of the copper mine and smelters can still be seen on the edge of the gorge.

Kidston, known originally as the Oaks, was a latecomer to the Etheridge. The first claim was worked by two prospectors, Charles Mack and William Barry. They would have kept their find a secret, but Mack went to a nearby mining camp where he over imbibed and showed the gold to another prospector. Within a few months 1500 miners had flocked to the field, but by the end of 1908 there were only 500. Prospectors could travel part of the way by train; however, many still came on foot, pushing wheelbarrows along the tracks. Official reaction was guarded as it was considered only as a poor man's field, though a reasonably remunerative one.[10]

Main street, Charleston, 1907;
now only a few stones are left.
(Courtesy Etheridge Shire)

By 1908 the mining camp had been transformed into a township, with wood and iron buildings replacing tents. Three hotels, six stores, two bakers, a butcher, post office, blacksmith, saddler and two billiard rooms were open for business, and by the following year a Chinese market garden had been established. There was also a temperance movement that, for the first few months at least, succeeded in excluding hotels and grog shops. The school-house also served as a dance hall, but there was no courthouse and the court of petty sessions was held in the policeman's bedroom and the warden's courts convened in the open or under a bough shed. There was also a sub-branch of the Cairns ambulance brigade.

Before long, conflict arose between the alluvial and reef miners, the latter wishing, understandably, to be granted larger claims, but this request was initially rejected for they were in the minority. However, the establishment of two crushing plants by the middle of 1909 gave them the edge and by the end of the year the vast majority of the men were working on the reefs. Many of the men had little, if any, mining experience, which proved to be a serious limitation until approval was given to amalgamate two of the larger low-grade properties in 1911. The amalgamation allowed them to be worked more profitably by open-cut methods, and other companies were formed in turn to mine on a large scale.[11]

By 1911 the town had a police barracks and courthouse, Jansen's Hotel, hall and billiard room, two other hotels, a bakery, two butchers, a hairdressing and billiard saloon, various refreshment rooms, boarding houses, stores and the union office. But by 1919 there were only three stores left, and the field was in decline. A state-owned battery was erected in 1921 to assist in the crushing of the lower grade ores, but by 1922 there was only one hotel, the Shamrock — a sure sign of hard times — though there were still several other businesses. By the 1930s gold production had fallen substantially, and in 1942 the state battery was closed for the duration of the war. In 1985 the Kidston

The old town of Kidston presents a most desolate appearance.

mines were reopened for working by modern mining methods, with the miners resident in a mining village with all facilities, on a fly-in, fly-out basis. But the old town remained abandoned.

Further to the south, Percyville benefited from the Kidston rush and the Chillagoe Company's purchase of a nearby mine. In 1912 a hotel, butcher, three stores, a post office and bakery served the town. A hessian-enclosed dance hall provided a venue for entertainment and a race club had been formed. The remains of the town are located on Allyn and Natasha Zabel's Percyvale Station, and include a boarding house, butcher's shop, police station, and several miners' homes and graves. Mount Hogan also experienced a brief revival in 1910, and Mount Jackson experienced two bursts of growth. In 1912 it was described as bustling with cottages and tents, but six years later the town was deserted.[12]

The old town of Kidston presents a most desolate appearance, dominated by galvanised iron, dust and long lank grass. Along the main street there are few buildings left. One hut had a broken-down car outside, appropriately scribed with the words 'help' painted on the doors, and across the road an even more dilapidated iron structure, possibly the Shamrock Hotel, carried a painted message on its walls: 'The pub with no beer.' Further along is the police compound, which includes the police station and house, the cells and a telegraph office. The main building in the town is the government battery, housed in a large galvanised-iron shed; the battery manager's residence is located several hundred metres away.

The fastest way of getting to Irvinebank from the Etheridge is from Mount Garnet via the appropriately named Mount Misery Road, as long as one can navigate the confusing myriad of tracks and lack of road signs in the area. On this occasion there was also the added challenge of a number of bushfires in the hills. These hazards successfully negotiated, we arrived in the village of Irvinebank, once the jewel in the crown of John Moffat's mining empire. By 1883 Moffat was one of Queensland's leading mining entrepreneurs, with successful tin mining and milling enterprises at Herberton and Watsonville. He embarked on a program of mine purchases and established a permanent headquarters near these properties, naming it Irvinebank in honour of his home in Ayrshire, Scotland.[13]

In 1884 he established a smelting works and in December of that year christened the mill 'Loudoun' before a crowd of 150 luncheon guests. The mill was the largest tin battery and smelter in Australia for decades. John Moffat displayed what historian Ruth Kerr has described as a 'strong sense of family and commonsense outlook' and a desire to create community cohesion. As part of this process his home, 'Loudoun House', was built very close to the smelters and battery.[14] On Saturday nights his house was open to all his staff and small dance parties were held, but no alcohol was allowed. His humane and philanthropic attitude is demonstrated in his report in 1884 on a nearby massacre of Aboriginal people, which resulted in the closure of the local Native Police camp. There were very few people in Irvinebank who did not owe their livelihood to him, which gave rise to the story that parents taught their children to pray at night, 'God bless John Moffat', in appreciation.[15]

Moffat acquired several silvermining properties in the late 1880s and in the depressed 1890s bought up every prospect he could find in the hinterlands, such as Stannary Hills, Mount Garnet, Coolgarra, Watsonville, Lappa, Koorboora, Wolfram Camp and Mount Molloy. His most astute purchase, however, was the Vulcan tin mine, which was the first to pay dividends on the field. The profits from this mine shielded him to an extent from some of his more injudicious investments, such as the Chillagoe mines and his network of private railways.[16]

Irvinebank was an urbane and progressive community. A progress association and coach and mail service were established in 1884 and in the following year a school of arts, library, post and telegraph office and police station were constructed. Most workers at Irvinebank owned their own two-roomed iron and timber houses, although in the boom construction period large numbers boarded in the hotels. From the outset Irvinebank was regarded as a 'pretty little town' with private residences surrounded by Chinese gardens and the local dam. Originally there was only one general store, which was flanked by two hotels, with two more in an adjoining street, and two butchers.

Irvinebank smelters and town
(Courtesy Loudoun House Museum, Irvinebank)

The town also had a vibrant social life. Women's activities centred on Loudoun House in the early years and dances were held in the hall attached to the Commercial Hotel. Community activities included racing, cricket and football, and for the less sporting there were bazaars, concerts and other events. The school of arts ball and concerts in aid of the churches and sporting associations, such as the cricket clubs, rounded out the social calendar. Many of the functions took place in the cooperative hall and attracted large numbers from nearby communities such as Watsonville.[17]

In 1903 a *Town and Country* correspondent described Irvinebank as the province of the Scots, for they constituted the bulk of the 800 residents. He was particularly taken with the mode of transport, which at that time was entirely dependent upon donkeys and packhorses. Irvinebank had the only tin-smelting works in Queensland, and the ore was transported there from all directions, the transport teams making a 'most picturesque sight, long files toiling along steep passes over hills'. Some of the buildings such as the National Bank's premises were very impressive. The shops and hotels included Gordon's saddlery and boot repair shop, Armstrong, Ledlie and Stillman's store, Jack and Newell's store and Moran's hardware and grocery store.[18]

By 1907, however, Moffat was in a precarious financial position. He was frustrated by overdrafts, declining assay values, management difficulties and transport costs, particularly for firewood, and was forced to link Irvinebank with the Chillagoe railway system. This would guarantee firewood supplies, speed up delivery of tin ingots to Cairns and reduce transport costs generally. It also had the side benefit of providing train excursions on social occasions. Conversely, Moffat's faltering financial situation increased the fear of a wage reduction and led to increased union activity. Two of the union leaders were Edward Theodore and William McCormack, both of whom were to become Premiers of Queensland. In 1907 there was a two-month strike at the Vulcan mine and two years later a four-month strike at the Vulcan, Loudoun mill and several mining camps such as Wolfram Camp and Koorboora. Moffat retired in 1912 and in 1919 the mill, mines and tramway were purchased by the State Government. The smelters were dismantled in the early 1930s.[19]

Today Irvinebank is only a fraction of its former size. However, over the last few years a new hotel has been built, and the town has been embraced by many people wishing a quieter lifestyle. Some of the older buildings such as the National Bank building, post office and police station are now local residences, the school of arts is a community centre and John Moffat's Loudoun House acts as the local museum. The school building is still used for its original purpose, but unfortunately the Loudoun mill complex is 'out of bounds'.

On our way to Chillagoe we detoured via the Emuford battery, which has been lovingly restored by John Fitzgerald. It is larger and more complete than the Kidston battery complex, and includes a rail line running from the hopper bins to the back of the battery, where it deposited its ore for crushing.[20] Next on the agenda was Lappa, a small town built around the railway junction of the Mount Garnet and Chillagoe railways. There are only three buildings in the town: a house, a small railway building and a hotel known as 'L'Espagnol'. We pulled up some distance from the hotel and were almost immediately greeted by a youngish-looking woman, who was relieved that we were not going to drive past without stopping. Our hopes of refreshments were dashed, however, when our host, who wished to be known as 'Lappa Liz', declared that there was not so much as a soft drink available, for this was truly the 'pub with no beer'.

Our disappointment was appeased by Liz's stories of the Lappa ghost, whose visitations included the tapping of morse code on the doors, stamping around in hobnail boots, slamming of doors and keeping them shut while people were trying to open them. When these events occurred the room felt like it was considerably cooler, but after a few choice words to the ghost, calm would return. In one instance a person bedding down at the hotel reported seeing a child peeping through the door and another time someone saw a little dark-haired girl in a white nightie at the foot of the bed. There are, however, no children in the town.[21]

Chillagoe, like Irvinebank, is something of an enigma. It has two hotels, a store, a cafe, an arts and crafts store, laundromat and bakery, and has gained a second lease of life as a regional centre and as a visitor destination for the caves and smelter site, which is one of the icons of North Queensland. Other

The copper smelters at Chillagoe are an icon of North Queensland.

than the smelters and the many vacant blocks in the town, there is little to suggest that it once had several thousand residents. Chillagoe is, however, one of Queensland's legends, not for any great contributions to the development of Australia's natural resources, but rather the spectacular collapses and scandals of its various companies.

For a time Chillagoe was part of John Moffat's empire. He was involved in promoting and developing the Chillagoe field as early as 1889, and in 1897 he formed a syndicate to further develop the field, the economics of which depended on the location of the smelters. However, government intransigence caused them to be built inland, near the Chillagoe mines, which meant incurring huge transport charges for fuel and other raw materials. Worse still, the ore reserves were found to be far less than originally stated, and this caused a serious slump in share prices. The smelters closed down in November 1901, the month they were opened. To say the shareholders were less than impressed would be a gross understatement. Ruth Kerr has commented that part of the Moffat legend is attributable to his holding more shares in the company than when it was formed, thus he could not be accused of profiting from promotion of a barren field.[22]

After 1901 Moffat ceased to have any further interest in the Chillagoe mines other than as a shareholder; the company was reformed and the smelters were reopened in October 1902. Once the financial crisis of 1901 was resolved, hotels and other businesses were established, in addition to a courthouse, hospital, school of arts and library, banks and two newspapers. Nonetheless, problems still plagued the company. A shortage of ore supplies led the company to invest in the Etheridge field, and for a while the gamble paid off as commodity prices were high. But in 1909 the Zillmanton mines were flooded and later that year a fire seriously damaged two copper furnaces as well as other plant and equipment at Chillagoe. In addition, falling ore prices and the vast distances over which the ore and coke were carried were ruining the company's finances. Unable to pay interest on its loans, the company closed the smelters in 1914.

The company's property was purchased by the Queensland Government in 1919, but there were numerous misgivings and questions about subsequent operations, and in 1930 the incoming government set up a Royal Commission. The commission concluded that Edward Theodore, then federal Treasurer in the Scullin Labor Government, and a former Premier, William McCormack, together with several other men, were guilty of fraud and dishonesty. The inquiry destroyed the careers and reputations of these men. During the 1930s, smelting continued haphazardly, serving an increasingly depressed mining community, and in 1943 the smelters were finally closed. By this time the government buildings outnumbered the private homes and businesses, of which only Jack and Newell's store and the two hotels remained.

There were several other mining towns in the area, almost all of which are now totally abandoned; for example, Zillmanton, where there were two hotels, three boarding houses, two shops and a post office; Koorboora, where there were 500 people at one time; Calcifer and Muldiva. At Calcifer there were five hotels, five stores, a branch of the Bank of Australasia, two dairies, a cordial factory, a butcher and the inevitable race meetings and cricket team. Muldiva had three stores, two bakers, two butchers, a blacksmith, wheelwright, cordial factory and a school. Another town was O.K., which at one time boasted five hotels, a police station, school, hospital, butchers, two stores, miners' cooperative, baker, confectioner and fruiterer and several dressmakers. All these towns are now abandoned.

Mungana was another such ill-fated but somewhat more resilient town. In 1896 there were three hotels and there were eventually two stores, a restaurant, draper, butcher's shop and bakery. The town also boasted a cricket club, amateur turf club and progress association, courthouse, library and reading room, and religious services were held in one of the stores. Because it was the railway terminus it lingered on much longer than the other towns. However, by 1959 it comprised just one hotel, a store, the post office and seven residents.[23] Today the foundations and floors of some buildings remain, along with galvanised water tanks and parts of rusting car bodies, and the beam pump at the Lady Jane mine. But like so many other North Queensland mining towns, Mungana is totally abandoned and likely to always remain so.

A Brooding Mountain

OUNT MULLIGAN LIES AT THE FOOT OF THE MASSIVE SANDSTONE mountain of the same name, about 54 kilometres north of Dimbulah in North Queensland. It is a place of legend and beauty, for the mountain was regarded in Aboriginal legend as the creation of the great rainbow serpent Goorialla.[1] But perhaps it is better known as a place of tragedy, for in 1921 it was the scene of one of the worst mining disasters in Australian history, when 75 men were killed in a mine explosion. Mining continued for another 36 years before the town was abandoned to the bush and the mountain.

All that is left of the main town area are the stumps of the houses, some concrete pads, the brick oven and floor of the bakery, gutters, street kerbing, water tanks and rusting car bodies. The brick-built Mount Mulligan hospital is still intact, but now its guests are backpackers and other visitors. Closer to the mountain stand the large brick chimneystack, the railway platforms and several buildings, including a beehive-shaped brick kiln. Further uphill the boiler for operating the tramline to the mine, wash and change rooms and the magazine are scattered through the bush. The cemetery provides a poignant reminder of the 1921 tragedy.

Coal was found at Mount Mulligan in 1907, and in 1912 the government agreed to the construction of a branch line from Dimbulah to Mount Mulligan for transport of the coal to the Chillagoe Company's smelters at Chillagoe. A township was surveyed, and by 1914 tents and modest houses lined the main streets. A brick-making plant and dam were built and work commenced on the construction of a powerhouse. By the time the railway line was completed, however, the company had run out of money and was forced to close its smelters. Mining at Mount Mulligan ceased and the town was deserted. The government pressed upon the company its obligation to continue to supply coal for the railways and the Irvinebank smelters, and the following year work started again. In 1919 construction work commenced on

Copperfield River, upstream from the old copper smelters at Einasleigh, is a cool contrast to the dusty hills and plains.

The now silent Loudon Mill at Irvinebank on the banks of the mill dam

A hive-shaped brick kiln set against the towering backdrop of Mount Mulligan

Discarded bread tins at the Mount Mulligan bakery site

The 1921 Mount Mulligan mine disaster was one of Australia's worst mining accidents, killling 75 miners. Many families lost more than one relative in the tragedy.

The Canton Hotel is the only original building left from the days when Thornborough was one of the busiest goldmining towns in the north.

These concrete pylons for the Cooktown-to-Maytown railway were never used; Laura River was as far as the train ever travelled.

workers' cottages, coke ovens and sorting and washing equipment.[2]

By 1921 the town had over 300 residents, most of whom lived in iron-roofed and timber-framed houses. Others lived in corrugated-iron huts or tents, and the senior management in more substantial homes closer to the mountain. There were two hotels (one of them two-storey), five stores, including a drapery and cafe, a billiard saloon and an outdoor cinema, a school and a church. Services were held in the church by visiting clergy, but it was destroyed in a cyclone in 1921 and not rebuilt until 1947. The damage to the hotels was repaired almost immediately. No one owned a motor car and the only way in and out was by the twice-weekly train or, over shorter distances, by a pump car.

In his book on the Mount Mulligan coalmining disaster, *If Anything Too Safe*, Peter Bell describes the town's social life as 'somewhat rough around the edges', with frequent fist fights and plenty of drinking. One old-timer recalled, 'We lived on beer mostly.' A more important focal point was the piano, and dancing and singing occurred regularly at homes and the hotels. Young female dancing partners were in high demand and could command a certain level of decorum from the menfolk. Because of its isolation and lack of any form of communication other than the train, there was a close-knit loyalty.[3]

The Mount Mulligan miners were paid by piecework, that is, by the weight of coal produced per man. Four times each year the miners cavilled or balloted for positions in the mine. Those working the cutting machines and others who were not directly involved with coal extraction were paid a day rate. Monday 19 September 1921 was the beginning of a new cavil or ballot for positions in the mine. Seventy-four miners reported for work that day, all with their carbide lamps and exposed flames. There was little enthusiasm for safety lamps because of the wage loading on their use, their effect on the miners' eyesight and, critically, the absence of flammable gas in the mine.[4]

At 9.25 am there was a sudden eruption of black dust at the foot of the mountain, and from the town pieces of timber and iron could be seen flying through the air. Then they heard the explosion. The women and surviving men of the town converged en masse to the mine. George Morrison, a blacksmith and tool sharpener who occupied a hut near the mine entrance, was seen stumbling down the track. He was dazed, coal-blackened and badly shocked. Peter Bell has described the scene that met the townsfolk:

> Heavy black smoke rolled from the mine's two openings. The steel winding drums, two tonnes in weight, which had worked the old haulage system, had been blasted from their timber framework above the mine entrance, and lay 20 metres down the ropeway. A mound of stone, earth and broken timber blocked the mouth of the adit, and it appeared that a massive collapse had occurred in the mine. The fan had been ejected from its shattered concrete housing and lay twisted among the trees, 40 metres in front of the ventilating tunnel. The whole area before the mine entrance had been coated with fine coal-dust and seared by flame — grass was burning 60 metres from the entrance.

Chimney stack of coke works with Mount Mulligan looming in the background

JT Watson, the mine manager, was one of the first on the scene. Standing on top of a shale dump near the entrance he yelled to the crowd, 'You'd better all go home. I hold out no hope for any man.'[5]

A few bodies were immediately recovered before bad air and rockfalls caused the mine to be evacuated. Two men were found alive near the entrance, one of whom died shortly after. Those at the surface were ill-equipped to enter the mine, even in normal conditions, for most of them were surface workers. Further, the mine had no rescue devices. The Queensland Mines Life Saving Brigade was at Ipswich, several days journey away. Local volunteers poured in and soon there were 300 on site, but only the skilled miners were allowed to enter the mine; the others were engaged in grave digging and other work. Caged canaries were commonly carried in the mines to check for the presence of toxic gases, but in the absence of these a family pet, a painted finch, was used.[6]

The removal of the bodies was a gruesome task. Many of the men were badly mutilated and most were burned, and before long their bodies began to decompose. The rescuers wore eucalyptus-soaked masks, and the bodies were disinfected with phenol. A report in the *Brisbane Courier* described in journalistic detail the grim scene that greeted the volunteers:

[T]he corpses bore the appearance of having been suddenly struck by a terrific heat flame. The surface of the bodies was carbonised, the skin peeling off in flakes, all the hair was black and frizzled, and a number of the men's heads had been crushed by falling stones. One victim apparently had been pushing a truck, which upset, and, in falling down, crushed his head. Another victim was found to be practically standing on his head, propped up by fallen timber. The most gruesome sight of all was several men whose position suggested that they had seen some awful object coming, and had their hands raised to ward off the danger.[7]

Identification was impossible in some cases, and as the days wore on the coffins had to be enlarged to accommodate the increasingly decomposed and swollen bodies. The press, as would be expected in such circumstances, waxed lyrical at the drama of it all. One of the more memorable of these accounts concerned the reaction of the women:

Brave-hearted women, whose dead husbands and sons had been brought out of the mine, were trying to comfort each other, and urging those whose menfolk were amongst the entombed not to lose hope, as surely some of their loved ones would be rescued alive. All through the night and day they stayed at the mouth of the pit … making tea to refresh the men, and cheering and urging them to greater efforts. Here, indeed, were true mothers of men — some of the wonderful women who, as their sisters have shown in the past, possess the British blood that makes heroines who can meet Death face to face and not flinch.[8]

For some the aftermath was grim indeed. The inspector attempted to keep the elderly Dave Hutton from the mine, for he had two sons and a son-in-law in the mine, but he insisted on continuing with the recovery work. Others who normally would have been in the mine on that fateful day were afterwards afflicted with intense guilt. A number of legends grew around these men concerning the survivor who had a premonition of disaster and did not go to the mine that day. There was also a belief that one man had unaccountably disappeared in the explosion and out of this grew the story of 'Morgan's ghost'. Ironically, the cemetery had only been established a few months earlier and it had just been cleared and fenced the weekend before the explosion.[9] Now, on the Tuesday after, it was to receive the first of many occupants.

Following the last burial there was an immediate evacuation of the town and a gradual reoccupation over the next few weeks. However, some never returned, including the deceased miners' families and some business people. Legislation was passed soon after providing that payments for the relief of the miners' dependants were to be vested in trustees. All up the widows would receive £770 each, in addition to a continuing annuity for each child. The payments can be compared with the average wage of the miners, which was then between £200 and £250 a year. By today's standards these provisions may not seem generous, but they appear to have been acceptable to the

Mine entrances at Mount Mulligan

recipients. The origin of the explosion was never clearly established, but was probably triggered by a neglect of elementary safety precautions, such as the handling of explosives.[10]

The mine reopened for production early in 1922. Repairs were effected relatively quickly and a cokeworks with 14 brick retorts erected, and the mine reconstructed. However, the new employees did not appear to have the same sense of community and common purpose as before, and there were two lengthy and crippling strikes, one in 1922 and the other a year later. These events finally tipped the scales against the company and it was wound up in late 1923, and the mine sold to the State Government. Most of the mine's plant was found to be in a poor condition and the cokeworks were in need of extensive repairs.

Following the mine's acquisition by the government, 12 new four-roomed houses with electricity and piped water were built for the miners, together with large coal storage bins, which would allow continuous coke production. 1924 was the high point for production at Mount Mulligan, when about 160 men were employed. From then on, however, it was a process of steady decline. The mines were soon overshadowed by the development of other more promising coal deposits on the Bowen River, and when the Chillagoe smelters closed in 1927 the mines lost their best customer.

The onset of the economic depression in 1929 would have been the last blow for the mine, but for a union proposal to work on a tribute basis. Under this arrangement the tributers, represented by a union comitttee, would sell the coal and pay wages to themselves, and pay the state government a royalty. This arrangement lasted for 18 years and demonstrated a new-found community loyalty. But these were not halcyon days for the miners. The committee's main concern was to provide employment for as many men as possible, and wages were lower than for state employees elsewhere. In addition, men occasionally had to be laid off. The population gradually fell away and the township was left mainly to the older married men.

In 1941 the town was rejuvenated by the opening of a new mine, the King Cole, and in the early 1950s the township expanded with the construction of a post office, a Catholic church, a new hospital and a few substantial private homes. Domestic electricity was also installed for the first time and a road built from Dimbulah and the streets properly formed.[11] A visitor to the town in 1954 commented that:

> The first impression on seeing Mount Mulligan township is one of solitariness ... The one hotel structurally and socially dominates the township's life, whilst close at hand are a few small stores, the post office, a cafe and wooden hall where a picture show provides occasional escape into the outside world.[12]

The mine was closed in October 1957, the government blaming the inability of the mine to keep up with demand, including the weekly order of about 200 tons of coal for Mareeba. As a sign that the end had really arrived, a fire broke out in the coal seam and all production ceased forthwith. Work began immediately on dismantling machinery in the mine and demolishing the houses before their removal, along with most of the families, to the coal mines at Collinsville further south. Within a few weeks of the closure announcement all homes had been demolished and removed to Collinsville at government expense.[13]

Other more personal matters were not so straightforward. A meeting of parents was convened by the school committee to consider bringing forward the setting up of the Christmas tree, which had been set originally for 9 December. It was agreed that the adults would join and make it a farewell party for everyone, to the accompaniment of Santa Claus, jingle bells and the school fife band and piano. For most residents the decision to leave was relatively easy, for they had jobs to go to, but some decided to live elsewhere, for instance, Cairns. Most of the townsfolk left on the train with their homes, others made their way south by car, but others stayed on pending the rebuilding of their homes at Collinsville.[14] A few months after the town had been abandoned, the mountain had the final say when approximately 255 000 tons of sandstone, which had been tilted beyond stability by the King Cole workings, fell into the gorge below.[15]

Mount Mulligan was named after James Venture Mulligan, one of Queensland's foremost mining explorers, who discovered the nearby Hodgkinson goldfield in 1876. The access road to the Hodgkinson is located near the Thornborough cemetery on the Mount Mulligan road. At Thornborough, the main town on the field, the only building left standing is the Canton Hotel, although the foundations of several others can be seen, such as the police station, courthouse and post office, and one of the other hotels. Considerable restoration work has taken place at the Tyrconnell, which was the most profitable reef mine on the Hodgkingson. This labour of love has been undertaken by Andy Bell and Cate Hartley, who have rebuilt the poppet head over the mine, restored the large crushing and concentration plant and renovated several of the mine officials' buildings such as the manager's cottage.

Mulligan predicted that the Hodgkinson would be a large reefing field. Of the reef prospects he commented that he had never 'seen such a show'. He warned that it would take some time to develop them and obtain results, but he had 'no doubt respecting their payability in this instance'. Of the alluvial he was far less enthusiastic. He described it as:

> very patchy, and the patches are very small in the gullies, and miners must not expect the gold to be got without working hard for it — I never worked harder for the little we got, and was never more than about two days in one gully or ravine.[16]

However, these warnings were totally ignored by the diggers, who flocked to the field from the south and from the Palmer field to the north. There were at this time about 2000 men gathered at Byerstown on the Palmer field anxiously awaiting the opportunity to travel to the Hodgkinson.[17] A subsequent report was provided by 'several reliable persons' who had returned to the Palmer field 'at considerable risk to their lives' to purposely stop their mates. The correspondent lamented that the 'utmost misery and starvation must ensue if people will insist in pouring in from the south'.[18]

Legend has it that these vicissitudes led to an extraordinary confrontation between Mulligan and a mob of malcontented diggers, who threatened to lynch him

Legend has it that these vicissitudes led to an extraordinary confrontation between Mulligan and a mob of malcontented diggers, who threatened to lynch him. On their approach to his horse he warned them not to touch the bridle as the man who did so would be shot through the arm and the man who laid hands on him would be shot through the heart. He then levelled his rifle at the ringleaders, reminding them that he had shot in self-defence before and would do so again. One man said that others could shoot as well as Mulligan, to which he replied that he would take out half a dozen of them before they killed him. This display of bravado impressed the mob and he had no difficulties thereafter.[19]

By June the main township on the Hodgkinson was described as a 'primitive mining camp' comprising some 300 tents, including butchers' and traders' tents. The correspondent wrote that the

> everlasting brandy bottle was here found in abundance, and it being Sunday, and the butcher having arrived with fifty head of cattle, its potent influence was soon generally diffused among the crowds who came pouring in for a supply of beef.

There were 2500 European miners and one Chinese person on the field, and the main form of mining was overwhelmingly reef. A subsequent report declared that as a payable alluvial field it was an 'unmistakeable failure', and men could work a week without making a living.[20]

In March 1877 Mulligan provided a full report on the field, which had only just acquired a post office and mail service to Cooktown. There were nine crushing machines on the field and near each one a small township was establishing itself. The main town was at Thornborough, one of the 'liveliest and most flourishing towns in north Queensland' according to Mulligan. A warden's office, police station, post office, a newspaper, two banks, a stock-broker, several hotels and a large number of stores were doing a busy trade, and a large crushing plant had been set up near the centre of town. The next largest town was Kingsborough, where there was also a large number of businesses. There were about 2500 men on the field.[21]

By May the residents of Thornborough had collected funds towards the establishment of a hospital and the goldfield's first horserace meeting. But there were many needs: a school, churches, a good dray road to Cairns, a new courthouse, police station and warden's court. The former was a bark slab humpy and the police were housed in a tent. One of the main concerns on the field was the lack of access to a port other than distant Cooktown, with its attendant costs. An interesting aspect of the Hodgkinson was the presence of large numbers of Chinese who were engaged in commerce, stock raising and gardening rather than mining. In August they introduced 500 pigs, which meant that the field would have an abundance of animal food at very low rates.[22]

In September the field was visited by the Under Secretary of Mines, who met with the Thornborough Progress Committee and other residents. He was presented with a long list of needs. Particularly vexing was the lack of any government financial assistance towards the local hospital, for which the residents had already collected £500 in subscriptions. Mining activity was subdued, largely due to the lack of water for the crushing plants and the lack of feed for the carrying teams. However, Thornborough's social life was more vibrant. The local amateur dramatic club had given several entertainments at Swan's musical hall, and a banquet and ball had been held for the departing warden. A grand hospital ball was planned for the near future.[23]

Good rains in December led to a resumption of mining activity and additional crushing machinery was introduced. There were now 13 crushing plants on the field, but against this there were still inadequate water storage facilities and an almost entire absence of gold-saving devices, which meant that the tailings were allowed to wash away into the creeks and rivers. There were also inadequate local roads for the carrying of ore, which had to be carried out on the backs of the Chinese, who had formed teams for this purpose. There was a high degree of confidence in the field, the warden remarking that the 'business establishments on the field appear to be fully equal to the requirement of double the population'. There was at least one church, and committees had been formed to finance others.[24]

Very few of the reef mines were successful for any period of time. In the early to mid-1880s the field was affected adversely by drought conditions, the greater attractions of tin and silvermining on the tableland, and a consequent lack of capital. In 1881 the population fell from 1134 to 935, and the gold yield halved. There were over 270 Chinese on the field, but none were engaged in mining. Most were involved in gardening pursuits, and the remainder worked as cooks, woodgetters and water carriers. The warden commented that they had found the cutting of timber for the boilers to be more profitable than goldmining.[25]

By 1883 the population had fallen to 789, and the gold yield was almost half of what it had been in 1881. In 1886 the population was down to just 393. It seems that the mines were worked by men with very little money and not much credit, a situation which, with the exception of mines such as the Tyrconnell and General Grant, was to remain that way.[26] These two mines were the only ones to ever develop comprehensive mine and crushing plants.

An infusion of British capital brought a revival during the 1890s, and a number of new companies were floated. In 1898 the warden reported that 'the field in general appeared to be steadily progressing and the population daily increasing'. There was a demand for houses and new buildings were being constructed at Thornborough and Kingsborough. However, this boom was short-lived. The Tyrconnell was worked almost continously, with varying results, until 1924. It was reopened in the 1930s, but all mining ceased during World War II.[27]

Thereafter, until the arrival of Cate and Andy, it was left to the elements and, perhaps, to the ghosts of the past. Cate recounted how a prospector arrived at their house one day, quite shaken and pale. He had been camping out at Kingsborough with his wife and daughter and had been walking in the dawn while they were asleep. He heard the sound of children playing, and on closer investigation could find no one. Returning to the tent he awoke the others, but there were no further incidents. It was only some time later that he found that where he had heard the children was the old schoolhouse site.

Cate also told the story of another couple who were camping out at the foot of Mount Mulligan. There wasn't enough room to sleep in the car so the mother slept outside, only to be awoken later by the sounds of a voice crying 'help me'. When I heard that story I shuddered a little, for several years previously I too had slept out in the open at the foot of Mount Mulligan. Next time I will partake of Andy and Cate's accommodation at the Tyrconnell. Despite Peter Bell's reassurances on this subject, the combination of Aboriginal legend and latter-day tragedy is eerie enough without camping beneath this sombre, brooding mountain.[28]

The Road to the Palmer

THERE IS PROBABLY NO GOLDFIELD IN AUSTRALIA SO ABOUNDING IN myths and legends as the Palmer River in far North Queensland. Nor would there be a goldfield where it is so difficult to distinguish fact from fiction. To complete a trilogy of exceptions, there would be very few significant mining fields that are so difficult and daunting to access. A trip to the Palmer is a journey into the past, for the perils of isolation, flood and drought are as real today as they were almost 130 years ago.

Although not located on the Palmer goldfield, Laura is an integral part of the Palmer story, for it became the terminus for the proposed railway from Cooktown to the goldfield. It was an impressive engineering feat, for the line passed through rugged mountainous country, and crossed numerous wooden bridges and culverts. At the Laura River a massive five-span steel bridge supported by concrete pylons was built, but this was as far as the line went. By 1888 the Palmer was in irreversible decline, and the financial crisis of the 1890s put paid to plans to extend the line to Maytown, the 'capital' of the goldfield. The only train ever to cross the bridge was the test locomotive.

The Aboriginal rock art galleries at Jowalbinna and Split Rock near Laura are also an integral part of the Palmer story, for the descendants of these artists were to bear the brunt of the gold rush. These art sites are among the most varied and extensive in Australia and proof that there was a rich and dynamic Aboriginal presence in this area long before Europeans arrived. A generation of Australian children has been enthralled by the stories and drawings of spirit figures such as the Quinkan man, which have been popularised by Dick Roughsey and Percy Trezise.[1]

South of Laura is the relatively new Lakelands Hotel, where we were advised to travel to the Palmer via the track to the Dianne copper mine. This was good advice, for the track was in much better condition than the normally recommended route. We travelled slowly, but comfortably, to the junction with the Palmer track. It was slower going after that, but bearable. Nevertheless, the 70 kilometres to the Palmer River took a little under three hours. On the way we detoured to look at the site of a Chinese village on Granite Creek, the most impressive remains of which are two well-preserved pig ovens. Only the stone foundations of the hut sites are left, however.

After some time we came to a halt at the crest of a hill at the site of an old miner's hut, in full view of the Palmer River. This was as far as we were to get. The river below was a raging torrent. My brother Chris volunteered to wade in to test the depth, but it did not look promising. The river was running swiftly, and although Chris was only a few metres from the bank the water was almost up to his knees and still rising. Crossing the river was out of the question. It had been an interesting, albeit time-consuming experience, for the sudden rising of the Palmer and its tributaries was one of the hardships that the early miners had to face, sometimes with fatal consequences.

I was now thrown back on my reminiscences and photographs from an earlier trip, which was easy as I can still recall my first impressions of Maytown. A more forlorn aspect could hardly be imagined, for none of the original buildings remained. The only immediately visible evidence that this was once a town were the stumps on which buildings such as the courthouse, post office and school of arts stood, the streets, gutters, a few huddles of stone and several telegraph poles. To add to this general scene of ruin a fire had passed through recently, blackening the stumps and trees and burning much of the grass.

But there was more to the town than immediately met the eye. Discreet plaques had been erected along Leslie Street, which was the main street, by the Palmer River Historic Preservation Society, identifying the various business enterprises, most of which had been Chinese. The original slate-slabbed gutters and pavements had been exposed and the remains of a brick oven could be seen. A short distance from the main town area were the hospital and cemetery sites and two charcoal burners, which supplied charcoal for the forges.

The most notable relics were further out and related almost exclusively to the reef-mining phase of the field. At the Louisa mine there was a four-metre boiler and two steam pumps. The nearby Enterprise mill, erected in 1941 and the last battery on the field, is one of the best-preserved battery sites in North Queensland. The Mabel Louise mill site includes the dismantled remains of a 15-head battery dating from 1877, but at the nearby Perseverance mill only the frame and stamper remain. The other items were relocated to the Enterprise mill in 1941.[2]

At the Comet (Canton) mill there is a large stone-encased boiler with its engine and gearing. The mill shed was re-erected and the flywheel moved back into place by the Palmer River Historic Preservation Society in 1987. Examples of stone-built races and dams are located nearby. At the more distant Queen of the North site there are three large boilers, a stationary steam engine and a large flywheel.[3] These sites are among the best pickings on the field, but they are by no means the only ones. The Palmer was a large and scattered field, with townships such as Maytown, Ida, Uhrstown, Lukinville, Palmerville, German Bar, Echotown and Byerstown, and numerous Chinese camps and other settlements. Many of these are accessible only to the most persevering and hardy travellers.

Alluvial gold was discovered on the Palmer River by the explorer James Venture Mulligan in 1873. News of Mulligan's discovery reached Georgetown on the Etheridge in September 1873 and within seven days 200 men had set off for the field. Miners in towns such as Ravenswood and Charters Towers soon followed. One correspondent described the rush from Georgetown on the Etheridge:

> Drays conveying swags, provisions, cradles and sundry other essentials for a new rush are leaving every day, charging 6d. per lb. freight; storekeepers are rushing post haste to meet teams originally destined for this place ... publicans are joining the universal skedaddle; sawyers and other tradesmen are packing up the implements of their respective callings; and local stocks of 'Port Mackay' and other stimulants are largely drawn upon, and waggoned off, to meet the anticipated heavy requirements for goods of this description at the new rush.[4]

Pavement and fire-blackened stumps at the school of arts site, Maytown

A charcoal burner on the Palmer goldfield; it is one of two burners that supplied charcoal for the forges.

Within a month unfavourable news filtered back with the return of unsuccessful diggers driven away by the lack of rations and general hardships of the field.

These difficulties influenced the government to establish a route and a goldfield's administration before the onset of the tropical wet season. An expedition, led by Gold Commissioner Howard St George and including 86 miners, left on the SS *Leichhardt* in October 1873. Their first task was to establish a port and an access road to the Palmer, difficult tasks given the limited labour and equipment on the boat. The lack of horses also meant that the diggers had to walk to the Palmer during the hottest and driest month of the year, and many of them had to discard their clothing, blankets or tents to keep up with the expedition. To make matters worse they suffered several attacks by Aboriginal people, and the subsequent reprisals led to a government enquiry. In a letter to a local newspaper it was stated somewhat casually that 'whoever the black troopers came across they made short work of them'.[5]

St George spoke in glowing terms of the goldfield. He stated that miners were making £1 a day and more and one man had discovered gold worth nearly £200 in three days. The Palmer field was not only attractive for its obvious riches, but also because it could be worked by miners without much capital and equipment, usually only a pan and cradle. They were assisted by the floods, which uncovered new alluvial deposits and allowed the working of gullies and creeks that had previously been dry. The first wet season on the field, however, was ultimately calamitous, for the miners were unprepared and hardship and distress were commonplace. Some were forced to kill their horses for food and others stewed the greenhide leather on their saddles. One report described the men as skeletons, frequently barefooted, with mud up to their knees.[6]

Back in the new port of Cooktown, prospective miners were warned that food was scarce and expensive, and that packhorses and several months' provisions were essential. They were also warned that the track was heavy and slow, but they pressed on regardless. Even after abandoning their less essential items on the track and confronted with emaciated and haggard diggers returning from the field, many still took little heed. There were some who, desperate to continue mining until the last possible moment, left their departure too late and became stranded by floods. Others were too sick to move. In some instances the ground was so boggy that the horses sank up to their ears, and had to be unloaded before they could be extricated. In other cases this was not possible and the horses were left to perish.[7]

Nevertheless, reports of success and new discoveries spurred on eager new miners. On one occasion, a reporter from the *Cooktown Courier* was despatched to Sandy Creek to check the recent rush to that locality. He reported that he had travelled over several miles of the creek and that every 'foot of the ground' had produced heavy, water-worn gold. He claimed he had seen washings as high as an ounce in a pan and in another he observed an average of half an ounce in four pans. In all instances the miners allowed him to stand next to them while they were washing. By August 1874 there were about 3000 on the field and a significant number of Chinese miners were arriving.[8]

At the beginning the main settlement was at Palmerville. A report in 1874 stated that the Chinese population was considerable and that every Sunday morning between 200 to 300 came into the town for their week's supply of meat. They were forming their own townships and erecting substantial buildings. Within a few months the focus had shifted to Upper Camp, which was also known as Edwardstown, and later as Maytown. The accommodation was reported to be substantial and that thanks to the Chinese gardeners, 'the want of the diggers is to be found in the cultivations round about'. German Bar was also reported to be heavily populated with Chinese, who had their butchers' stalls, restaurants and doctors. There were at that time an estimated 6000 miners on the field, of whom about 40 per cent were Chinese.[9]

By mid-1875 Maytown was the centre of attention, with business people rushing there, encouraged by the prospective development of the nearby reef mines. The number of Chinese on the field had grown to about 5000. Palmerville, by comparison, was becoming a deserted village, although there was still a notable Chinese presence, for they owned nearly every store, hotel, bakery and butcher. By November, Maytown was assuming the proportions of a populous and prosperous township, 'with stores, hotels and shops of every description'. Sunday was the main business day, when all the miners, Chinese and European, would come into town to sell gold and buy stores.[10]

Maytown continued to thrive, and by October 1876 it had a courthouse, police barracks, telegraph office, three banks and numerous public houses, of which there was 'one every third door and to every 20 adult male inhabitants'.

In that month a successful ball had been held for the hospital, and there had been a grand farewell supper to one of the bankers. Palmerville, by contrast, was nearly abandoned. Charles Bowly commented that it was 'falling into ruins rapidly', and the few stores and public houses were in a dilapidated state.[11] By the end of the year a new township had sprung up in the Revolver Point District at Echotown and buildings were being erected rapidly. In time a hospital, school and miners' institute library were established at Maytown. Remarkably, there were no churches, although there were two Chinese temples.[12]

In 1878 Maytown was described as 'not the most imposing-looking place in the world'. Mimicking Warden Selheim's style, the writer stated:

> There are the usual concomitants of a bush township — bark, galvanised iron, and policemen; a Warden to settle gold-fields' disputes and tell men not to make 'swine of demselves' when he is fining them for imbibing too much of the rosy; a butcher's shop, several stores, twice as many pubs, a quack doctor or two, a blacksmith's shop, Hospital, one billiard saloon and a variety of banks and their aristocratic-looking clerks in snowy moleskins and paper collars. But Maytown is the best place that I have yet seen in the North — for the main thing: money. Everybody complains of the dull times here, but I have seen more money change hands, and more spent over the bars, at a bob a nobbler, than I have seen in any other towns in the North — and I have visited them all — Island Point and the famous Hodgkinson included.[13]

The Hodgkinson rush in 1876 caused an almost total abandonment of the alluvial workings by the Europeans. Warden Selheim reported that

> as a consequence of this rush, Oakey, Stony and Sandy Creeks, which had been forbidden ground to the Chinese, at once fell into their possession and has [sic] practically remained so ever since, the Europeans (mostly sluicers) barely numbering 200 as against 6000 Chinese.[14]

This exodus interrupted the development of the reef mines, and from thence on it was never possible to obtain the necessary capital to fully develop the mines. Apart from the difficulties of travelling during the wet, or the lead up to the wet, it was all but impossible to maintain and upgrade the tracks, most of which were effectively washed out each year. These challenges added to the cost and delays in obtaining supplies, and led to the construction of the ill-fated Cooktown to Maytown railway. Skilled labour was also in short supply and expensive, and the mines generally poorly managed and over capitalised.[15]

By 1877 there were an estimated 18 000 Chinese on the field and, as Peter Bell has commented, the prospect of indulging in an 'old-fashioned roll-up' with its associated violence along the lines of that in Lambing Flat in New South Wales, was bleak in the extreme. Attempts to eject Chinese from their claims were also unsuccessful because of their superior numbers. They were, however, subject to a certain degree of official harassment and their involvement in reef mining was strongly discouraged. Following the opening up of the Canton Reef (later the Comet) by Chinese enterprise, the European reef miners formed a union and went on strike. The battery owners agreed not to crush ore from mines employing Chinese labour and the owners were left with no alternative but to sell the mine to the Europeans.[16]

In addition, while official instructions stated that licence revenue was to be collected from the Chinese 'without undue violence', considerable discretion was given to the goldfield officers.[17] The assistant warden, WRO Hill, took great delight in recounting his experience in forcing the Chinese to take out miners' rights. On several occasions he rounded up and arrested groups of between 100 and 150 Chinese, escorting them over long distances to his camp and retaining their swags until they found the money. He carried a long light chain on a pack horse with 75 pairs of handcuffs, and secured one of the chains around a tree whenever they stopped to camp. On the occasion of his departure from the Palmer, the Chinese farewelled him by letting off a cart load of crackers, but whether this was for 'joy or sorrow' he was not sure.[18]

Many miners and small business people, particularly the packers, disliked competition with the Chinese and in 1877 an Anti-Chinese League was formed in Cooktown.[19] Despite this, many business people in Cooktown considered the Chinese an asset, for they could import many of their goods direct from China, and they were the biggest customers for enterprises such as shipping agents, merchants, cattle growers and banks. Some European carriers, such as Corfield, made agreements with Chinese storekeepers to carry goods for them. While the European business people did not oppose restrictions on Chinese coming onto new goldfields, they were swift to denounce any measures which impoverished themselves.[20]

On the goldfield itself there appears to have been a considerable degree of forebearance and acceptance between the Europeans and the Chinese. By 1877 both races were working in different spheres, the Chinese in alluvial mining and the Europeans on the reefs, which no doubt lessened the prospects for racial antagonism. Furthermore, the European population on the Palmer was dependent upon the Chinese, who ran most of the stores and all the gardens. Charles Bowly wrote in November 1876 that:

> The whole district is crowded with Chinese who keep stores, butcher shops, gambling houses and also grow vegetables at every different settlement. You might almost fancy yourself in China there are so few whites to be seen.[21]

The generally benign relationship between the two races is supported by the reminiscences of J Binnie. He noted that the Aboriginal people usually made their attack on the miners at about 4 am, believing that at this time people were in their soundest sleep. One morning at that hour, his parents saw Aboriginal people about 100 metres from their bark house. The intruders were interrupted by his parents' dogs and by his father calling out to warn a

... the goldfield officers carried a long light chain on a pack horse with 75 pairs of handcuffs, and secured one of the chains around a tree whenever they stopped to camp

The cemetery near Maytown, forlorn admist the fire-ravaged bush

Chinese miner who was camped about 50 metres away. His parents were unarmed, but lost little time in getting a rifle from Echotown. Later that day Aboriginal people attacked a Chinese prospecting party a few kilometres away, but they were driven off by gunfire.[22]

Binnie also recalled that at the small town of German Bar, about six kilometres from Maytown, there was a small general store and a butchering business, both of which were run by Chinese. Sunday was the big shopping day and the only day in the week that fresh meat was available. The butcher killed a bullock every Sunday morning at daybreak and this event attracted most of the neighbouring residents. Most of the carcass was cut up, boned and sold by midday, and the balance salted for other customers. He remembered that the Chinese sundried their meat.[23]

New Year's Day was a very special occasion, for their family was treated to a Chinese feast with the tables laid out with a plentiful supply of poultry and pork and other European and oriental dishes. After they had eaten, the table was cleared and laid out in 'full Chinese style', with a great variety of their national foods, including their own liquor. The leading Chinese of the district were invited. Following the feast, everyone adjourned to the sports ground, where there were performances by young Chinese acrobats and the exploding of hundreds of packets of crackers.[24]

The Aboriginal art galleries at Split Rock, near Laura, are among the most impressive in Australia.

Despite the passage of time, the mobile boiler and ten-head Enterprise stamp mill near Maytown have lost none of their regal splendour.

Stone kerbs and gutters are almost all that remain of Maytown, the capital of the Palmer goldfield.

Abandoned shops at Cracow; at night-time the silence and solitude are unnerving.

Like so many ghost towns, the Cracow cemetery is better populated than the town.

Boarding houses at Cracow provided temporary homes to many miners and other workers.

Once a bustling shopping arcade, these empty shops bear witness to a time when Cracow was one of Queensland's largest goldmining towns.

A family promenade in Maytown,
Palmer Goldfield
(*Queensland Department of Mines Annual Report*, 1902)

The main act of violence involving the Chinese was at Lukinville in 1878, when disputes broke out between rival Chinese groups. Over about two weeks there were three separate incidents involving several hundred Chinese, which resulted in at least four deaths, possibly more. Noreen Kirkman speculated that this incident coincided with the vast increase in the number of Chinese on the field and dwindling gold yields. Already many Chinese had been unable to pay for the new and more costly miners' rights.[25]

While relationships between the Chinese and Europeans were relatively benign, the same could not be said of the relationships between the miners, both European and Chinese, and Aboriginal people. The Etheridge experience was repeated on the Palmer with unrelenting ferocity. Faced with the loss of their lands and impending starvation the Aboriginal people attacked the miners and carriers at every opportunity, harvesting their horses and bullocks as a food source. Reprisals, or as they were termed in those days 'dispersals', followed swiftly. Taking the side of the Europeans the *Cooktown Herald* commented in 1874 that 'When savages are pitted against civilisation, they must go to the wall; it is the fate of their race.'[26]

The savagery of these reprisals, which also involved the killing and kidnapping of women and children, led to an equally fierce response by the indigenous people.[27] Following the killing of the Strau family at a place known thereafter as Murdering Lagoons, and the death and alleged cannibalism of the Macquarie brothers, the racial conflict became even more savage. In his reminiscences, Corfield describes a 'dispersal' carried out by the native troopers. He stated that if at any time he felt a compunction in using his rifle, he lost it when he thought of the Strau and Macquarie murders.[28]

One historian, Noel Loos, has remarked that the effectiveness of the Aboriginal resistance in this area can be gauged by the number of Europeans killed in the Palmer–Cooktown district, for there were twice as many

Europeans killed here than on all other North Queensland frontier mining fields. Both he and Peter Bell have, however, questioned strongly the claim that hundreds, if not thousands, of Europeans were killed. Both have commented that these conflicts have given rise to fanciful stories that have found their way into popular literature and into popular folklore. Some of the more lurid accounts concern alleged cannibalism by the Aboriginal people who, it is alleged, preferred Chinese flesh to European because it was less salty. It has been claimed that the Aboriginal people herded the Chinese into an area known as the devil's kitchen, where they were strung up until needed for culinary purposes.[29]

Peter Bell's research indicates that there are no credible accounts of cannibalism by Aboriginal people. In particular, he strongly disputes the alleged cannibalism of the Macquarie brothers.[30] However, the stories were clearly popular among contemporary observers, and certainly believed by some, including the Chinese. These apprehensions were apparent in the reminiscences of Taam Sze Pui, who was on the goldfields in the 1870s:

> We resumed our journey. Walking sometimes slowly and sometimes briskly, we kept close to the group not daring to detach ourselves lest we should be set upon by the black natives, and probably be devoured by them. The fear of such a fate kept one and all together and no one dared tarry behind to rest or to regain his breath.[31]

By the 1880s the Palmer was in decline, hastened by a mining scandal in 1884, and by the 1890s alluvial mining had ceased and only a few profitable reef mines were left. In 1892 Maytown was described as 'in an almost torpid state', and the entire population of the field was only a little over a thousand. Thereafter, mainly fossickers worked the area, although some efforts at large-scale mining were made.[32] A photograph taken in 1902 shows that the town was still in existence at that time.[33]

The railway to Laura continued for some years after the evacuation of all remaining residents from the field during World War II, but it has long since been abandoned, and only the large concrete pylons remain. On the Palmer, the stumps of the buildings, crumbling stone walls, stone ovens, the remains of slowly rusting machinery and the lonely graves are left. The Maytown District was proclaimed a reserve by the Queensland National Parks and Wildlife Service in 1986, so at least these relics will stand as a memorial to those years of hope and aspiration, turmoil and conflict.

A Stockbroker's Paradise

THROUGH A CURIOUS PROCESS OF NEGLECT THE TOWN OF CRACOW HAS not, like Ravenswood or Maytown on the Palmer goldfield, become one of outback Queensland's icons. Few know of its existence, let alone its history. To a degree this is understandable, for Cracow, about 300 kilometres west of Gympie, is a long way from any sizeable town. It was, however, the scene of one of Australia's last gold rushes and brought employment and sustenance to many men and their families during the trying years of the 1930s Depression. It was also probably one of the first Australian mining towns where miners and prospectors arrived by aeroplane.

Along the dusty drive from Eidsvold beckoning signs attached to trees proclaim variously, 'Are you thirsty?', 'Are you still thirsty?', 'What about your mate?', and finally, close to the traveller's goal, the welcoming sign, 'Relax, you are almost there', or words to that effect. Very thoughtful. A few scattered farms adorn the approaches to the town. The first town building to be met is a derelict boarding house, and along the main street almost every building is abandoned, with the more recent ones displaying an optimistic 'for sale' sign. Even the more recently painted Cracow store is abandoned. Periodically it is resuscitated, only to fall from grace not long after.

The signs on some of the shop buildings are faded, but it is still possible to discern the Bank of New South Wales buildings, the butcher's shop, billiard saloon, frock shop, newsagent and gift shop, Hamilton Motors and another boarding house. Beyond the hotel (now the only operative business in town), is the courthouse, a church and several other buildings, including the bowling club (now used as a community centre) and the old community hall. The most substantial complex of buildings is the hospital with its grand stone façade. Slightly out of town are the mine relics, currently the scene of exploratory work by the gold-mining company, Newcrest. The old mining area includes a large complex of cyanide vats and the manager's house.[1]

The focal point of the town is the hotel, run by Stan and Jenny Brophy. On my visit I was the only guest, and was looked after by the chef, Stan Dunwoody, and several other staff members, who entertained me with stories of the hotel's fiery past. And, of course, everyone was adamant that there was a ghost. It is not clear exactly who the ghost is, but there are two prime candidates. Legend has it that in room number one upstairs an angry husband dispatched his faithless wife to the nether world by shooting her through the floorboards from below, sight unseen.

Almost all the apparitions occur on the first floor and most of them in or near that particular room. Cassandra van Nooten, one of the staff, told of the occasion when she and a girlfriend were watching the TV on the landing outside room one when they saw on the wall the shadow of a person heading towards them; they did not sleep well that night. On another occasion some backpackers were descending the stairs for breakfast when they looked up at the wooden railing and saw a pair of legs in boots.[2]

There are many other unexplained phenomena, such as finding doors that were firmly latched at night open by the morning, even when there is no one staying in the hotel. As my room was on the first floor just down the corridor from room one, I thought it best to sleep with the lights on. I awoke at 7 am after a reasonable sleep, but I was soon assailed by a myriad of noises. Firstly, there was a loud thump on the wall next to me, then the brief sound of footsteps on the floorboards, and next an incessant rattling of the latch on my bedroom door. Finally, and most eerily, there was the unmistakable click of a key in an old wooden wardrobe, not unlike the one in my room. I was the only person on that side of the hotel corridor. Perhaps it was no more than the creaks and groans of an aging timber building … but who knows?

Tommy Mulhall, who is now a resident of Theodore, has confirmed that there was an altercation in the hotel concerning the aforementioned woman, and that a gun was used, but the incident took place in the dining room, not the bar, and no one was killed. There were other shootings in town, and a few other incidents such as throat cuttings, some of which were suicides, or attempted suicides. Several shootings were carried out by women, apparently retaliating at their husbands' partaking of the pleasures of the flesh. In one instance the shot missed its intended target, but the husband had a sore groin for some time, and in another instance a sore backside was the result.[3]

The first gold find in the Cracow area was by a part-Aboriginal stockman, Jacky Nipps, who worked for the Cracow Station in the early 1900s. Mines sunk in this area failed completely, but undeterred, he continued looking and some years later found a lump of gold-bearing quartz in a spot not far from the present-day town of Cracow. On a hurried but more extensive search, he found that almost every lump of quartz was gold-bearing. This information was passed on to a well-sinker, Charlie Lambert, who detected colours in almost every dish. However, dry weather and a lack of funds discouraged him and he did not return until 14 years later in early 1931.

On this occasion Charlie returned with two partners, and after a few weeks of prospecting the party hit upon a very rich quartz lode. The find was registered and the news broke out quickly, for this was clearly one of the most important gold finds in recent years. Other prospectors were attracted to the field and claims were pegged out along the line of the lode.[4] Officials greeted news of the discovery with considerable scepticism, for the geological maps indicated that this was an unlikely area for mineralisation. Consequently, a junior officer was sent to inspect the locality. Alan Denmead was chosen for this task. The miners received him enthusiastically, for his presence was taken as an indication of government interest, although the intention was exactly the opposite. When he arrived in April there were some 40 or 50 men on the field, including several families, and many of the men were unemployed.[5]

Denmead returned to Cracow in June and took a particular interest in a prospect worked by John Mohr and George Ryan, who were in receipt of £1 a week government assistance to unemployed prospectors. On his earlier visit to Cracow he had stayed with the Mohr family and, as he recalled, had the opportunity of showing his gratitude in a practical way. Mohr and Ryan were disappointed with the yield on their claim, but Denmead persuaded them that it might be the prelude to something more promising, and lent them £54 to register the claim as a lease, sealing the contract by 'emptying a bottle of over-proof rum'. As he was planning to get married in a few months this was a big slice out of his savings.[6]

By July there were 200 men on the field. At that stage there was still no crushing machinery, and the evenings and early mornings were given over largely to dollying by pestle and mortar, much as their gold-seeking forebears would have done some eighty years or more before. It was already clear that

Hotel Cracow is the one remaining business in town, and it's haunted!

Cracow was not a poor man's field and that capital was needed to work it successfully.[7] By the time that Denmead returned in June 1932 very good values had been obtained on Mohr and Ryan's lease, and companies had been formed to purchase both theirs and Lambert's lease. The former was to be known as the Golden Mile and the latter as the Golden Plateau, the richest of them all.[8]

The first attempts at civilising the diggings did not occur until April 1932, when a road was constructed through the bush to Theodore by the joint effort of the miners and business people. A weekly mail service was in operation and the first store had been erected by a Theodore businessman, followed by a butcher's store and a small sawmilling plant.[9] A few months later the field was booming. The Golden Plateau company had offered 500 000 shares to the public and within an hour many times that number of subscriptions had been received. Within a few weeks the population had multiplied tenfold.[10] In July, as many as four planes had arrived on the field in one day. A football match between Theodore and Cracow was played and a free dance was held on Cracow's new community floor. An amusements' committee had also been organised.[11]

Denmead's task was to sample all the mine workings, which also required a survey. He asked for an assistant but was refused. However, he found a happy way out, for six months earlier he had married a graduate geologist, and she agreed to work as a chainman on the survey, while at the same time sampling the outcrops as they were working. Writing in 1976 he recounted that the government still had not recompensed her for these services. Denmead also recalled that they were not the only husband and wife team on the field. Ernie Sleep had erected a horse whim at his shaft. Normally the whim was worked by a horse, but Ernie could not afford one, so Mrs Sleep got into the harness and trotted around the track in response to Ernie's signals from below. The buckets were only half-filled, which meant that she worked long hours, but she claimed that it kept her fit.[12]

By September the concerns of the town were turning to questions of roads, health and water. A doctor had taken up residence, an ambulance committee had been formed, and the Department of Health had selected a hospital site on the outskirts of town. A 'talkie' theatre had been erected, and two more butchers, a chemist, a second laundry and new dining rooms had been established. By this time the Rockhampton business community was keen to secure a share of the flow of trade from Cracow, and a delegation was formed to visit the main towns concerned. An important aspect of the discussions was the construction of a road between Cracow and Theodore and the establishment of a tri-weekly train service between Theodore and Rockhampton. The *Morning Bulletin* praised Cracow as a 'Stockbroker's Paradise'.[13]

Not long after, a meeting of local business people decided to form a local chamber of commerce. A school was urgently needed, as there were about 100 children of school age. It was also expected that a sanitary service would be in operation shortly. A dance had been held at the new billiard saloon to raise funds for the Theodore ambulance service. At a public meeting it was agreed to form a Theodore–Cracow–Rockhampton League, to further the claim of Theodore as the railhead for the goldfield and of Rockhampton as the port, and to obtain improvements in road, rail and telephone facilities.[14]

Although there were no pubs, there appeared to be no shortage of drink. Denmead recalled that when one visitor asked where he could get a drink he was pointed in the direction of the church. The incredulous traveller was told that the church was the only place in Cracow where he couldn't get a drink. On the other hand, water was in short supply and expensive, and it was some time before a regular supply was obtained from the Dawson River. There were 10 companies actively mining, with the Golden Plateau clearly the most important.[15]

In E Watson's souvenir booklet, published in 1932, he estimated the population as between 2000 and 3000. Some of the businesses he identified included 17 stores, five bakers, two butchers, eight fruiterers, one stockbroker, two laundries, one machinery house, two cordial factories, three drapers, two chemists, two picture shows, five plumbers, three tailors, two blacksmiths, two newsagents, three billiard rooms, five garages, eight barbers, three sawmills, one brickworks, a sanitary service and a chamber of commerce. Despite this apparent affluence, most of the mines were still poorly equipped and used only windlasses or wheelbarrows for transporting the ore. The buildings were constructed of galvanised iron and timber, although some businesses, such as Scholes' newsagency, Benwell's garage and Hunt's picture theatre, were conducted from tents.[16]

Another account on the Cracow field at this time was by Noela Denmead, Alan's wife. She estimated that the population was between 1200 and 2000 and on either side of the town were 'suburbs' of tents and a few shacks set up in a haphazard manner. In the main street the buildings were almost wholly of iron and canvas, and few could boast of anything more than a dirt floor, while still fewer were furnished with glass windows, but rather a system of wooden shutters. A more superior building would have measured about four metres square with iron walls and roof, a wooden floor and a lock on the door. The furniture would consist of a table supporting a basin and small spirit lamp, and along one wall would be two stretchers, the remaining space serving as a combined dining room and office. One of the largest buildings was the Regent Cafe, which possessed one of the very few glass windows in the town.[17]

The range of businesses was very similar to that described by Watson, but there were three picture theatres, one silent and two talking. In addition, there was an open-air dancing floor and a shooting gallery, occasional boxing matches and visits by theatrical companies. Tennis racquets could be purchased, football and cricket clubs were in full swing and a swimming carnival had been held recently on the Dawson River. Air services were frequent and every conceivable variety of vehicle could be seen, from the most dilapidated to the latest sedan. The traffic was ceaseless and gave an air of liveliness. One

Although there were no pubs, there appeared to be no shortage of drink

result was the continual presence of dust, at times aggravated by small whirlwinds.

Noela was particularly concerned at the plight of the housewives, of whom she was one. The endless dust was testing for those trying to keep their clothes and camps clean and tidy; conversely the mud was particularly sticky and adhesive. In addition, while most houses had wood stoves, a great many of the camps had only open fireplaces. The dirt floors were a particular challenge, for sweeping was an endless and hopeless task; the only remedy was to sprinkle the floor with water. In addition, the furniture suffered from 'black feet', for the legs of chairs, tables and everything else were permanently discoloured. However, many of the houses were neat and well arranged and in the afternoons some women appeared in silk frocks, with accessories such as shoes, stockings and necklets. Occasionally evening dresses were worn.

Of course, some were better set up than others. About three kilometres out of town was a camp owned by Mrs Gorringe. Her camp had the advantage of being away from the prevailing dust and was situated near a small dam, so water was plentiful. It had its own compound, a canvas town of many tents, so that there was a tent for a bedroom, lounge, dining room, guest room, bath, kitchen and store. Between two of the largest tents was a type of fernery lounge surrounded by plants and ferns in pots and a canopy of overhead creepers. Between the tents the ground had been sprinkled with water and trampled down hard, and inside the tents the floors were scoured with an elaborate system of leaves, papers and rush mats. She had a picturesque garden consisting of a number of rockery-like beds in which almost every flower known to the garden lover was growing.[18]

By January 1933 a post office with postal note and money order facilities was open for business. Tennis courts had been erected and there were about 100 members and plans afoot for regular competitions. Following the Anzac Day celebrations in May, a sub-branch of the Returned Soldiers' League was formed. Card evenings during the winter months were planned to raise funds. A basketball club was also formed with the intention of an additional club later. In July a Mr Jarvis announced plans to build an up-to-date theatre, cafe and shops complex of fibrous cement and three-ply lining, hailed by the *Bulletin* as 'a decided improvement on the present structures in the town'. The race to domesticity continued into the latter part of the year. In November a ballet and two plays were held and a welcome to Miss Winifred Jeynes included music provided by the Joy Boys.[19]

By the end of 1934 many of the unprofitable claims had been abandoned, but the Golden Plateau mine continued to expand, and in the process acquired adjoining leases. Working costs had been reduced and to date the company had paid £130,000 in dividends and over the last eleven months it had produced about a ton of gold. None of the other Cracow mines were payable, however, and those that were still operating were handicapped by the lack of adequate crushing facilities. Cracow was described as a well-established township with business places, cafes and a 'very creditable picture

An expectant throng on mail day in Cracow, 1931
(*Queensland Government Mining Journal*, April 1976)

theatre'.[20] In 1935 the Gympie team of Archibald and Runge took over the Rose's Pride and Klondyke leases and erected highly efficient crushing plants, which allowed them to mine low-grade ore at a profit. However, Lambert's old mine, now known as the New Golden Mile, could not find enough ore to keep its mill working.[21]

The late 1930s were the high point for the field and the town. In 1937 continued agitation by the prospectors' association for the erection of a public battery to treat the low-grade ore from the smaller mines led to a conference between the government, the association and owners of the Klondyke mill. The government agreed to subsidise the miners for their own labour, the cost of explosives and cartage to the mill. There was a considerable demand for residential sites outside the surveyed area of the town, and arrangements were made with the Golden Plateau Company for a supply of water from their Dawson River reservoir to the town.[22]

By 1938 the Golden Plateau was firmly entrenched as the most important mine. Up to that date the Cracow field had produced gold to the value of £1.3 million, of which over 96 per cent had come from the Golden Plateau, and employees of the company far outnumbered the prospectors and small miners.[23] Alan Denmead recalled that most of the married men had permanent homes, but that the needs of the single men were not altogether overlooked. Late one day he was on his way back from a survey when he passed an isolated house below the town and spotted a queue of 15 or 20 men waiting at the door. He was a little puzzled until he realised that it was payday at the mine, but that this was not the pay office![24]

1938 was a busy year for Cracow. By this time there was a progress association, a branch of the Country Women's Association and a hospital committee. In May the Minister for Health and Home Affairs attended the opening of the hospital, which had been fully paid for by the government. The Ladies' Guild was a particularly active organisation, and seemed to be continually organising fetes, afternoon teas or concerts and baby shows. A branch of the ALP had also been established by this time and there were sporting associations such as a cricket club and football clubs.[25]

Other organisations were the welfare committee, which was formed to financially assist employees and other members during sickness, accident or death, and the Pioneers of Cracow, which had held annual reunions since 1935. There was a Cracow band and also a number of other musical groups, which played at functions such as benefit evenings. The new courthouse was opened in August by the police magistrate, who commented that Cracow was a very law-abiding community. An Oddfellows Lodge was formed in the same month. Concerts and dances were also organised in aid of the school.[26]

The war years were difficult for Cracow, as they were for almost all gold-field towns. There were continued shortages of manpower due to a large number of miners having enlisted or been called up for military and other services, and also due to men seeking more lucrative employment elsewhere. During 1943 only the Golden Plateau mine operated, and even this mine had only sufficient men to keep the mills going part time at two shifts for a five-day week. Several houses had been sold for removal and some businesses had ceased to operate. The population was 410, compared with more than 800 in peacetime.[27]

By 1959 dwindling ore reserves were causing the company to have serious misgivings about the future of the mine, but fortunately an extensive drilling program located substantial ore reserves.[28] In 1976, however, the mine was closed. In its 43 years of operations the Golden Plateau had produced almost 592 000 ounces of gold. It was one of the largest lode mines in Queensland, and with its closure the golden era of Queensland mining was virtually over, for the once-fabled Mount Morgan mine had closed just a few months before. At the end Cracow was no more than a shadow of its former self, for there were only 65 adults and 50 children, and whilst the closure may have been a sad day for some, it does not appear to have come as a surprise.[29]

NEW SOUTH WALES

Valleys of Oil

MOST OF THE TOWNS THAT GREW UP AROUND AUSTRALIA'S HISTORIC oil-shale industry in the nineteenth and early to mid-twentieth centuries are located in stunningly attractive ravines and valleys, bordered on two or more sides by towering sandstone cliffs. Access is not always easy or straightforward, for although the mines and towns are only a few hours' drive from Sydney, in some cases they are on the fringe of the wilderness areas of the Blue Mountains. Some of the towns and industrial sites have been restored and preserved whilst others have been left to the mercy of the bush.

In the latter part of the nineteenth century oil shale was used to manufacture kerosene, oil and paraffin. The kerosene was used for lighting and the paraffin for candles. The manufacturing processes were complex and involved retorting, distillation and refining, which required substantial capital investment in plant, equipment and labour.[1] In turn this led to the establishment of sizeable towns and villages.

Oil-shale refining in New South Wales commenced at Mount Kembla and Hartley Vale in 1865. In 1874 the *Town and Country Journal* correspondent described the manager's house at Hartley Vale as a 'conspicuous and pretentious building … a pretty and bright looking residence surrounded by a garden filled with gay flowers'. At the back were offices, stables and sleeping apartments for visitors. A school and other homes with neat gardens were nearby. Today a few walls of the retorts and refinery can be found amidst dense scrub on the fringe of a small cluster of buildings and farms. Hartley Vale allegedly had a peak population of 1500, but now there are only a handful of residents.[2]

Another early oil-shale mining venture commenced at Airly Mountain in the Capertee Valley in 1883, where a small village was established along the valley floor and along the main track to the mines. Retorts were constructed in 1900, and the private township of Torbane followed. The mines on Airly Mountain were connected by a tramway and cable haulage system with the retorts, which were in turn connected to the government railway at Torbane siding. After processing in the retorts, the crude oil was transported by rail to the company's refinery at Hartley Vale.

Following serious industrial problems at Torbane in 1911, the company decided to restrict operations in the area and focus on Newnes. In 1913 the retorts were closed, and a steady exodus of men and buildings took place from both Airly and Torbane. The last big social event at Torbane was in July, when an Eight-Hour Day picnic and social were held. Operations recommenced in 1916, but two years later the works were closed and by 1920 the company houses had been dismantled and sent to Newnes. The retorts and other plant were progressively but slowly dismantled over the next ten years. Shale mining recommenced in 1944, but activity did not rise to any great heights.[3]

At Airly some of the building remains are in good condition and in almost all instances the chimneys are still standing. Some of the huts were built adjacent to and adjoining large granite boulders, which gave some protection from the weather. One miner constructed his home in a small cave under one of the boulder overhangs, and in another even more notable case, a miner constructed a two-roomed house under an overhang, and used mud bricks to build the outside wall. An external kitchen chimney and fireplace adjoined the overhang, with the whole edifice reminiscent of the Anasazi cliff buildings in Arizona and New Mexico. There are only a few buildings left at Torbane, such as the manager's house, the brick-built railway station (now a stables) and the somewhat ornate oil works.

Glen Davis is located at the eastern extremity of Capertee Valley. During the 1930s the Commonwealth and State Governments established a committee to investigate the feasibility of re-establishing a refinery in the Carpertee Valley, making use of equipment from the abandoned works at Newnes. The part private, part government-owned National Oil Company was formed, and a new town, Glen Davis, was built. A pipeline was constructed to convey the finished petrol from Glen Davis to the railhead at Newnes Junction.

According to an account by Allan Cargill, the first residents lived in appalling conditions and suffered from a lack of water, sanitation, food supplies and an inability to obtain building materials. The nearest large town was Lithgow, which was a bone-jarring four hours away, much of the trip along a bush track from Capertee. A well-laid-out town with prefabricated houses was eventually built, and by 1947 there were 11 brick staff cottages, a brick hostel for 30 junior employees, 100 permanent and 50 war-type emergency houses, a hostel accommodating 300, a 'bagtown' of 125 substandard buildings, three churches and a large hotel. Other businesses and facilities included a doctor, chemist, community hall, school, two general stores, barber, butcher, garage, post office, bank, police station, picture theatre and ambulance station.[4]

In 1942, the Commonwealth Government assumed control of the enterprise and the retorts were reconstructed and the plant extended. Unfortunately, the output of shale from the mines could not keep pace with the plant's requirements. Oil production fell, and the plant operated at a loss. The shale deposits became less economical to work, and the Miner's Federation was concerned that efforts to increase output could threaten the safety of the miners. By 1951 the plant was producing only half of one per cent of Australia's petrol consumption. It was clearly an uneconomical proposition, and in the light of continuing manpower shortages in the coal mining industry it was decided to close the plant.[5]

There had been 1800 people living in the town, but uncertainty over the future had caused many of them to leave. Development ground to a halt. By the middle of 1951 businesses such as William Ferguson's bakery were already feeling the effect. He had intended retiling the bakery and had bought tiles for that purpose. The chemist had almost finished building his new shop, but work on that had now ceased. Jack Henderson, the publican, had sold his hotel in Bathurst and sunk his life savings into the hotel. The Country Women's Association had spent five years raising money to build a new baby welfare centre. They had spent half of the proceeds on the new building, but work on that too had ceased. The scouts had raised funds for the building of a new gymnasium, but that was also shelved.[6]

However, in its death throes Glen Davis achieved the fame and glory that had eluded it in its heyday. In protest at the closure 54 miners began a stay-down strike in the mine in June 1952. By the tenth day the strike had already surpassed the Australian stay-down strike record. While several men left the mine for medical reasons, the remainder stayed. Some continued to mine the shale, and otherwise passed most of their time reading, playing cards, listening to the gramophone and wireless and even playing billiards on a small table erected for that purpose. The women of Glen Davis stood by their men, running a soup kitchen at the pithead to supply meals. Following the withdrawal of support by the Australian Council of Trade Unions, the strike ended. The men had spent 26 days underground.[7]

Other than the hotel, which became a seminary and then a boarding house, the main relics in Glen Davis are the various buildings at the refinery, which include a tall bank of brick retorts. Although it has been gradually reclaimed by the bush and blackberries, the refinery still looks like a bombed out wasteland — a bush version of Berlin or Stalingrad. Several fibro and brick houses and shopfronts are strung out along the now largely deserted streets of the town. Some have been reoccupied and a few newer homes have been built relatively recently, but not enough to counter the overall air of desertion. According to Leonie Knapman and many others, the ghosts of Glen Davis are not confined to the buildings. An unexplained priestly figure can be seen in a video clip filmed for a rock group on the refinery site. Stories of a suicide and the sudden abandonment of the seminary have since come to light, but I will leave these for Leonie to tell in her forthcoming book on Glen Davis.[8]

... in its death throes Glen Davis achieved the fame and glory that had eluded it in its heyday

At Newnes, in the nearby Wolgan Valley, large scale oil-shale mining commenced under the auspices of the Commonwealth Oil Corporation in 1906. Many of the early miners were Scottish immigrants, who brought with them their expertise and experience in mining and refining. A retorting and refining complex was completed in 1911. The works were elaborate and comprehensive, and a full range of by-products was produced, such as kerosene and fuel oils, fertiliser, paraffin wax candles, coke and oil pitch. Both the coke and the locally made bricks were used in Lithgow.[9]

In his history of Newnes, Lawrence Salter described the town as having a haphazard appearance. Houses and huts were scattered around the adjoining hillside, and were not connected by roads but by a maze of tracks, with a small number of shops arranged at odd intervals along the main road. In 1906 Newnes had a population of about a hundred people, and there were two places where groceries could be bought and a butcher's shop. The streets had still to be formed and the inhabitants lived in buildings with frames made from saplings, with canvas, bagging or galvanised iron fixed over the frame.[10] Tony Luchetti observed that some homes 'were very sad places', while others were comfortable, with bark roofs, slab sides, ant-bed floors and mats. Some were 'beautifully decorated' with the pictorial pages from newspapers and magazines.[11]

By March 1907 the population had increased to about 800, but facilities were limited and access was very difficult with the main road little more than a bridle track. Salter has commented that there was a conflict of interest between the company, which was preoccupied with the works, the government and the Blaxland Shire. The council failed to make arrangements for the provision of roads, water and sanitary arrangements until 1910 when the company brought the threat of a typhoid outbreak to the attention of the Board of Health. While some form of sanitary arrangements was provided, no move was made to construct a second main street or to provide a piped water supply.

Other areas of neglect included the post office and school. A regular postal service was not inaugurated until late 1907, following the construction of the railway from Newnes Junction. The post office was constructed on the railway platform near the oil works, and on the opposite side of the river to the township. However, the light traffic bridge across the river was washed away in floods, and despite numerous representations, it was never rebuilt. This meant that the townsfolk had to ford the river by horse before reaching either the post office or oil works. Neither was there a school until 1907, though there were some 50 or 60 children in the town.

At its peak the town contained about a dozen shops, while at other times there were only two. As well as the grocery stores, there was also one baker's shop and two butcher's shops, one of which was operated by a branch of the Lithgow Co-operative Society. The co-op building was, unlike most others in the town, constructed of brick with sandstone foundations. In addition, the society also operated a general store. There were two hotels and a Parochial

The remains of the cyanide vats at the Golden Plateau mine, one of Queensland's most productive mines

The coke ovens at Newnes were built at a time when the town was Australia's leading oil shale producer.

Built on the slopes of a steep hill, the homes of the company executives at Newnes commanded stunning views of the valley below.

At Airly the miners built their homes wherever they could find flat ground and a bit of shelter.

Part of the ornate and stately oil shale refinery at Torbane, near Capertee

The remains of the schoolhouse at Mount Hope; there are now only a hotel and a few homes left.

The immense slag heaps at Mount Hope bear witness to a time when copper-seeking was the backbone of many towns in western New South Wales.

The paraffin sheds, Newnes

Hall, which was used for church services, a Sunday school and a men's read-ing room. The Sutherland family contributed most of the monies for the hall's construction, and it remained in use until the 1930s.[12]

Technical and labour problems led to the closure of the works in March 1913 and the following week most of the population left the town on two free trains. By July the two general stores and police station had closed, and the remaining population was dependent for their supplies on a visiting grocer. The train service between Newnes Junction was also restricted to once a week. By February 1914 the population had fallen to a mere 96 persons, but help was on the way, for the retorts were redesigned and operations re-commenced the following year.[13]

Continuing industrial problems led to the closure of the works in 1924, by which time the population had fallen to 200. By May of that year there was only a handful of men working at the distillery. Ironically, the council's road gangs had only just repaired the town's roads and streets for the first time since its establishment, and the teacher's residence was nearing completion. In June 1927 a visitor to the valley described it as a scene of stagnation, 'utter and complete'.[14] A few months later another visitor reported:

Scores of one-time cottages, rendered neat and trim by those who resided in them ... have fallen into a state of decay. Broken windows, doors nailed up with rusting iron, tumbledown fences, out-houses, and neglected gardens, present a very depressing aspect.[15]

Between 1929 and 1936 there were three more attempts to take over and operate the works, but none were successful. In 1931 Newnes was inundated by unemployed men looking for work, but when the project failed they too left.[16] The *Lithgow Mercury* described the scene thus:

Picture a long, winding and dusty road — motor cars and motor lorries, all laden with men ... horsemen canter by, leaving a cloud of dust in their wake, motor bikes ... are seen for a moment and then disappear amongst the trees and ferns. Cycles, laboriously propelled by perspiring men, take a more sedate pace and last of all men with swags on their backs trudge wearily along the roadside, all with intent faces, making for the Mecca of Newnes.[17]

The plant was taken over by the National Oil Company in 1937, dismantled and removed for later use at Glen Davis. By 1940 there were only four families living at Newnes.[18]

Today the Wolgan Valley is still isolated and difficult of access. On entering the valley the persevering traveller is, however, rewarded by stunning views of the sandstone ramparts to the Blue Mountains on either side. The road into the valley is less enchanting, a mixture of very indifferent and potholed bitumen and an occasionally graded dirt road, which in the wet weather would be impassable for some vehicles. On reaching the valley floor one of the first sights is the weatherboard hotel, but within its doors no succour can be found, for it is now closed. Further down the track the Parks and Wildlife Service has created a large camping area.

The main residential part of the town is reached by a foot track, which follows the course of the Wolgan River up to its junction with Petrie's Gully. Some house sites, including the remains of a brick kiln, can be seen from the main track, but most of the houses are located on a steep hillside overlooking the gully. The largest buildings, as evidenced by the tall and still largely intact stone chimneys, were located at the very summit of an even narrower footpad. Obviously these were the homes of management and other dignitaries, for in the early 1900s trees and other vexatious forms of vegetation would have all been cleared for use in the oil works, leaving unimpeded views of the valley from several vantage points.

To access the oil works it is necessary to cross the river, a task that can either be accomplished on foot or by vehicle, but obviously not when the river is in flood. The remains of the oil works are still relatively intact, not withstanding the demolition of many of the buildings. My favourite has always been the paraffin sheds, looming out of the bush like some huge Aztec ruin, and downhill from those, several banks of beehive-shaped oil washers. Above

Joadja refinery (foreground) and
Carrington Row (background)
(Courtesy Leonie Knapman)

these stand the remains of a substantial bank of coke ovens, and further
downhill a prominent brick retaining wall, which is about 10 metres high.
The retorts and other associated works are located on flatter ground near the
river. It is to the credit of the Parks and Wildlife Service that so much has been
done to stabilise the structures and to provide access tracks and interpretation
signs.

Perhaps the most renowned and picturesque shale-mining site is in the
Joadja Valley near Mittagong, south of Sydney. Mining commenced in 1876
and soon there were 300 to 400 residents in the valley. Transport was difficult, however, with access into the valley by a narrow packhorse track. To
overcome these difficulties a tramway was built on the main incline using a
winch worked by horses. In 1878 a steam-powered railway was constructed
to operate on the valley floor, and an inclined railway was built to link the
valley floor with the newly constructed branch line from Mittagong. Another
inclined railway was built on the other side of the valley to transport shale to
the processing plant. Passengers and freight were also carried by the inclined
tramway. Open-air carriages were often used on the trip to Mittagong, ensur-
ing that the passengers received a good dousing of cinder, ash and smoke.[19]

Subsequently, the company erected large retorts and a refinery. In 1879 a
Town and Country Journal correspondent noted that there were 150 men
employed in the valley. The manager was provided with an 'excellent home,

and the miners, mechanics, and others, with very comfortable cottages'. There was also a company store, a post office, two butchers, two bakeries and a school.[20] To overcome labour shortages, experienced workers were recruited from Scotland, and Scottish retorts, distillation equipment and locomotives were purchased. In 1880 a correspondent described the manager, Mr Brown, as a 'shrewd determined-looking Scotchman'. Of the workers it was commented that their 'language is the broadest and sometimes the most incomprehensible, the dress in some cases the quaintest, and the habits peculiar'. There was a population of 300.[21]

The migrants entered into a two-and-a-quarter-year contract at good wages. However, the conditions in the valley must have shocked many of them. In her book, *Joadja Creek*, Leonie Knapman provides several accounts of the housing which, for the main, consisted of slab houses and earthen floors, the main collection of which earned the title 'Stringybark Row'. Worse still, to prevent fire, the company had cleared all vegetation from the floor of the valley to the top of the hills. With the refinery and retorts belching steam and smoke the valley must have presented an awesome sight. Understandably, some of the miners reacted by absconding.[22]

In 1882 there were 20 new brick cottages built, most of which had between three and five rooms, a washhouse, kitchen and toilet, and white-washed walls. Outside, the area was liberally planted with deciduous trees. Originally named 'Brick Row', the name was changed to Carrington Row after a visit by Governor Carrington. Nonetheless, many of the homes at Joadja remained small and cramped. One correspondent remarked on the resplendent hall used for concerts and meetings and the houses of the managers and directors, but the overall impression was of an indiscriminate, irregular jumble of buildings, works, shops, kilns and equipment. Jumbled it may have been, but it was a large town, and in 1891–92 the population would have exceeded 1200, more than the combined population of nearby Mittagong, Bowral and Moss Vale. Despite its size, the town did not have a hotel until the mid-1880s and most of the alcohol was supplied by illegal stills. Police raids were often well known about beforehand, however, and the stills hidden in time.[23]

Although Joadja's population was 90 per cent Presbyterian, there was no consecrated church, as the population attended St Paul's in Mittagong. However, Sunday school and services were held in the school of arts after its construction in 1886. There was also a very strong Masonic Lodge, a Band of Hope, a branch of the Oddfellows and a wide array of sports, for example, soccer, cricket, fencing, boxing, quoits and shooting. Concerts and balls, often attended by the Mittagong Brass Band, were held in the school of arts. In January each year the Oddfellows celebrated Robert Burns' birthday with an athletics sports day, ball and supper.

Organised picnic days were an important part of community life, particularly over the Christmas and New Year period, which many residents spent in Mittagong. One aspect of life at Joadja that set it well apart from many other

colonial communities, was its relative immunity to epidemics of cholera, influenza, diphtheria and typhoid. Leonie Knapman attributes this to the valley's isolation and lack of through traffic. Possibly more important was the water supply. Originally the water had to be carried to most homes. Later, it was stored in reservoirs and then piped to the refinery and village.

Fruit growing was another important industry in the valley. The company planted extensive orchards in the valley and at the top of the incline; the surplus crop was packed and railed to Sydney. During the 1880s production of kerosene, gasoline, benzine and paraffin was maintained at a high level. But by the early 1890s production began to fall in the face of competition from cheaper North American products and increased mining difficulties. Men were occasionally laid off and many families began to leave the valley. By 1900 the railway had ceased to run, and in 1903 the mine was closed indefinitely. The final blow to the company was the removal of import duties on kerosene. In 1905 fires destroyed many buildings.[24]

Thereafter, the only industry in the valley was from the company's extensive orchards, which by then contained over 6000 fruit trees, though this too ceased in 1924. The plant and buildings gradually fell into disrepair, and were subject to vandalism and souvenir hunting. Cedar woodwork in the school was used for campfires and a door was used as a makeshift bridge. Some of the mines and structures in the valley were further destabilised by a severe earthquake in 1973. According to a visitor in 1941 'trees have grown up through the floors of the houses and vines are entwined around the retorts and tanks ... The whole scene has a poetic quality hardly to be expected from a place so recently in commission'.[25]

On my trip to Joadja I was fortunate to be accompanied by Mark Longobardi and Greg and Leonie Knapman. Mark is the new owner of Joadja and has put a herculean effort into clearing the sites and constructing improved access paths for the public. For some 10 years prior to his purchase of the property public access had been restricted. Leonie for her part can quite rightly claim title as the 'Queen of Joadja'. She has written about the valley extensively, and with her husband Greg has been to the forefront in promoting it for many years. The good news on Joadja is that after many years of seclusion, it is back in business as a visitor destination.

There is still much to see at Joadja; indeed it is probably the best-preserved nineteenth-century industrial and residential complex in Australia. In front of the mines are the chimneys used in furnace ventilation, and inside the mines the fire grates and the incredibly narrow shale seams. The remains of the two benches of retorts with their chimneys and part of the refinery works and their chimneys can still be seen on the valley floor. Of particular note are the remnants of the director's house and its associated buildings, the school of arts, the school and the houses in Carrington Row. These commodious and well-built brick buildings with their whitewashed walls stand under the shady bows of spreading deciduous trees. They are a restful contrast to the arid surrounds of so many other Australian ghost towns.

Along the Kidman Way

PRIOR TO THE DISCOVERY OF COPPER AT COBAR IN 1870, MUCH OF western New South Wales north of Hillston was little more than a poorly populated sheep run, for there were few towns or even roads of any consequence. European settlement and the development of much of the west were almost entirely dependent upon the discovery and exploitation of minerals such as copper and, subsequently, gold. Cobar was the most significant of these towns and remains so today. Indeed, almost all other towns in the region have either vanished or are close to so doing, their future having waxed and waned with changing copper prices or, in the case of gold, with the depletion of ore deposits. The Kidman Way links many of these towns.

Copper mining first commenced in 1874 at Mount Hope, north of Hillston, and by the following year a manager's house, store and men's huts had been built.[1] Six years later the company was reorganised and smelters were built. By 1882 the mine employed 200 men and boys and the town had a population of 800. It was served by four hotels, a post office and savings bank, a billiard room and boxing saloon, four stores, with two being built, two or more butchers and three bakers. The same year, 100 men were employed at the Great Central mine at South Mount Hope, where smelters had also been constructed. A police station and public school were erected at Mount Hope in 1884.[2]

By 1885 the population had reached well over a thousand residents in both towns. At Mount Hope a Roman Catholic chapel was the only place of worship. Other denominations used the Good Templars Hall, which seated between 30 and 40 people. There were two cells at the police station, a comfortable cottage for the senior constable, a surgeon, chemist, produce merchant, watchmaker, bootmaker and saddler. Not long after, however, plunging copper prices brought an end to this prosperity. Both mines were closed and the towns abandoned.[3]

In 1888 there was a resurgence of mining activity sparked by an increase in copper prices. At the onset of this revival a *Town and Country Journal* correspondent portrayed Mount Hope as a long, straggling town:

> Near the mine are numbers of ruins where mud or bark huts once stood, while the street is lined by a number of weatherboard stores and shops, many of which have been closed for the past two years and are not yet opened.[4]

Nevertheless, the population was gradually returning, some of the deserted shops had been reopened, and a barber, bootmaker and a saddler had also set up business. According to the postmaster, several months before Mount Hope had consisted of 70 adults and South Mount Hope 80, but now the adult population had almost doubled. If children were added the total population would have been even higher. Sixty-eight pupils attended the public school, a solid weatherboard structure. There was a Roman Catholic chapel that was used only once every three months, the Protestants continuing to contend with the Good Templars Hall.

South Mount Hope was described as a long, scattered township running along two sides of the company's fenced land. Inside the fence were several miners' huts, the manager's residence, a store and the public school, while outside were three hotels, another store and several homes, nearly all built of timber. There was little cultivation around the township, other than a few flower gardens, some of them with fruit trees. Many of the stores were closed, but new arrivals were coming every day, and a revival was expected.

Both mines were highly capitalised. The Mount Hope mine included four smelters and a refinery, and there were plans to expand the plant, while at the Great Central mine at South Mount Hope there were two smelters and a refinery. Large numbers of men were employed in wood gathering, and at Mount Hope the timber was cleared for about five or six kilometres around the township. At the Great Central, steam-powered hauling machinery was to be installed for the first time.

By 1889 the New Mount Hope mine, as it was now called, employed 62 men, who were working on tribute, and the Great Central employed 90. Mining continued throughout the 1890s, but at a slower pace, for there were rarely more than 40 men employed at either mine. By 1902 both mines were again closed and Mount Hope was 'well nigh deserted'. In response to higher metal prices the Mount Hope mine was reopened in 1906, but for the Great Central it was the end of the line — the mine was abandoned and all machinery removed. By 1909 metal prices had again fallen and the New Mount Hope mine was abandoned. A small-scale treatment plant was erected at a later stage, but it only employed a few men, the stop-start nature of mining by then having taken its toll of the town and its businesses.[5]

The collapse of copper prices towards the end of World War I brought an abrupt end to the prosperity of all copper mines in the region, including those at Cobar. Where the copper occurred in association with gold, mining continued. But for Mount Hope it was the final straw. Today there are only a handful of homes left, and the only business still in operation is the Royal Hotel, under the amiable management of Annie Hamilton. The ruins of a bakery can be seen across the road from the hotel, and elsewhere in the town are the abandoned schoolhouse and police station. Extensive remains of the mines and the slag and waste dumps are a reminder of busier days.

Between Mount Hope and Nymagee there were several other even more ephemeral mining settlements. Two of these were gold-mining towns. Gold was found at Mount Allen in 1894, but by 1902 the small town was 'another practically deserted village'. Rather more resilient was Gilgunnia, which had the fortune to be located astride the road from Mount Hope to Cobar (now the Kidman Way). Gold was found at Gilgunnia in 1895, and there were soon about 185 men on the various claims and about 60 more in the vicinity. The rush was, however, short lived, and by the end of the following year only 51 remained. A large battery had been erected, but it operated spasmodically because of a lack of stone for crushing.[6]

In her history *Gilgunnia, a Special Place*, Leila Alderdyce recounts that water or the lack of it was a major concern. The schoolteacher, Mr Helm, had a particularly trying time. He had to requisition the Education Department for a water barrel for the children's needs, and subsequently he requested a small allowance so that he could supplement this supply with water purchased from the water carter. In time the bark roof of the school cracked and split, and the rain, when it came, fell onto the children below. Eventually the school and teacher's residence were located in part of a vacated hotel. However, there were large gaps in the floorboards and the schoolroom was cold and draughty and did not possess a fireplace or stove. He made several requests for a transfer, but these were declined.[7]

By 1900 the drought had taken a terrible hold on western New South Wales, one observer commenting that there were scarcely any sheep on any of the holdings and that even the rabbits had almost died out. At Gilgunnia there were few men on the field and most of the business places and private dwellings were empty. By the middle of 1901 there was one hotel, a post office, butcher's shop, two small stores, and a few scattered houses, most of which were empty. One resident who stayed until the end was a Chinese gardener known as Charlie Chin, who excavated a large underground tank on his property, and later supplemented that with water carried from the battery tank some 400 metres away. He grew both vegetables and fruit, including grapes and peaches, and transported his produce to Mount Hope on a bicycle.[8] Today all that remains of the town is a stone plaque and rest area.

Copper was discovered at Nymagee in 1880, and within a short time four reverberatory furnaces, brick kilns, a large powder magazine, storeroom and 20 wooden, iron-roofed huts for the workmen were under construction. A hotel had opened up in the area some time before the discovery of copper. Five more opened for business during the year. Two general stores, with two more under construction, three butcher's shops, a steam saw-mill and

In time the bark roof of the school cracked and split, and the rain, when it came, fell onto the children below

119

a multitude of trades and professions serviced the population of around 500. One farmer took up a lease to establish a large vegetable garden and a dairy.[9]

By 1882 there were 500 working the mine and the population had jumped to about 2000, but the fall in metal prices in the mid-1880s led to a reduction in output, and by 1887 there were only enough hands retained to keep the works in order and the mine open.[10] Work resumed later that year, and by May of the following year a correspondent of the *Town and Country Journal* reported that there were about 430 men employed, including miners, surface hands and wood carters. The timber demands were enormous, for the eight smelters and three calciners consumed about 5000 tonnes of wood a month.[11]

South-west of the main town, at Cornish Town, the houses fronting the street were built by the company and rented to the miners and their families. Other miners set up their own humble abodes, using calico, bark and kerosene tins. The correspondent commented that the huts were much more comfortable than might be supposed because the Cornish men and women were 'very clean in their habits and rather particular about their habitations'.

Other buildings included a bank, a public school with 180 students enrolled, a police station, cells and a courthouse, all three of which were to be rebuilt. The most imposing building in Nymagee was the two-storeyed post office, which also provided accommodation for the staff. A brick-built cottage hospital, with a separate kitchen and accommodation building, was located about three kilometres from the town. The hospital was supported by a government grant and by local people, who had raised £100 at a bazaar and fair the previous year. There was a Roman Catholic church, convent and school and a Wesleyan church and five hotels. It was remarked that there was much less hard drinking in Nymagee than many other country towns, and the police were not called upon very often.

The population was estimated to include about 1200 Europeans and a large number of Chinese, of whom there were between 800 and 1000 in the district. They had about a dozen bark houses and huts in the eastern part of the town, and were engaged primarily in scrub-cutting and ring-barking, although they also had several market gardens around the town. They were generally under the control of two or three headmen, who took contracts on the various stations at prices which 'literally defy competition'. There were about 200 Chinese who were cutting and burning scrub on Goan Downs near Mount Hope, while 24 000 hectares were to be cleared at Yathong, and large contracts had been let on various other runs. One squatter had commented that Europeans were no good at that type of work.

> They can't do it at the price; and if they take a contract they only do so to get draw of rations and then clear out and take the tools with them. It's quite different with the Chinese; we only deal with the head man, and whatever price he accepts the work is always done, even when they can't earn tucker at it. And then they don't get drunk, and kick up rows.

It was remarked that there was much less hard drinking in Nymagee than many other country towns, and the police were not called upon very often

It seems that the working men in the district were not so kindly disposed towards the Chinese, but this did not manifest itself in any overt way. An account by the late Mr E McKay, retold in the *Nymagee Centenary 1879–1979*, stated that there were about a hundred Chinese scrub-cutters camped behind Ah Moy's store.[12]

In 1896 the Nymagee mines were acquired by the Great Cobar Mining Syndicate, and the following year major changes were made to the mining and smelting plant. Modern water-jacket blast furnaces, which used coke for fuel, were erected to replace the old brick reverberatory furnaces, electric lighting was installed and a tramway constructed from the roasting kilns to the furnaces. The acquisition by Great Cobar obviously heralded in a new period of prosperity for Nymagee, and may also have been instrumental in leading to the discovery of rich copper deposits at Crowl Creek in 1901, where a new town called Shuttleton was established and furnaces and a refinery erected.[13]

The early 1900s were prosperous and active years for Nymagee. In August 1901 the Reverend Kelly visited the Church of England congregation for several days, during which time there was a tea meeting and concert, and an announcement that the debt on the new church building had been further reduced and that it would open shortly. A mission was also held by the Roman Catholic church, with the ground between the church and convent transformed into a sacred grove of transplanted pine trees around which the adults and children paraded. In 1902 a new brick-built courthouse, police station and cells were built. Bicycle racing was a popular sport in the town. Shuttleton had by this time a hotel, with another under construction, five storekeepers, two butchers, a wine shop and newsagency, sawmill, two boarding houses, a billiard room, progress committee and a branch of the Wrightville Amalgamated Miners' Association.[14]

In 1907 the Shuttleton mines were closed and the Nymagee mines were sold and all the old plant, with the exception of the blast furnace, was removed and replaced with new equipment and buildings. The decision to sell was obviously a wise one, for the increasingly poor quality of the ore and the high costs of cartage for coke and wood were seriously affecting profits, and later that year the new owners were forced to close the mines. There had been constant but fruitless calls for an extension of the main railway to Nymagee to help alleviate transport costs.[15] The effect of the closure on some individuals and businesses was devastating. In one account the writer recounted the misfortune of his brother, a chemist at Nymagee

who left his comfortable home to rot and went to Canbelego to a horrid damp shack to try to eke out a livelihood. There he contacted [sic] cold and pneumonia set in and he died, leaving in my charge a daughter of 19 years.[16]

The Nymagee mines were sold again in 1909, but it was not until 1913 that work recommenced on any scale. In that year new plant and equipment were installed and by 1915 the mines were again in full production. Mining

The abandoned Nymagee
Post Office

also recommenced at Shuttleton. Carting continued to be important, and at times there were about 50 carriers transporting coke from the railway to Nymagee. By early February 1917 additional accommodation had been provided for the workers, and in June the town was described as 'moving along'. A bazaar had been held in aid of the convent debt and had raised £250, and a doctor had been appointed with a view to reopening the hospital.[17]

This new burst of prosperity did not last, for by December 1917 the Nymagee mines were closed. Lack of railway communication, freight charges and labour troubles were regarded as the main causes, and by March the town was described as 'almost deserted'. A month later the inhabitants welcomed the sound of the old traction engine, but it had been sold and was on its way out to Girilambone. Though not connected with copper mining, the settlement of Gilgunnia was 'a deserted camp', with just a hotel, a deserted store and a Chinese garden. In June it was Shuttleton's turn. The mine was closed and smelting operations ceased some months later. In September the one remaining store closed its doors, leaving the town without a store for the first time in its existence. The Cobar mines closed in early 1918, but were reworked subsequently for gold.[18]

Today at Nymagee there is a school, police station and hotel. The most prominent buildings from Nymagee's heyday are the hospital and post office, now both private residences, and the police station and courthouse. Scattered around the town are a few miners' cottages, some occupied, some abandoned. According to residents such as Pat Dunn there is an air of civic pride and progress in the town, and an annual festival attracts hundreds of visitors. Shuttleton is completely abandoned.

Canbelego, some 60 kilometres north of Nymagee, was the main town on the Mount Boppy goldfield. It has fallen on much harder times than Nymagee, for only a few houses are left, and there is no hotel. But it was not always so. Incredible as it may seem now, from 1901 to 1909 Canbelego was by far the largest gold-producing centre in New South Wales, rivalled only by Cobar. Gold was first found in 1896, and production commenced in 1901. The mine could access water from the government bore, which enabled it to withstand the withering drought conditions in the early 1900s.[19]

In 1904 the *Town and Country Journal* described Canbelego in the following glowing terms:

To one who has had experience of very many embryonic mining towns throughout Australasia, Canbelego appears as though having 'come to stay'. The hessian and iron buildings, so common a feature in the above, are absent here, all the houses being generally built of weatherboard. One of the proprietors of a sawmill in the outskirts of the township informs me that they cannot, with their present appliances, cope with orders for timber. In the main street are three well-built hotels, six stores, two butchers' shops, a baker's, blacksmith's, and billiard saloons, cool drink shops and boarding-houses innumerable. A courthouse is in course of construction and will be visited periodically by the police magistrate and warden from Cobar.

There were 158 pupils enrolled in the school, compared to 36 in 1901, but the school building was now 'altogether inadequate to its requirements'. The Presbyterian church was the only place of worship, although the building was used by other religious bodies when the occasion required. J Bryant, a wholesale and retail fruiterer and tobacconist, had erected a large marble soda-water fountain and a soda water and cordial plant on his premises. The town also possessed a 'very nice little library' and a doctor. There were 900 residents, 180 of them employed in the mines.[20]

By 1908 the population had risen to 3000 and there were about 400 men working at the mine. A convent and convent school had also been erected. With the inevitable depletion of the easily treated ore bodies in the upper levels, a change in treatment processes became necessary and an extensive new plant was constructed. By 1912 the town had between 2000 and 3000 residents and boasted four churches, a public hall and a one-ward hospital with two resident doctors. The mine owners had provided a reading room, library and band-room within the mine enclosure. During World War I, labour shortages, increases in wages and material costs led to the introduction of open-cut mining. Today, the few straggling houses and vacant blocks bear

Miner's dwelling with rusted kerosene tins nearby, Mount Drysdale

scant witness to these years of glory. However, there is a faint glimmer of hope courtesy of Polymetal Mining Services, which has recommenced mining with a work force of 20, using the old post office as the mine office.[21]

One of the more intriguing ghost towns along the Kidman Way is Mount Drysdale, north of Cobar. It is located on Mount Drysdale Station, which is owned by Michael and Shirley Mitchell. Gold was discovered in 1892, and the early yields of 100 ounces to the ton were described as phenomenal. Fortnightly dividends of £20 a share were paid. The Government Geologist considered that the mine was one of the most remarkable yet discovered in Australia. Before long a township was established with over 150 residential areas and some substantial buildings, including hotels, stores and other business places. A school and police station were also under construction. There were about 600 on the field, of whom 300 were miners.[22]

By 1895 some of the claims had been abandoned in favour of the Gilgunnia rush. However, there was still a population of about 600, a progress committee, and numerous businesses, including a post office and government savings bank, three commodious hotels, butchers, blacksmiths, a baker, boot maker, hairdresser and newsagent, and a school with room for more than 90 children. By 1896 the prospects were less encouraging, for the easily worked and very rich gold was depleted and the mine owners had to turn their attention to further exploratory and development work, a process

124

which should have been undertaken from the outset. There were still 100 miners on the field in 1901 and at the annual races in January of the following year there were 300 spectators. Regular cricket matches were played with teams from Cobar.[23]

The Mitchells' association with Mount Drysdale goes back many years. Shirley's grandmother, Nell Bennett, was born at Mount Drysdale, or more accurately West Drysdale, a small mining township located to the west of a ridge separating both towns. Nell's father worked at Rankin's general store at Mount Drysdale and drove the daily coach to Cobar. Nell married Joe Harvey in 1913 and moved back to Mount Drysdale when Shirley's mother (Dolly) was only 18 months old, and lived for a time in the former police station. This sojourn came to an abrupt end when they went into Cobar to await the birth of one of their children, only to return and find that the station had been pulled down and all their possessions taken out and put under a tree. It was then that they moved to the caretaker's cottage near the government tank. The house is now Shirley and Michael's home, although it has been considerably extended since that time.[24]

Today the townships of Mount Drysdale and West Drysdale are completely abandoned. However, a large number of house sites are still visible, including the remains of a hotel, the oven from one of the baker's shops, and the mine manager's house. The mines are located on the ridge separating the two towns and include several steam engines, which were used to power the mine machinery and the crushing plants. West Drysdale was both the oldest and most recently settled of the two. Small dams can be found near some of the old house sites, along with an array of artefacts such as pots, pans and the remains of bicycles. Several huts, including the assay office and oven, clearly date from the 1930s or 1940s and still have the shelving in place. One of the most interesting sites is the Chinese market garden, which still has its underground tank, irrigation channels, fences and main entrance gate intact. According to Shirley and Michael up to 200 Chinese at a time were employed in scrub-cutting on some of the neighbouring stations.

Caring for their property and its heritage treasures, Aboriginal and European, has been an intense and occasionally frustrating labour of love for Shirley and Michael. At times they have been confronted by an unsympathetic bureaucracy and predatory mining companies. Nor has their task been made any easier by the cowardly visitations of local shooters who have left rotting animal carcasses in the mineshafts and tunnels. Like many other property owners in the west, they have had to diversify and develop off-farm incomes. They consider that the only way for the property to become self-sufficient is to diversify from pastoralism to tourism, based on both its Aboriginal and European heritage.[25]

Boom and Bust on the Barrier

FUELLED BY INCREASINGLY HIGH, AND AT ITS PEAK ALMOST OUTRAGEOUS, silver prices, mining turned the harsh, craggy landscape of the Barrier Ranges into a hive of activity in the 1880s as one rich surface deposit after another was discovered. This activity gave rise to a number of towns, the most significant and enduring of which was Broken Hill. The most important of the other towns was Silverton, though there were many settlements, such as Thackaringa, Purnamoota, Day Dream, Euriowie and Tarrawingee, all of them now slowly reverting to the dust and stone from whence they came.

Silver was not mined in the Barrier region with any great endeavour until the early 1880s. The earliest mining centre was Thackaringa, located about eight kilometres east of the South Australian border. Work commenced on the Umberumberka mine near present-day Silverton in 1882, and by August of the following year John Penrose had built a hotel and Mrs Downey was erecting a store. However, the nearest post office was at the Thackaringa Hotel.[1] By March 1884 Silverton had begun to take shape. There were four stores, with one more under construction, two licensed hotels, with two large stone ones being built, plus bakers' and butchers' shops; about 60 buildings in all, besides the tents. By May the Chinese had commenced work on a market garden.[2]

The mines in the Silverton area attracted early interest from the South Australian newspapers, and the early reports were encouraging. However, the accounts of the miners' behaviour were far from that. The first beer arrived in February, and most days by 8 am more than half the town was drunk, with the numbers gradually increasing as the day wore on. By 8 pm almost everyone was drunk, and there were 'special and free fights in every direction'. In the circumstances the police had no alternative but to let things run their course. The gaol facilities consisted of a tree, a chain and some handcuffs. Although accustomed to a 'somewhat knockabout life', the reporter was appalled.

This Huntington mill is an example of the many pieces of abandoned mining machinery scattered around Mount Drysdale.

An old car rusts outside the remains of the Mount Drysdale bakery.

Ancient Aboriginal engravings adorn the sides of Byjerkerno Gorge near Euriowie.

The Day Dream smelters near Silverton were built in the 1880s, when silver prices reached astronomical heights.

These building foundations at the foot of Mt Pintapah are almost all that is left of the once vibrant, but short-lived, town of Euriowie.

The scattered miners' huts at Day Dream are a reminder of fleeting prosperity in the arid outback.

Mine shafts and snow-white quartz litter the ground in all directions at Mount Browne.

Milparinka was the main town servicing the Mount Browne diggings in the 1880s; the courthouse and police station were two of its most prominent buildings.

Every second word among the drinking men was an oath, and, subtracting the oaths and obscenity, I really believe fifty English words would cover the entire vocabulary. There are no Churches, no Salvation Army, no spiritual guidance of any sort … No finer opening exists for the Salvation Army and, if they really want work in a good tough vineyard I can honestly advise them to go there.[3]

The reporter also referred to the miners' habit of travelling with 'about forty-five different sort of rocks', or slugs. Much of the ground in the Silverton area was worked by merely 'scratching' or 'pig rooting', with almost everyone on the lookout for rich surface 'slugs' of pure silver.[4] Alfred Hales, in his whimsical account of life on the fields, referred to the practice of 'travelling on the slug'. With an eye to future profits the storekeepers supplied rations to the miners on whose claim the slug was found. However, in some instances the slugs were pilfered from someone else's claim and the storekeeper ended up out of pocket.[5]

Some years later, the *Town and Country Journal* correspondent recalled that within a short time

the scum of the country began to be attracted to the new and prosperous field like blowflies to a carcase. Horse-stealers, cattle-duffers, mining sharks, and rogues of all descriptions rolled up from the various colonies … after the 'scum' made its appearance things began to be decidedly rough. Robberies, and the jumping of claims and allotments, were things of daily occurrence. It was nothing unusual to see from ten to twenty culprits chained together to a tree at the rear of the police camp; some of the more refractory members having bells fixed on to their backs, so that should they attempt to get away the police would be warned.[6]

In June 1884 Sub-Inspector Hitch reported that Silverton had 'wonderfully increased' in size and importance since his last visit in December. There were three hotels, blacksmiths, bakers, butchers, barbers, a dancing saloon and auctioneer's offices, and a branch of the Commercial Bank was to be opened soon. The population of Silverton and surrounding areas was 1500, and people were 'flocking in daily from all parts'. He instructed the senior constable to have someone patrolling the public house at Mount Gipps every other week, staying a night and returning the next day, if convenient, and also once a week to Thackaringa 'for the purpose of preserving order amongst the unruly ones'.[7]

Living conditions were, however, still basic, for there were very few large homes. Under the lease arrangements, each home-owner in Silverton had to erect improvements to the value of £10, which was just enough to have a galvanised tin shed set up. Other miners lived in stone huts or tents. A visitor in July 1884 commented that, 'A stranger, on first seeing the township, is struck by the rows of small galvanised iron houses, about 10 feet square, which are being erected as fast as timber and iron arrive.'[8]

Meanwhile there were also rich finds at Day Dream, with the assays running as high as 13 000 ounces to the ton, and Purnamoota, also known as Leadville, or the Soakage. Assays at one claim on the latter field had been as high as 20 000 ounces to the ton. One of the main claims on this field had the distinctive name of the Terrible Dick. Some of the claims in the Silverton area were passing hands at very high prices. Overall there were between 1200 and 1500 in the district, with large numbers travelling from Adelaide, some on foot, others on horses or in buggies. A visiting member of parliament worried that so many new arrivals were poor men, 'absolutely ignorant of mining, and with no more capital than was represented by their last cheque for wages'. He recounted that many earlier arrivals had exhausted their food and money and had already left as it was impossible to gain employment. The miners were living partly in tents and partly in houses halfway hidden in the ground with only the roofs and upper parts of the walls showing as a protection against the very high temperatures.[9]

Before long Silverton was 'crowded to suffocation', with numbers arriving daily and not even half enough accommodation for those who were there at the time. There was a 'whole army of auctioneers and brokers ... and rivalry in every calling, including shoe-blacking'.[10] On entering a certain hotel, a visitor found the

> barroom was literally crowded with men more or less intoxicated, some already overpowered by the liquor had sunk helplessly on the floor and lay there muttering unintelligibly. Some were propped against the walls and in corners, not quite so far gone. In an adjoining room were to be seen one or two lying restlessly on their faces evidently suffering from an overdose of stimulants.

Elsewhere there were other crowded bars and billiard rooms, a bowling alley and shooting gallery and a man selling pies. In the morning this gentleman would visit homes, and later the hotels, blacking boots, hawking oranges and acting as town crier for concerts, balls and auctions.[11]

At Purnamoota more than 20 iron buildings had been erected and a number of others were under construction. Although a wit at the *Adelaide Observer* referred to Purnamoota as 'another city of sardine-boxes', some felt that this place would soon rival Silverton. There were no hotels and the nights were more peaceful, and 'from the prospectors' camps could be heard 'strong voices singing love songs'. By December 1884 there were two hotels and seven stores, and a branch of the Commercial Bank.[12] At Silverton there were 1745 people, which, combined with the town of Purnamoota and the villages of Lake's Camp (probably Day Dream) and Mount Gipps, brought the population of the Barrier Ranges up to about 4000. There were between 400 and 500 people at Day Dream and two hotels.[13]

Silverton was clearly the main town. At that time there were seven large stores, a number of smaller shops, butchers, bakers, six hotels (with another on the way), a hospital, jockey club, progress committee and a Masonic Lodge, which was under construction. A bond store had been built recently and a newspaper, the *Silver Age*, was published weekly. One of the hotels had 63 rooms and another 23, but the majority of the houses and shops were still little more than galvanised huts. One observer in 1885 claimed that the only substantial building was De Baun's Hotel, followed by the newly erected stone courthouse.[14]

The lack of solid buildings was not the town's only problem. By early 1885 there was still no warden, magistrate, justice of the peace or telegraph station. Thus a person charged with a minor offence of drunkenness had to remain confined until the arrival of a magistrate or be released altogether. The lack of a reliable water supply was also a serious concern, with the town residents dependent upon soakage and well water. By April 1885 there was a round of acrimonious correspondence concerning the prevalence of typhoid, one of the doctors, HW Brownrigg, attributing the outbreak to the dependence upon contaminated soakage water. He claimed that the high death rate was due primarily to the generally debilitated state of many of the victims, and their habit of not presenting themselves for help until too late. Others claimed that the reports were exaggerated. However, the hospital had been very full, and additional funds and assistance were urgently requested. It was not until the visit of a ministerial party in late May that steps were taken to remedy most of these defects.[15]

Silverton had the distinction, relatively rare in the Australian outback, as a place where many people of note either lived or visited. For instance, a wholesale and butcher's shop was owned by Sackville Kidman, a brother of Sidney Kidman, who was to become Australia's 'cattle king'. A son of Charles Dickens, the famous English novelist, had been the manager of nearby Corona station some years before. Now another son, EBL Dickens, opened a branch of his Wilcannia-based stock and station agency. He was subsequently elected to the New South Wales Parliament.[16]

Other important personages were the Resch brothers: Edmund, Richard and Emil Carl. They had already established a cordial-making plant and brewery at Wilcannia, an important port on the Darling River, and in 1885, in partnership with John Penrose, they built another brewery at Silverton. Eventually they entered the Australian beer drinkers' hall of fame as manufacturers of Resch's beer. Another notable identity to spend her formative years in Silverton was Mary Jane Cameron, otherwise known as Dame Mary Gilmore, a poet, author and journalist. She was an assistant teacher at the school in the late 1880s.[17]

Silverton eventually had all the trappings of 'civilisation'. A brick and stone hospital was built, and there were three medical practitioners in the town, one of whom was Chinese. All the major churches were well represented, but it was not until August 1885 that the first church building was constructed, in this instance by the Bible Christians. It was noted that there was 'a large number of children and ladies who were present', taken as a sign that the town was 'making progress towards a more permanent settlement'.[18]

A miners' association, which was more akin to a friendly society, was also

Another notable identity to spend her formative years in Silverton was Mary Jane Cameron, otherwise known as Dame Mary Gilmore, a poet, author and journalist

formed in 1884 to assist members who had been injured at work. In 1886 a branch of the Amalgamated Miners' Association (AMA) was formed, but six months later the office was transferred to Broken Hill because of the exodus of members to that town. A municipal council was also formed in that year. Sporting and recreational interests were amply catered for, and in addition to the jockey club, there was a football club, lawn tennis club, gymnasium, skating rink, brass band, gun club, mechanics' institute and literary society. One of the literary society's active members was 'Miss Cameron' (later Dame Gilmore).[19]

Transport in such a remote region was always a challenge. The South Australian Government saw the benefits of closer contact with the Barrier silver field and built a narrow-gauge line to the South Australian–New South Wales border. However, requests for an extension over the border were repeatedly refused. It was then decided that a local privately owned company should be formed to build the railway and in 1886 the *Silverton Tramway Company Act* was passed. Construction of the line took 12 months.[20]

By 1886 Silverton was in the first stages of genteel decline, largely as a result of the burgeoning growth of Broken Hill to the south. In that year Silverton had a population in and around the town of about 2000, and boasted several substantial new buildings. Although the population at Broken Hill was close to 3000, due to the unsatisfactory land tenure arrangements, the buildings were not as substantial as those at Silverton. By the following year these impediments had been removed and the population of Broken Hill had risen to between 5000 and 6000. There had also been a decided improvement in the style of architecture of the buildings.[21]

A reporter of the *Town and Country Journal* travelled to Silverton in September 1887. In rapturous tones he reported that there was a 'thriving town of nearly 2000 inhabitants, from whose roofs the blue smoke is rising uninterruptedly heaven wards in the clear morning air'. There were many fine buildings and its inhabitants obviously had a 'practical faith in its permanency'. Churches, banks, breweries, a newspaper office, and the 'other adjuncts of a civilised community' were all represented. He reserved his most enthusiastic hyperbole for Tantram's Hotel, with its 'aesthetic wall papers, high art draperies, canaries, haughty barmaids, luxurious saloons, simpering mashers!' Of lesser note, however, were the government buildings, which he considered a disgrace. For instance, 140 children and two teachers were 'unhealthily cooped' in the one-roomed public school.[22]

Notwithstanding these generally glowing comments, by 1888 Silverton's population had dropped to 1700. A special correspondent from the *Adelaide Observer* referred to the refreshing and soothing aspect of Silverton compared to the noise and bustle of Broken Hill. Business at Silverton was healthy, properties still fetched favourable prices and claims were still worked. There had been a necessary exodus of businessmen to Broken Hill, but nobody wished to live at the 'Dustholia' of the Barrier at present, no matter how much it may improve in the future.[23] This was, however, wishful thinking, for many

families had already transported their small wood and iron cottages to Broken Hill by horse, camel, bullock or donkey.

At Thackaringa the population was between 200 and 300, and for the time, on the rise. It was described, like all other Barrier towns, as belonging to the 'Iron Age, the structures being erected of that friend of hurriedly built settlements — galvanised iron'.[24]

However, the reporter was less generous in describing the 'shrunken township' of Day Dream.

> Now one may frequently travel from Silverton to the Day Dream without meeting a person on the forsaken track, while at the township the loquacious prospector who has seen better times bears testimony in the solitary public-house to the glory that has departed. To the right are seen the smokeless rust-accumulating smelters, which in an unhappy hour the Barrier Ranges Association erected, and round and about are the sites of houses which have been carried off, probably to witness some other mushroom town.[25]

Today, the tall multi-hued smelter stack at Day Dream stands in regal splendour atop a high hill, overlooking the stone walls and flues of the smelting plant and several hut sites on the valley floor. The mines and town site are located a little further on. At the town site are the remains of a large number of hut sites with their chimneys, ovens and parts of the walls still intact. They constitute a nearly complete and visible, albeit crumbling, township, a reminder of fleeting prosperity in the arid outback. Beth and Kevin White conduct underground tours of the main mines.

By 1889 the refreshing and soothing aspects of Silverton so lovingly described the previous year, had been replaced with obvious signs of decline and decay. Owing to the poverty of the district the Anglicans could not raise a stipend of £600 per annum for a clergyman.

> Six years ago 'a mighty throng of restless, moving humanity of all nations, all colours, and all creeds bustled about — some laughing, some sorrowing and many cursing — all busy, and each intent on making money somehow.' Today it was as quiet as a South Australian farming township.[26]

The correspondent attributed this decline largely to the failure of the Euriowie field, but this was not the only problem, for the Day Dream mines were all but abandoned, and Purnamoota was also in trouble. By 1886 no mines at Purnamoota were paying dividends, and a great many were either abandoned, under suspension, or operated by only a few men. The town's population had dwindled considerably and it retained only a remnant of its former prosperity.[27] Later that year the town was described as melancholy and deserted.

> Many of the buildings have been carted away and re-erected in Broken Hill; while others have been allowed to fall into decay, and, with their ragged canvas flapping about their ruined frameworks, make a weird and gruesome picture. Here a stone fireplace and chimney are all that remain of a dwelling. There a heap of empty bottles tells a story of prosperity departed.[28]

Unlike Day Dream, Purnamoota's fortunes improved for in 1888 it had a rising population of 380. At the Terrible Dick mine there had been an extensive investment in mining machinery and a smelter was under construction. A stone assembly hall was also built in that year. By 1891 the town still retained two hotels, two bakers, two stores, four butchers, a shoemaker and an aerated water factory, as well as a police station, school and telegraph office.[29] However, this improvement was temporary only, and its demise was not far off. Today the only building left standing is the assembly hall, which has been preserved as the kitchen complex of David and Cynthia Langford's shearers' quarters. Several other structures have been incorporated into the farm buildings, and the scant remains of hut fireplaces are spread over the property.

By late 1887 tin was all the rage, and about 800 men were on the Poolamacca (or as it was later known, the Euriowie) tin field, about 80 kilometres north of Broken Hill. On the day of the *Town and Country Journal* correspondent's visit the Euriowie Hotel was crowded to overflowing, and all the space on the dining room floor was taken up with 'shake-downs' (blankets). At nearby Byjerkerno Gorge the correspondent noted the ancient Aboriginal rock engravings cut into the rock surfaces.[30] By the end of the year there were 500 persons in the locality and the town boasted of a police station, two banks, six hotels, and numerous stores and other business places. The following year the population was estimated at 700 and there was a racecourse, but no church building. Every building was made from galvanised iron, although it was considered that more substantial buildings would soon be constructed. Another nearby settlement was the Lady Don.[31]

The Euriowie field benefited enormously from the involvement of John Reid, one of the founders of BHP (Broken Hill Proprietary), who with his reputation preceding him, had 16 000 shares in his company fully subscribed within three hours of listing. Prices in allegedly tin-bearing ground rose at high prices and for some created instant wealth. It was commented that such individuals could be seen 'marching along the main street of Silverton or Broken Hill, dressed in a new tweed suit, with the creases of its folds still plainly visible ... their hats at a rake, and withal an air of importance that betokened some sudden change of fortune'. Some, 'more cautious than their fellows', took to the banks rather than the hotels, 'not a few taking to themselves wives'.[32]

Historic buildings, such as churches, lodges and old miners' homes, almost outnumber the people in present-day Silverton.

A few scattered headstones in the saltbushes are all that remain at Euriowie cemetery.

To visit Euriowie is to step back in time. The crushing plant for the Mount Euriowie mine is set into the side of a steep hill, overlooking barren but colourful hills on the opposite side. Euriowie township is located at the foot of picturesque but equally barren Mount Pintapah. Building foundations and chimney remains, including a stone water tank, are found in profusion in this area. The journey to Byjerkerno Gorge is along a rough track, which for the most part follows a stony creek bed. Several hut and mine sites are scattered along the track, with the main cluster still having their stone chimneys intact. The winding creek bed passes several more huts and mines, terminating abruptly at a 20–25 metre high concrete dam wall wedged between the narrow gorge walls. Engravings are located on either side of the gorge and on the flat rocks on the floor. A hundred and twenty years ago the *Town and Country* journalist described the wallabies perched above the gorge. On this occasion we had goats for company.

The massive wave of speculation in tin and silver mines ended almost as abruptly as it had begun. Outside of Broken Hill most of the silver lodes did not reach any great depth and were soon exhausted. Perhaps more devastating was the cataclysmic fall in silver prices. By 1891 they were only a third of their peak a few years earlier, and they were to fall even more in the next few years. At these prices the mines were clearly uneconomic. Even if they had been viable it would have been difficult to find the capital to sustain them during the economically depressed years of the 1890s. At Silverton the Umberumberka mine closed in 1892 and by the end of the century the town's population had fallen to 600. In the previous year the furniture belonging to the council, which had not met for four years, was sold by auction.[33] Euriowie, Purnamoota and Day Dream were stones and dust.

One mining town with a difference was Tarrawingee, about 70 kilometres north of Broken Hill. Not for it the glamour of silver or tin, but only humble limestone. Uninteresting as they may seem, the high-grade limestone deposits were an essential part of BHP's operations at Broken Hill, for they were used as a flux in the smelters. The cost of transport was, however, prohibitive and to overcome this the Tarrawingee Flux and Tramway Company was formed and a railway constructed in 1891.

But Tarawingee's beginnings were less than impressive. Late on a Saturday night in February 1891, half a dozen coaches from Broken Hill landed 100 men who had been brought via Adelaide from Sydney to work in the quarries. Within a few hours a small town of canvas tents sprang up and teams from Broken Hill were soon arriving with stores and appliances for the company. However, in its haste to commence production the company did not provide the men with sufficient water, cooks or boarding accommodation. At one stage the men became so agitated that guns were produced. Nevertheless, work did commence and within a short while business premises, including the company's store, were erected.[34]

Before long the residents had forwarded petitions to the government asking for a dam, schoolhouse, teacher and a post office with savings bank and money order office. A progress committee was appointed. The railway opened in June 1891 and there were between 200 and 300 men employed out of a total population of between 400 and 500 people. There was a hotel, assay office and manager's residence, and in 1892 the police station was transferred from Euriowie to Tarrawingee.[35]

In 1898 BHP decided to close its Broken Hill smelters and produce concentrates for further processing at its new works at Port Pirie in South Australia. This should have spelt the end for Tarrawingee, but the town lingered on for many years as a supply centre for the northern pastoral stations. Supplies were transported to the stations by camel train, and for this purpose a small Afghan camp was established at Tarrawingee.[36] Today, little remains bar the quarry, hotel site, the foundations for what was probably a boarding house, and several house sites.

Silverton fared much better than any of its siblings, for at least people still live there, albeit not very many. There is a large number of historic buildings, most of them restored, for instance, the gaol, courthouse, municipal chambers, Methodist and Roman Catholic churches, Masonic Lodge, public school and hotel, and some houses. The more inquisitive visitor will find other reminders of the past, such as the remains of abandoned buildings, including Resch's brewery. Silverton is probably one of the most photographed outback towns in Australia, and has been used as a setting for many Australian and international films. In its twilight years Silverton has found the glory which eluded it so many years ago.

Corner Country

MILPARINKA AND MOUNT BROWNE ARE LOCATED IN THE ARID CORNER country of north-west New South Wales. In the early 1880s they were the focus of a wildly optimistic gold rush, at a time when there was no Broken Hill to the south and only a few hardy pastoralists in the north. For many years now the population of Milparinka has varied between one and four, depending on the size of the family running the Albert Hotel, the only original building that is still inhabited in the town. More recently there has been a 'population explosion' with the establishment of a small kangaroo abattoir, but the town is by any standards still nearly deserted. Mount Browne is totally abandoned, and has been that way for many years.

Other than the Albert Hotel, Milparinka has many reminders of the past. Across the road from the hotel are the ruins of the Commercial Bank building, and further away the more solid remains of the courthouse, police station and post and telegraph office. The cellar of Baker's shop, and the foundations of a number of other buildings, including one of the hotels, are clearly visible. Mount Browne is located about 14 kilometres south of Milparinka. It is difficult to imagine a more uninviting landscape, for the ground is strewn with quartz pebbles and gibber, and barely a tree is to be seen. At the main diggings shafts and piles of quartz pockmark the ground. The foundations of the main group of buildings in the former township are clearly visible, and in some instances part of the walls — particularly those of the bakery — are still standing. Overlooking everything is the cemetery, bare and stark on a rocky hill.

At the historic site of Depot Glen, about 12 kilometres north-west of Milparinka, the deep waterhole and majestic gums contrast with the surrounding barrenness. But this site's importance does not rest with aesthetics, or even its brief acquaintanceship with the gold rush, but with Charles Sturt's Central Australian Expedition of 1844–45, and the grave and tree carved with the name

Majestic and roofless, the post office, Milparinka

of one of Sturt's officers, the unfortunate James Poole, are still there today.[1]

Sturt and his expeditionary party were the first Europeans to visit Evelyn Creek, near present-day Milparinka, and Depot Glen. The expedition was conceived by Sturt as a means of discovering an inland sea and, hopefully, a fertile interior, though the official instructions were rather less ambitious. Sturt and his party left Adelaide in August 1844 with 16 men, 11 horses, 30 bullocks, several drays and carts, a boat and boat carriage and 200 sheep.[2]

As Sturt's party moved north and summer approached, their position became increasingly perilous. Water was at a premium, and much of the exploration was conducted by small groups travelling from base camps or depots, which were located near a waterhole. After one such trip from Evelyn Creek, Sturt returned to find the creek dry. Fortunately, Poole had located a large body of water in a small rocky gorge, which was named Depot Glen, and it was there that the party set up camp on 27 January 1845.[3]

By late February it was clear that the party was marooned, for there was no prospect of either advancing, or retreating the 400 kilometres to the safety of the Darling River. The heat was excruciating. During December, January and February the average temperature was over 100 degrees Fahrenheit. So intense was the heat that the ink dried up in their pens as they were writing, the lead dropped out of their pencils, the teeth of their combs fell out, handles of razors split, boxes were warped, nails and screws worked loose and tyres fell off the carts. The wool on the sheep and the men's hair ceased to grow, and their nails became as brittle as glass. The flour and bacon lost much of its weight and even the once prolific bird life at the Glen departed.[4]

To overcome the heat an underground room was constructed, though this was only a partial solution. The greatest danger was from scurvy.[5] For Sturt and others the scurvy to some extent abated, but Poole suffered terribly. By the end of April he was confined to bed, and by the following month Sturt recorded grimly: 'He lost the use of his lower extremities, the skin of his legs turned black, large pieces of flesh hung down from the roof of his mouth.'[6]

With June approaching the water level in the creek fell alarmingly, and it was at about this time that Poole suggested building a cairn on the small mountain as a means of keeping up the party's morale. Despite their privations, Sturt was determined to press on with the expedition as soon as the drought broke. He had decided to split the party and send Poole and a number of others back to Adelaide as soon as rain fell. He wrote:

I would rather that my bones had been left to bleach in the desert than have yielded an inch of the ground I have gained at so much expense and trouble.[7]

On 12 July it rained, and it continued almost without interruption for two days until the creek was filled to the brim. The Adelaide party left with Poole and Sturt's group headed further north. A day later, however, one of the Adelaide party caught up with Sturt, bringing the news that Poole had died. Both parties returned to the Glen, where Poole was buried.[8]

Sturt set up a further base camp at a spot called Fort Grey to the north. From there, with Browne, Stuart and two others, he crossed Strzelecki Creek, Coopers Creek, and the gibber-strewn plains to be known as Sturts Stony Desert. West of present day Birdsville, they were finally driven back by the impenetrable sand hills of the Simpson Desert. On their return to Fort Grey they made one more trip to Coopers Creek, only to return and find that their companions had been forced to retreat to Depot Glen because of water shortages.[9]

A few days later Sturt's party returned to Depot Glen, but now their plight was desperate. Sturt was disabled by scurvy and the heat was even more intense than that of the previous summer. A dash south by two men confirmed that water was still available, but only for a few more days. Four bullocks were killed, skinned and loaded on the carts for use as water casks, each holding about 600 litres, and as a farewell gesture the boat was launched on Preservation Creek. Travelling at night for much of the way they reached the remaining waterholes and eventually the comparative safety of the Darling River. Sturt reached home in January 1846.[10]

In the intervening years, prior to the discovery of gold in early 1881, the area was settled by pastoralists. The nearest town was Wilcannia, a river port on the Darling River, several hundred kilometres away. From there, coaches ran direct to the diggings, but many miners travelled by their own means. At the diggings water was scarce, although there was water at Evelyn Creek and Depot Glen. By March there were about 800 men on the field. The most popular location was a waterhole on Evelyn Creek, where the township of

The epitaph of James Poole is carved in a grevillea tree at Depot Glen, near Milparinka.

Sketch of Mount Browne,
near Peak Hill
(*Australian Sketcher*, 20 May 1882;
by permission of National Library of
Australia)

Milparinka was beginning to emerge. There were good reports of gold at
Mount Browne, but the lack of water was a major setback, and some miners
stacked their dirt in anticipation of rain, in the meantime returning to
Wilcannia.[11]

By June there were reports of serious food shortages at the diggings and
impending riots. Grog had been sent out to the diggings in preference to flour
(probably because carters and storekeepers could make more money on the
more costly liquor), and the miners at Mount Browne had signalled their
intentions to destroy the liquor supplies unless the Wilcannia storekeepers
sent out a sufficient supply of food. Some miners were reported to be starving for want of flour and a number of them had abandoned their claims as a
consequence. There were around 2000 men on the diggings, several hundred
of whom were begging for food at adjacent stations.[12]

An account by E Murphy provides a graphic account of the Mount
Browne diggings at that time. When he arrived at the diggings the only food
supplies he and his companion had were what they could carry: a few pounds
of flour, some tea and sugar. Murphy camped by a nearby creek, and obtained
a small supply of water by digging in the creek bed. There were two shanties
and a butcher's shop on the field, but no store, and before long the men were
living on meat alone. Not long after, their water supply also dried up. Water
was available for sale at the Four Mile diggings, but it was a long walk there
and back each day with two four-litre water bags, which had to last the two
of them 24 hours for all drinking, cooking and washing. On hearing that a
wagon had arrived at Milparinka with some flour, he and many others
walked the 19 kilometres there, but they arrived too late and he only procured
half a tin full. It was, however, the first flour he had tasted for eight weeks.[13]

Not long after, a two-roomed iron store was built at Milparinka in anticipation of further teams arriving. In due course there was another wagon, so
the men tramped off again, about 200 in all. The wagon master refused to
unload until the morning, so the men camped and waited, only to find that

one of the Mount Browne shanty owners had arrived and was loading cases of whisky and other goods. On this occasion the men took possession of the wagon and helped themselves to anything edible, although they paid for it. The next rush for flour was to the Four Mile diggings, where the storekeeper saw fit to make his fortune by charging outrageous prices. At this provocation, hundreds of irate miners threatened to put a rope around his store and pull it down. In the end they took possession of the store, put three men in charge and distributed the flour in equal shares, again after paying for it.[14]

By late 1881 the *Town and Country* correspondent, 'The Raven', had arrived in Milparinka. There were three general stores, two of which were owned by branches of Wilcannia firms, a police barracks, and two public houses, the owners of which were erecting stone buildings. The post office was at Depot Glen. Referring to the Afghan cameleers, he commented that not long before his arrival eleven camels had arrived from South Australia with a load of drapery, the town assuming an 'oriental appearance'. Although many of the Mount Browne miners had left for the granite rush, near present day Tibooburra, the town was still lively enough. He was particularly taken by the Mount Browne coffee palace, which was owned by a gentleman who went by the name, 'Frank, the Pieman'. His fare of coffee, pies and tarts was eagerly sought after by the miners and his premises were crowded nightly, whilst the shanties were completely deserted.[15]

Another visitor at that time was J Johnson, who rode to the diggings in 1881. His first sight of the diggings was hardly encouraging; two large vans containing no less than 50 or 60 returning diggers, and a large number of men on horseback and foot. They were 'despondent and wretched … emaciated, and with eyes bound up, groping their way along, or being led by a compassionate companion'. The mining population was described as comprising a few making good wages, a large number 'making tucker', and the rest starving. He considered Milparinka a good place for grog and he fancied that 'a considerable number of its inhabitants would never know whether the creek had run dry or not unless somebody told them'. Nevertheless, there was very little rowdyism, and the shanty owners appeared to be 'highly respectable men'.[16]

At Milparinka there was a population of about 300, several stores and six unlicensed shanties, a butcher, baker, chemist, two blacksmiths and a barber, who played the banjo in his unofficial hours. At night Milparinka presented a novel sight: 'camp fires all over the place glinting through the trees, tents (big and little), diggers, ditto, music of various sorts, violin and concertina principally, with snatches of song'. He doubted, however, that there was much real jollity, for there was not enough gold-getting. Also in town was a squad of gamblers, including a *rouge-et-noir* man, a gentleman with a wheel of fortune, and a ring-and-spike artist. Several days later he visited Depot Glen, where the remains of one of Sturt's carts, a boat and the excavation for his underground hut could still be found.[17]

Whatever the state of affairs in 1881, the diggings were soon beset with much worse woes. By March the following year supplies of flour were down to a few days rations, while at nearby Tibooburra there was no beef and the residents were living on rice and pigweed. Scores of miners were sick and destitute, lying unattended, and there had already been several deaths from typhoid. There were numerous representations for assistance, and before long a formal request was made by the New South Wales Government to the South Australian Government for the use of camels stationed at Beltana to transport food supplies to the diggings. Because of the drought and the lack of feed and water, camels were the only practical means of transport.[18] Within a week of the request, food supplies and Dr Wilkie from Wilcannia were on their way to the diggings.

Reports of the unavailability of flour were mixed, some claiming that they were exaggerated, and others telling stories of imminent shortages, with the miners rushing the hawkers when they came to the diggings. Because of a scarcity of water, many miners had been prevented from working and obtaining gold to pay for their supplies. Dr Wilkie had seen 25 patients who were more or less destitute, procured a house and a man to attend to them, and recommended the construction of a hospital. The diet had been very indifferent and the weather and some of the remedies 'very trying'.[19]

Murphy vividly described these troubles, which he labelled, a 'tidal wave of general disaster'. He attributed the typhoid outbreak to men drinking the soakage water brought down from the stony slopes by the occasional rainfall. According to Murphy hardly anyone recovered from an attack, but the heaviest toll was among the strong young men. The burials were crude and hasty, with the men wrapped in their clothes and blankets and deposited in an unmarked grave. Murphy also contracted this illness, but with the help of chlorodyne, which his mate managed to buy from a hawker, he was soon back on his feet. A doctor visiting the diggings (presumably Dr Wilkie) attributed the high death toll in the young men to their teetotaller habits. The older men drank spirits, and he himself did the same while there.[20]

By the end of April the famine at least was over. A caravan of camels and two wagons, each drawn by 10 camels, had arrived from South Australia, and eight teams from Wilcannia has also arrived within the last few days. By the following month, however, there were still 45 persons sick with typhoid, scurvy, ophthalmia or dysentery. Those in the hospitals were totally destitute and most of the other sick were unable to pay for their medicine. Hospitals had been set up at both Tibooburra and Milparinka in galvanised-iron buildings rented for that purpose. Dr Wilkie stayed two weeks at the diggings, and after his departure the local chemists attended the men.[21]

By September Milparinka had a large number of impressive stone buildings, in particular, Connor's Royal Standard, McIndoe's Royal and Penrose's Albert Hotel. Prentice's Hotel was an iron building. There was also a branch of the Commercial Bank, three stores, two butchers, a baker, blacksmith, chemist and carpenter. Government services included a goldfields' warden,

The burials were crude and hasty, with the men wrapped in their clothes and blankets and deposited in an unmarked grave

police, post office, and a well, from which water could be obtained for a fee. Chinese gardeners had also sunk a well near the town and had established a vegetable garden. The correspondent commented that they 'deserved the greatest credit as they had been the means of keeping the place open'. W Slee, who had been the goldfield warden in 1881, and was later the New South Wales Minister for Mines, commented a few years later that he had induced Jack A Poh and other Chinese gardeners to settle at Milparinka.[22]

Although the present population was only about 100, the correspondent saw a prosperous future for the town as a supply point for much of the border country and part of south-west Queensland. At Tibooburra, 41 kilometres north, there were 250 residents, served by four hotels, a number of stores, a bank, chemist, two bakers, two butchers and an underground coffee house dispensing coffee, pies and sweet music. A dry-blowing machine, the first of its kind, arrived at Milparinka the following month. By this time reef mining had commenced at a number of locations, and a post office and store had been established at the new town of Albert.[23]

The warden's report for the year is instructive, for despite the more settled appearance of the towns the reality on the diggings was quite different. There had been little rain during the year, and what had fallen had not lasted for more than two or three weeks. The miners had no alternative but to stack and register their wash dirt until such time as rain fell again. Reef mining was also hampered by the lack of water and timber. In autumn of that year there had been many deaths from typhoid and dysentery. A camel-wagon with sick men had been sent to Wilcannia, and all of them had recovered their health. The improvement since in the general health of the inhabitants was he felt, 'in some degree … attributable to the good supply of vegetables raised by the Chinese gardeners', of whom there were eight employed on two gardens. He also commented on the favourable conduct of the inhabitants, for sly grog selling and shanty keepers had been nearly eliminated.[24]

Continued dry weather the following year seriously retarded mining and led to a gradual decrease in the population in the district, which by July did not exceed 600. The most common means of working the fields was by dry blowing, which allowed the men to purchase only the bare necessities of life. If they could obtain a good water supply for washing, the miners felt that they could make good wages. Nevertheless, the warden commented that during the year, 40 town allotments were sold at Milparinka, and there had been a slight increase in the population. It was considered that the town owed its vitality more to the surrounding stations than the goldfields. Reference was again made to the Chinese gardens, which had been very successful in supplying vegetables at reasonable prices. They had grown potatoes and the following year they expected to have peaches, pears and grapes in bearing.[25]

By 1884 Milparinka had assumed a more settled and infinitely less frantic existence. In addition to its previously described establishments, it now possessed a courthouse, photographer's shop, three boarding houses, a timberyard, two sawyers, a saddler's shop, assembly room, billiard room, public school

Mount Browne cemetery, atop a bare rocky hill, is a stark sight.

and library, the latter of which had over 200 books and a healthy credit balance. The town also had a progress committee, jockey club and athletics club. Despite the seemingly perpetual presence of drought conditions there was a surprising air of prosperity, for at the last race meeting between £300 and £400 worth of prizes were distributed, together with the usual array of silver cups. Neither was the town without its more cultural distractions, for concerts and minstrel entertainments were held by groups of local musicians and amateur actors, and the funds raised by such functions went to the school and library.[26]

At Mount Browne, however, there had been an average of only 30 miners during the year and most of the reef claims at Albert had been abandoned. This picture of gloom was reversed the next year following very good rains. In 1884 there had been only one house left in the Mount Browne business area, but now there were three stores, a public house, a butcher, baker and several residences. But these favourable conditions did not last, for in 1888 Mount Browne had a mere 10 millimetres of rain. Some turned their attention to the reef mines at Warrata, which soon had a population of about 120, a public house and two boarding houses, but many others must have headed south to the potentially more prosperous Barrier silver fields.[27]

Good rains fell in 1890, but these were followed by over ten years of almost uninterrupted drought. A rabbit plague in 1891 further diminished the available fodder for stock and the carrying teams. Lack of capital and expertise was also a constant lament, with some of the more vaunted mining ventures falling on their own sword through mismanagement. For instance, the manager appointed by the Milparinka Goldmining Company in 1888 was derided for 'pottering about aimlessly, making a hopeless attempt to reset the table of the machine, and wasting no small amount of the company's funds', before his services were dispensed with.[28]

Despite these vagaries there were some positive developments at Milparinka. In 1893 William Baker commenced construction of a store, which featured a large underground apartment (built as a cellar). The enterprising Baker traded well into the twentieth century and had the last shop to close. According to Geoffrey Svenson, who has conducted extensive archaeological investigations at Milparinka, dances and socials were conducted on Baker's premises until World War I, when most of the young men enlisted. Another development was the establishment of the *Sturt Recorder* at Milparinka in 1893.[29]

There was probably no single cause for Milparinka's decline. Certainly, a lack of rain and poor mining prospects did not help, but added to that was the economic depression of the 1890s, which would have directly affected some of the businesses through the general hardships and foreclosures on neighbouring pastoral stations. Perhaps even more critical was the prevarication in building a hospital at Milparinka. In the meantime one was constructed at Tibooburra, thus directing further business away from the town. By 1912 the village was reduced to two hotels, two stores, the police station, a school and seven or eight homes.[30]

Apart from occasional dances one of the big events in these declining years was the arrival of the camels, decorated with fringed rugs and little bells, with the Afghan leader dressed in flowing robes and a turban. So momentous was the occasion that a school holiday was granted. Some of the Afghans were also hawkers, and there was much buying and selling as a consequence. With World War I, many young men enlisted and of those who returned, few felt inclined to return to the hardships of the outback. The death knell was the introduction of motorised transport — the town was often bypassed, and in 1950 the main road was relocated elsewhere.[31]

Today the social centre of Milparinka, and indeed the district, is the Albert Hotel. Recently the hotel was purchased by Phillip Young and his fiancee, Rebecca McMillan.[32] The hotel has always been one of my favourite spots. All the rooms face onto an internal courtyard, which has a small pond and a very content tortoise. The coolness of the courtyard and the soothing ripple of the water contrast sharply with the heat and dust outside.

And, of course, the hotel is haunted. A small lady with a white blouse, black skirt and high boots has been seen in the corner of one of the rooms. Although the rooms are regularly cleaned, the beds in this particular room often look like they have not been made up. On one occasion the cleaner felt as if someone was pushing her out of the room. Ghosts or not, the hotel is a veritable oasis, and Milparinka is one of the icons of the Australian outback.

SOUTH AUSTRALIA

From Waukaringa to Yudnamutana

AJOURNEY TO SOUTH AUSTRALIA'S ABANDONED OUTBACK MINING TOWNS is a visit to a world of rocks, dust and emptiness. West of Broken Hill and north of Yunta is Waukaringa. On my last visit, the town looked a little worse for wear. The hotel was still a grand sight, but it was minus a few stones from a side wall. Other buildings showed more obvious signs of decay, and in most instances only the stone chimneys or stone foundations were left. One building looked as if it had been more recently occupied, for it still had some of its walls standing, and not far from it was a rusty motor vehicle.

At the mines, the chimney, flue and furnaces of the Alma were still largely intact, but what particularly fascinated me was the large scattering of miners' huts in the vicinity. They seemed to be everywhere, and some of them had imposing views of the surrounding plains and hills. Obviously there had been a village in close proximity to the mine, in addition to the township itself. The village must have been a lively spot, for in 1894 the *Adelaide Observer*'s correspondent remarked that the top of the hill had the 'largest and best assortment of empty bottles to be seen anywhere near'.[1]

The first gold find at Waukaringa was in 1873. In August of that year a correspondent wrote that:

> The first impression that a person would get would be that he had arrived on a racecourse, to see the number of white flags in a row, extending on the course of the reef east and west ... and then there is another row going north and south.

The only drawback was the lack of fresh water, but there was a store on the field. By July of the following year the gold in the Alma was described 'as thick as currants in a pudding'. A crushing plant was erected in 1875 and doubled in size in 1881, the same year that the stone chimney and flue were built.[2]

An abandoned car,
store (foreground) and
hotel (background) at Waukaringa

From the outset the mine seemed to be bathed in controversy and there
was a frequent turnover in managers, several of whom came into conflict with
the directors, and they in turn with the shareholders. The disputes worsened
visibly in 1882, and led to an investigation by a shareholder representative,
and a round or two of acrimonious correspondence in the Adelaide press. The
report accused the previous manager of incompetence. Of the machinery it
was said:

> Everything appears to have been done without any system — all huddled up
> together and piled on top of one another in a state of grand confusion. The foun-
> dations of the batteries are very faulty, and have not been solid from the time they
> were put in. The ripple tables and buddles are the worst I have ever seen. They are
> simply useless for the saving of gold.[3]

Although some of these faults were rectified, there continued to be additions and alterations to the machinery. Nevertheless, for a while the mine
prospered, and between 1888 and 1891 £24,000 in dividends were paid.[4]

In 1888 it was commented that at Waukaringa 'Quite a town of galvanized
iron and stone houses has grown at the place, with the proverbial "pub" and
stores, as well as a small place of worship'. By the following year 475 people

were living in the town area, and by 1890 the trappings of civilisation had started to take a hold. In February of that year a grand tea and entertainment in the Wesleyan church in aid of the Circuit Fund attracted 200 persons, who enjoyed the tuneful sound of the Waukaringa brass band. By July there was a population of 700, and a parliamentary delegation was entertained at the opening of the new 20-head battery. Boxing Day sports, held at the racecourse in December 1890, drew a crowd of 400 people, again accompanied by the town's brass band. At its peak the town had two hotels, two stores, a school, a baker, three butchers, a wine saloon, billiard hall and dancing saloon.[5]

In 1894 the fortunes of the town were enlivened by gold finds at Lovely Gully, about 13 kilometres north. A small population of diggers had settled in at the Gully and two stores and a butcher's shop had been erected, with a greengrocer on the way. Despite this activity, Waukaringa's best days were behind it, although there was still hope for the future. The population was 250, one correspondent remarking that it boasted of the 'largest crop of babies in proportion to its population' that he had ever seen. The main buildings were the post office, telegraph station, school, hospital (with 12 beds), two well-furnished stores, a hotel, Democratic Club, two butchers, a Wesleyan church and a police station. The system of water conservation was described as 'commendable', and tanks roofed over by galvanized iron had been constructed in several places. But gold supplies dwindled, Waukaringa's fortunes faded, and the last business in town, the hotel, was finally abandoned in 1964 following the death of the publican.[6]

Blinman is located in the heart of the Flinders Ranges. Copper was first discovered there in 1859 and mining and smelting commenced several years later. When JB Austin visited Blinman in 1862 on his journey to the colony's mining fields, he found a village of substantial pine huts for the miners erected near the mine and a good store, as well as offices and captain's apartments. An early attempt at modernisation took place in 1863. There was an attempt to reduce transport costs by the introduction of three steam-powered traction engines, each of which would haul six wagons. On their arrival at Port Augusta the engines caused a sensation, and their trials were watched with consternation, and then some relief by the bullockies, who became quite enthusiastic when the vehicles met with any obstacle. The following year the engines ceased operations, for they were far too costly, as the drivers and steerers had to draw water from deep wells to fill their tanks and cut their own timber for fuel.[7]

By 1869 the population had risen to nearly 1500, and by 1872 there was a school, a doctor, a Foresters' Lodge and Rechabites' Lodge. However, by the following year the mines were closed. By 1881 the population was only 172 and many of the town's homes were empty. The arrival of the railway to Parachilna and then north to Farina led to a reopening of the mine, but not long after a visitor described it as the most primitive town in the colony. The ramshackle courthouse and school, and nearly all the houses, were built of native pine, and the schoolchildren, of whom theoretically there were 70, were 'stuffed together like herrings in a barrel' in a building seven metres by three. More substantial buildings were erected, but a slump in copper prices a few years later caused the mine to close again.[8]

Blinman's stop-start existence continued for many years. In 1888 the population was about 500, and a concert that year drew an audience of 120. The town had a post and telegraph office, substantial schoolhouse with master's residence, a Wesleyan meeting house, police station, two hotels, stores, blacksmiths and saddlers' shops and other businesses. Whilst some homes were stone or brick and looked 'commodious and comfortable', many were living in huts. The mines closed again in 1897, the population falling from 500 to about 260 in that year. A visitor to Blinman the following year commented favourably on the hotel, school and Foresters' Lodge, and the small household gardens, though he was surprised at the number of goats roaming about the town. He was also struck by the cleanliness of the town and the absence of bad language and drunken behaviour, though these characteristics were probably a reflection on the absence of most of the miners.[9]

Sentinels of despair at the once thriving town of Beltana

Blinman entered its last and most prosperous period of production in the early 1900s, when work was commenced by the Tasmanian Copper Company, under the enthusiastic management of A Henrie, an American. The company intended to treat ore from Blinman and neighbouring mines, and purchased a large number of them. Over 400 men were employed at Blinman, as well as 80 teams of horses each, and from 350 to 500 camels. The plan was ambitious — even grand — but copper prices slumped yet again, and by 1908 this venture had also collapsed.[10] It was the end of an era, and eventually almost all the mining plant and buildings were removed. Today you can still see the mine captain's cottage, built in 1862, as well as two other miners' cottages, the school, post office, library, memorial hall, police station and cells, butcher's shop, and the much renovated and very comfortable Blinman Hotel. A number of the other buildings are now private homes.

Blinman was to be our last brush with anything remotely approaching civilisation for some time. Nucculeena had beckoned for many years, and now I was filled with excitement and anticipation, and also a degree of edginess, for this was not a trip for the faint-hearted. From the turn-off from Glasses Gorge it was only another 14 kilometres, but it took almost an hour, as we drove our way slowly along the rock-strewn gullies and ridges. Eventually we arrived at the site of several stone buildings, one of which had been the hotel, and another a store. This was the surveyed, but sparsely occupied town site; the mines and miners' cottages were located on the other side of the creek.

Nucculeena was the site of one of Australia's, and certainly South Australia's, most famous mining scandals. The prospectus for the Great Northern Copper Mining Company was issued in London in 1859. It made a number of questionable statements; for example, that the country was well watered, with plenty of timber and feed for cattle, and that the South Australian Government was to construct a railway line to the mines. Worse still, the prospectus implied that the Governor of South Australia, in commenting upon the valuable northern mineral leases, had referred exclusively to the leases now held by the company. Not long after, the Governor visited the northern mines and strongly implied that the various owners had knowingly promoted mines of uncertain value. Even more embarrassing, the legality of the leases was later called into question, resulting in the appointment of a Select Committee to inquire into the matter.[11]

This news, however, came too late for the unsuspecting English investors, for the subscription list for shares in the company had to be closed almost as soon as it had opened.[12] The Great Northern commenced work the following year, and by mid-1861 some 85 men were employed. In that year the *Adelaide Register* described the company's headquarters as 'quite a township':

> On the Sabbath-day you may hear the chapel bell tolling ... During the week the lively music played by the miners' band, and generally finishing with 'God save the Queen', shows that there are some loyal subjects in these remote parts.

A public meeting of 40 miners was held for the purpose of forming a miners' institute. The miner appointed as chairman commented on the 'great need of literary recreation in these parts', and hoped that before long the institute would be opened and a series of lectures given.[13]

Austin, in his visit to the mines, waxed lyrical upon the miners and the mechanics' institute:

> The men seem to devote themselves after work to useful study, or to innocent recreation. They have established a judge and jury club, for the trial of petty offences amongst themselves, and it has been found to work well. There is, also, a good musical band, including some good singers among its members, the instrumental part consisting of a drum, triangle, bones, violins, and concertina. On the evening of my arrival the band was 'discoursing sweet music', the sound of which reverberated through the hills, was very enlivening, especially to weary travellers, who had been long absent from anything of the kind.

He also described the mine as presenting 'a more pleasing appearance as to its buildings, and all the arrangements at "grass", than any mine in the North'. There was 'an air of comfort as well as of business about the place, which its more recent competitors have not yet attained to'. The captain's apartments, office and three other stone buildings were erected on a terrace opposite the enginehouse. There were substantial stone stables, a good store, smith's shop, workshop, a general store, doctor's house and 'about 20 good huts for the men'. A hotel, called the Bushman's Inn, and a store, were built subsequently at the surveyed town site, but few other lots were sold.[14]

But by 1866 all this investment and activity had come to nothing. Hastened by the onset of drought conditions, which raised the transport costs hugely, Nucculeena, along with all other northern mines, closed. There were the usual accusations of over-expenditure and incompetent management, which were obviously justified in this instance. The Great Northern had produced copper to a value of £13,000, but at a cost of £57,000. Most miners and their families left the town, but the hotel lingered on for several years.[15] Preserved largely by its remoteness and recent restorative efforts by the South Australian Department of Mines and Energy, Nuccaleena is one of the state's treasures. The beautifully crafted engine-house, workshops and chimneystack are still standing, together with part of the captain's apartments and offices, assay office and smelter and several other stone buildings.

The mining town of Sliding Rock is located to the north of Nuccaleena, via a roundabout route through Parachilna and Beltana. Though not a mining town, Beltana was at the intersection of the Sliding Rock road and the old main road north, and played an important part in the town's development. Beltana came into existence in 1872, when it was decided to build a repeater station for the Overland Telegraph line a few kilometres from Thomas Elder's Beltana Station. A town was surveyed not long after. Ironically, Beltana received a fillip from the demise of Sliding Rock, for many of the businesspeople and others shifted there in anticipation of a brighter future. In the short run at least they were not to be disappointed, for the railway line reached Beltana in 1881, and it soon became an important railhead for the surrounding pastoral and mining properties.[16]

One important, and perhaps less heralded, feature of Beltana was the presence of camels and their Afghan drivers, or cameleers. The first commercial consignment of camels in Australia was sent to Elder's Umberatana Station and then to Beltana. In 1869 Elder formed a transport company to carry goods between some of his properties. He also set up a camel-breeding program at the station and exported the camels to other colonies. With the camels came the Afghan cameleers, who were on short-term contracts, and many of whom afterwards left to set up their own businesses.[17] The Afghans did experience racial tensions and the Ghantowns, as they were called, were always located on the outskirts of town, where the land was cheap and where they could be close to their camels. Nevertheless, their role in assisting in the development of central, western and northern Australia and western New South Wales is undeniable.[18]

According to Graham Aird and Nic Klassen in their book *Beltana: The town that will not die*, the peak years for Beltana were between 1875 and 1920, a considerably longer time than that enjoyed by most of the northern mining towns. During this time Beltana boasted a brewery, two hotels, post and telegraph office, school, police station, doctor, courthouse, church, baker, butcher, blacksmith, hospital, railway station, saddle-maker, carriage-maker, mining exchange, several hotels, and up to 500 residents. Religious services were held by several denominations, although a church building was not constructed until 1895. The church was called the Smith of Dunesk Mission, and one of the early churchmen was the Reverend John Flynn, founder of the Australian Inland Mission.[19]

Increasing use of mechanised road transport in the 1920s and 1930s led to the town's gradual demise. This decline was hastened by the establishment of a new town on the Leigh Creek coalfield, and the replacement of the old narrow-gauge railway with a standard-gauge line to the west of the town. The town's fate was sealed in 1983 when a new bitumen road was constructed 17 kilometres to the west.[20] Some of the old town buildings such as the railway station, post and telegraph office, school and the Smith of Dunesk Mission have been restored and some are used as dwellings. Other buildings are derelict or have only their chimneys remaining.

Sliding Rock is located near a creek of the same name. The first sight to greet the traveller's eyes are two tall and well-preserved chimneystacks. Further on are the ruins of the hotel and at least two stores. The remains of a number of miners' huts and a kiln are located between the mines and smelters. Copper was discovered at Sliding Rock in 1869, but unlike Nuccaleena the mine was wholly financed by South Australians. By the following year work had begun on the construction of the smelters. Despite all the other setbacks that copper mining had suffered in the northern Flinders over the last decade,

With the camels came the Afghan cameleers, who were on short-term contracts, and many of whom afterwards left to set up their own businesses

there was a conviction that the mine would be permanent. A small community developed around the mine and along the creek, where the miners lived in huts of pine or bark or in dugouts. Those that chose the latter mode of living had to contend with occasional flash floods. By June 1870 there were 50 men employed at the mine, and nearly 200 residents. The first store was Jones' 'Ready Penny Store', followed by two other stores, a carpenter, butcher, eating house and a contracting business.

Large machinery was installed in the first half of 1871 and hopes of success were high. Further capital was raised later that year, primarily to purchase a boiler and other equipment to cope with the underground water. Meanwhile it had been agreed to formally survey a town, to be called Cadnia, which was an Aboriginal name for the rock, and the shares had leapt from £7 each to £50. By late 1872 the boiler was installed, and within a few hours all the shafts had been de-watered.

The town lots went on sale in 1874 amid much excitement, for more than 90 per cent of them were sold, with some prices reaching extraordinary heights. All the buyers were businesspeople and storekeepers; not one was a miner or teamster. Nevertheless, there appeared to be no lack of confidence in the town, for that year two dividends were declared, a rare event in the north Flinders. During the year the residents successfully lobbied for a school, with a teacher arriving later that year. Another important social event was the first anniversary of the Wesleyan Sunday school, which was held early the following year. The tea meeting was presided over by the mine manager, Captain Matthews.

However, the prosperity did not continue. There were many difficulties, including the perennial one of obtaining timber and other supplies during the hot and dry summer months. In these conditions supplies of timber and other materials were hard to come by and often only at ruinous prices. Excess water in the mine still posed a problem and there were machinery breakdowns with costly repairs and delays. By the time that a director's meeting was held in early 1877 the men's wages were already in arrears, and it was proposed to wind up the company. The residents responded strongly, for they felt that the mine had never had a fair trial and that the prospect of a railway was by now almost a certainty. Despite these views the company was wound up.[21]

The effect on the town was immediate, since the miners had no alternative but to look elsewhere for employment. By February 1877 the community was described as 'very sparse now and daily and weekly our ranks are getting thinned, of the male portions particularly, the wives and children, or the "encumbrances" being left behind'. Provisions were becoming exhausted and the only way of obtaining animal meat was by shooting. Many miners had been paid by the company in IOUs, which were almost worthless. One of the first buildings to be moved was the school, which was rebuilt at nearby Beltana.[22]

By 1878 only two shops and the hotel remained. The stone chimneys and ovens of the miners' cottages were a poignant reminder of the town's brief

Dugout hut on the banks of the creek at Yudnamutana

heyday. Although the mines were reopened several times over the next few decades, nothing came of it. In 1907, Sliding Rock's fate was sealed when a fire burnt down the hotel, and the town was finally abandoned.[23]

Yudnamutana is perhaps the most intriguing of the northern mining towns, primarily because of its isolation and its location at the foot of a dark red, sharp-ridged mountain range, which Austin described as a desert alpine landscape without the snow.[24] The isolation and transport difficulties of all the other northern mines almost pale in comparison with Yudnamutana, for it was about 400 kilometres from the railhead at Port Augusta. Even today it is a daunting trip. The road to Arkaroola has been improved considerably in recent years, but it is still a long way from anywhere and Yudnamutana is about 40 kilometres further on over the usual bevy of ridges and stony creek beds. But the tough travelling is more than compensated for by the breath-taking scenery.

There are several hut sites near the main creek, one of which is a partial dugout, which on the description of Reg Sprigg would appear to be John Lander's store and post office. These were established at the town in 1901. The post office closed in 1918, but the store continued for several more years. The town also had a bakery. Over the creek are the remains of a row of six semi-detached stone houses, and one other large stone building. Further hut sites and a stone whim are located near one of the main mine sites, and at the smelter site are two bricked-in boilers set on a stone terrace.[25]

The original copper lode was discovered by an Aboriginal man. Austin, in turn, described the lode as a large boil that outcropped on the surface, and of which about 70 tons of ore was visible. On his journey to the mine he also described meeting about 20 drays loaded with about 50 tons of ore. One dray carried a four-ton block.[26] This may have been the block that was paraded through the streets of Adelaide in February 1863. On that occasion six wagons and drays with ore from the mines were led through the city by a band from Burton's Circus. Distance and drought, however, combined to bring an early end to this mining activity.

For the next few decades the only other mining activity of any significance in the area was the construction of the Bolla Bollana smelters in 1873. They were built to provide a central smelting facility for a range of small mines in the north-east Flinders Ranges. Permanent springs at Bolla Bollana were a deciding factor in the location. A small village was constructed of mud and slate buildings, which included a store, post office and huts for employees. However, the venture did not last more than about 12 months.[27] Part of the flue and several other buildings, including some miners' huts and the domed brick kiln, can still be seen.

Mining at Yudnamutana recommenced in 1901, and in 1904 the mines were sold to a London-based company, which intended to work the Yudnamutana and neighbouring mines. In 1908 work commenced on the erection of a smelter, which was not completed until 1910. The problem of transport was addressed by the ingenious use of a road train made by the Daimler Company. It had a petrol-powered four-cylinder engine that could draw several trucks. The trial run from Farina was promising and took only two days. Loads of 10–12 tons of timber and iron were also transported, but the vehicle could not transport large loads of ore, and breakdowns were frequent.

The smelter was fired in 1910 to help persuade the Premier, who was visiting the mines, to construct a railway, but to no avail. Yudnamutana lingered on for several more years, and efforts were made to improve and expand the processing plant, but these also failed. Before long the complex was abandoned and left to the elements.[28] It was an ignominious fate, all too common in the Flinders Ranges. Yudnamutana is one of several monuments to the boundless energy, but often-misdirected enthusiasm, of the early miners. The solitude and quiet, amidst the crumbling walls and slowly rusting boilers, is overpowering.

A lonely miner's hut at Mount Browne sits amid the gibber and quartz.

The beautifully crafted engine house, chimney stack and other buildings at Nuccaleena form the site of one of Australia's most famous mining scandals.

Now totally abandoned, Sliding Rock was once a bustling copper mining town.

Parachilna Gorge, near Blinman, is picturesque at any time of the year.

The Anglican church at Dawson,
one of South Australia's many
abandoned wheat-farming towns

The Transcontinental Hotel, Farina; once a cosmopolitan town, Farina is now a collection of ruins on the arid gibber plains of South Australia's far north.

The crumbling walls of the Exchange Hotel, Farina, with the bank building in the background

Leaving the Land

From the Flinders Ranges south to Peterborough, in South Australia's remote northern and mid-northern areas, the countryside is studded with relics from the past. Solitary farmhouses stand abandoned, surrounded by rusting farm machinery. Crumbling walls and tall chimneys are silhouetted again the skyline. In other parts whole towns are deserted, or almost so. The harsh but beautiful landscape with these bleak remnants invokes immediate questions of why and how.

Dawson, for instance, is all but totally deserted, though there are still two stone churches in good condition and a large but slowly disintegrating hotel. At the railway town of Black Rock there are several occupied houses, but also an abandoned mechanics' institute and church. Similar scenes of desertion can be found at the railway towns of Eurelia and Walloway. Cradock is one of my favourites. The hotel, with its small internal courtyard is still in business, but the store and petrol station across the road have been demolished and the police station is now a private residence. St Gabriel's church is by far the largest in the north, but it too is abandoned. Further west on the saltbush plains is Johnburg, where the empty buildings include a former hotel and a shop.

Hammond is one of the stand-out towns. Several streets can still be discerned, lined by the remnants of houses. On the main street are an abandoned hotel, several shops, the former Bank of Adelaide building and a little-used church. A handful of residents keeps the town alive. Further west on the railway line is Bruce, with its recently renovated railway station and a derelict hotel. It too has a few residents. Heading further north are the totally deserted townships of Willochra, Gordon, Wilson, Simmonston and Wonoka. In all instances some remains can be found, but the most prominent are located at Wilson, and even include a cricket pitch. Perhaps the most notable ruins south of Hawker are at the former pastoral station of Kanyaka, which was virtually a town in its own right. The most complete ghost town is Farina, just south of Marree on the Oodnadatta Track. Here is an abandoned town in its entirety, with hotels, bank, bakery, police station, railway buildings and several residences scattered over the landscape.

These towns had their origins in a general wave of optimism and expansion that swept through South Australia in the 1860s and 1870s, a process which has been extensively documented in Donald Meinig's classic work, *On the Margins of the Good Earth*. South Australia's wheat lands were located on a fertile coastal plain, close to the capital city, Adelaide, and a number of small ports. In the aftermath of the gold rushes there was a demand for agricultural land, which gave rise to a wave of land reform legislation throughout Australia. In South Australia there was also a growing population and a strong demand for farm land; however, it could not be satisfied under the existing farm purchase and land tenure arrangements. All the arable land not then occupied was held under pastoral lease, and few of the aspirant farmers could have afforded it, even if it had been available.[1]

Legislation was introduced in 1869, the essential feature of which was that unoccupied land and pastoral leases in selected districts were to be surveyed and offered for selection on credit, after payment of a 10 per cent deposit. Each farm was to be no larger than 260 hectares (a square mile), and the applicants had to live on the land and carry out prescribed improvements such as fencing and dams. Credit selection was available only for the purchase of land within designated surveyed agricultural areas. Outside these areas payment could only be made in cash. With closer settlement of the land came new towns, roads and eventually railways. Government policy was to survey one township within every Hundred (a survey area of 100 square miles or 160 square kilometres).[2]

Originally the legislation applied only to land south of a line drawn by the Surveyor-General, George Woodroffe Goyder, in 1865 and known popularly as Goyder's Line. The Line was drawn initially to assist in the appraisal of pastoral rents following serious droughts in the early 1860s. It designated the land that had been least affected by the droughts, and was based entirely upon personal observations, Goyder having travelled about 4800 kilometres on horseback for this purpose.[3] The Line was not initially intended to be used as a means of dividing agricultural from pastoral land, but was given wider significance during contemplation and passage of the 1869 legislation.[4]

Very good seasons in 1870 and 1871 were followed by a slump in wheat production in the following year. But the clamour for land continued and in 1872 the idea of agricultural areas was abandoned, and all land south of Goyder's Line was made available for selection on credit. This may have been the end of the story, but the wheat yields after 1872 were massive, and Goyder's Line was held up to popular ridicule, particularly by the local press. One newspaper editorial declared Goyder's Line to be 'all nonsense'. At Melrose a public meeting was convened 'for the purpose of getting Goyder's Line of rainfall shifted to about 64 kilometres north of its present position'.

At a Laura gathering it was proposed 'that Mr Goyder's line be shifted out of the colony'. Similar sentiments were expressed in the more distant northern towns of Sliding Rock and Blinman.[5]

By 1874 the government had drafted new legislation designed at abandoning the Line and throwing the whole colony open to credit selection. Goyder continued to contend that north of the Line the rainfall was unreliable, but no one was listening. In Parliament in November of that year the Chief Secretary stated that 'Hon. Members would see the necessity of doing away with Goyder's absurd line of rainfall — a line prepared for another object and not having anything to do with the matter under present circumstances'. Goyder's Line was duly abandoned, and all restrictions or guidance on further settlement of the land were removed.[6]

Heavy rains in 1875 were of unusual intensity and gave rise to the popular view that the climate was changing. The old folk-idea that the rain followed the plough was revived. One explanation put forward was that the breaking up of the soil resulted in the absorption of more moisture, and thence its evaporation into the atmosphere and thus more rain. These views were strongly supported by the rural press and endorsed by the Minister for Agriculture. The 'frontier' was now halfway along the salt bed of Lake Torrens and over 160 kilometres beyond the present settled limits.[7]

Abandoned churches at the deserted town of Dawson

A derelict farmhouse, north of Orroroo

Despite this frenzy of optimism Goyder remained steadfast in his views. As each new Hundred was proclaimed he declared that the rainfall was unreliable. In 1876 he urged that the surveys be halted. Recalling his observations of over ten years before, he stated prophetically that:

During the last twenty years I have crossed and recrossed the country in question during all seasons of the year, and have seen the surface in good seasons like a hay field, teeming with rich, rank, and luxurious vegetation; and during drought destitute of grass and herbage, the surface soil dried by the intense heat, in places broken and pulverized by the passage of stock and formed by the action of the wind into miniature hummocks, surrounding the closely cropped stumps of salt bushes ... and the soil blown away in places to a depth of several inches, the drift covering the fences of yards, troughs ... and so denuded of feed as to be altogether useless for stock of any description.[8]

These views found little support, although an experimental farm was established in the arid east at Manna Hill.[9]

Expansion of the agricultural frontier was reflected in an ambitious program of railway development. The northern railway from Port Augusta to Government Gums (renamed Farina) was originally intended to serve the mining and pastoral interests in the far north, and was now sited to ensure that it tapped the new agricultural areas along the Willochra Plain. Towns along the route included Willochra, Wilson, Gordon and Wonoka. Similarly, the line from Peterborough to Quorn was routed to serve the new wheat lands to the east of the Willochra Plain. It would have been difficult to envisage a more roundabout route. New towns along this route included Dalton (later Black Rock), Rye (later Walloway), Eurelia, Orroroo, Carrieton, Hammond and Bruce. Many towns were also laid out beyond the railway. These included Johnburg, Dawson, Cradock, Simmonston, Stephenston and Belton. There was a massive expansion in wheat exports, and Port Pirie suddenly became one of the major wheat ports of the world.[10]

Along with the view that the climate was changing was the slightly more credible opinion that the planting of trees would increase the annual rainfall. This view was of worldwide interest at the time and perhaps can be viewed as part of Australia's first, albeit somewhat primitive and at that stage decidedly lopsided, conservation and environmental debate. The new Conservator of Forests, John Brown, was an ardent advocate of the 'tree theory'. He argued in an official report that forests had a tendency to equalise rainfall and attract clouds. Goyder disagreed with Brown's views. As Donald Meinig pointed out, there was an inherent contradiction between the theory and the settling and farming of the treeless saltbush plains.[11]

This optimism ended abruptly. The 1880 wheat season opened with good rains, but unusually dry weather followed, and as winter proceeded crop conditions worsened. Heavy rains in September were followed by a long hot dry summer, and crop failures were reported throughout the north. Average yields were less over the whole colony, but nowhere more so than in the far north. It soon became obvious that the poor harvests were not a one-off occurrence. In the Willochra area the average harvest for the previous year had been only modest, but this obscured the reality that many farmers had obtained far less, and that all along the northern frontier only marginal crops had been obtained, and some had not yet harvested a paying crop.[12]

1881 was to be much worse. Rain was sparse and total production throughout the colony fell again, with the north the hardest hit. Complete failures were far more common. Petitions from distressed farmers calling for a cessation of interest payments and government mortgages on their selections were widespread, and public meetings were held seeking government support. Despite the failures most selectors were willing to hang on, bolstered by the memory of past yields. Their immediate problem was to obtain seed for the next crop, but the government refused to subsidise them, believing this would set an unfortunate precedent. In parliamentary debates on the matter it was commented that for all practical purposes Goyder's Line was 'quite correct'. Nevertheless, the need for seed wheat remained and the Farmers' Mutual Association set up a program to distribute voluntarily contributed seed wheat on loan.[13]

By early 1882 signs of distress were again beginning to emerge. The

Empty stores, houses and bank at Hammond

Adelaide Observer joined the call for immediate relief. It noted the almost universal desire by the selectors to try another season, for it was believed that good seasons would follow the drought. Subsequently, selectors in a number of northern areas called for a remission of all interest paid or due. In an amazing reversal of popular attitude one representative stated that Goyder's Line was 'no fancy line', and that 'it was as correct as it was possible to make it'.[14]

Relief measures were introduced in March of that year, allowing for a remission of interest payments and more importantly allowing selectors to surrender their holdings and reselect elsewhere or to reselect their own holdings at a reduced offering price. The editor of the *Adelaide Observer* commented that it was doubtful whether much of the land north of Goyder's Line was suitable for agriculture. However, he reminded his readers that the land was only thrown open for selection because of the demand of people who wanted to occupy it, despite warnings to the contrary. In the Hundred of Willochra North many farmers had no crop at all, for the little wheat that had grown had been destroyed by a plague of locusts. The reaping machines had not left the sheds since the harvest of 1880.[15]

The average yield for the entire colony in 1882 was the lowest on record, but the 1883 harvest was even worse. One correspondent stated that in his district 'not one farmer in ten put his machine in his paddock', another commented that it was the worst season that they had seen, and yet another remarked that although about 3000 acres were cropped, not a single bag of wheat was harvested. The editor of the *Adelaide Observer* commented rather optimistically that, 'Great hopes are entertained that we have seen the last of the drought years, and that we are entering upon a truly golden era.'[16]

But this was not to be, for the 1884 season was equally disappointing, and the return to favourable conditions in 1885 did little to reinstall the earlier optimism. In recognition that the agricultural advance was over, selectors were allowed to convert from credit purchases to long-term leases. Goyder's Line was now firmly installed. It was accepted reluctantly that by itself, wheat cultivation in the arid north, outside of the occasional favourable season, was not remunerative.[17]

The crop failures also signalled the end to the establishment of new towns in the north. Sale of township lots had not occurred until after the farm selections had been offered, and many lots were not put on the market until 1881 or later. Some of the more northerly towns, such as Cradock, Belton and Johnburgh, had a stunted start, and others were stillborn, for the lots were never purchased. In human terms the cost was high. However, the extent to which farms and ultimately towns were abandoned during the 1880s has been questioned. Geographer Michael Williams has stated that many farmers hung on grimly for the rest of their lives, and that the population in the north actually increased between 1882 and 1901, although it declined steadily from thereon.[18] Most of the northern towns lingered on for many more years, before succumbing to a multitude of circumstances in the twentieth century.

Williams saw these men as victims of their time, aspiring to a life on the land as independent farmers, with its consequent hardships and toils. By the early to mid-1900s, the selectors of the 1870s had either died or reached retirement age, and their children understandably did not have the same level of commitment or even opportunity to remain on the land. Farm incomes in the 1920s and 1930s were also very low and in some cases nonexistent. Williams has estimated that in every 160 square kilometres (corresponding to the old Hundreds), there were in 1974 about 30 occupied dwellings to 20 ruins and 10 abandoned houses, which in turn explains the overriding impression of visual decay that can be seen today. However, the final phase of abandonment occurred after 1920.[19]

During the two world wars shortages of labour and increased demand for wheat led to further mechanisation, which in turn encouraged a trend towards amalgamations and larger holdings, reducing the number of farms and the overall demand for farm labour. In turn this led to the closure of many businesses whose customers no longer had any money to spend. The introduction of large concrete grain silos also dispensed with the need for bagged wheat, further reducing employment. Improved vehicle transport eventually impacted on the railways, and led to the closure of the lines north from Quorn and Peterborough. Better roads and vehicles also meant that local businesses were bypassed in favour of larger and cheaper stores in the large towns. More recently, government and institutions such as banks have reduced their services.[20] Overall, the farming and town communities have found themselves in an increasingly unattractive environment.

A few examples illustrate this general process of decline and abandonment. For instance, Wilson was surveyed in 1881 and a hotel, store and several homes were erected. By 1884 it had three stores, a Wesleyan chapel, school, saddler, branch of the Commercial Bank of South Australia, a carpenter, builder, butcher, blacksmith and hotel. The school was conducted in the Wesleyan chapel. By 1886 there were growing concerns at the continued dry weather. Rabbits and dingoes were also a problem, horses and cattle were dying, and a number of farmers had abandoned their holdings temporarily for the Teetulpa gold rush. The harvest was again poor in the following year, which was described as 'the hottest summer since agricultural settlement'.[21]

From 1889 to 1895 good seasons were the norm, but for the next six years, the rainfall was below average every year. By 1890 there were two green grocery businesses, one of which was run by a Chinese person, who bought vegetables from a Chinese friend who had a market garden at Kanyaka. Kanyaka was a pastoral station with an area of 608 square kilometres, but its size was reduced dramatically when it was resumed and subdivided for agricultural purposes. A town of the same name was established about four kilometres away, and had a hotel, post office, store, blacksmith's shop and a few buildings, but it could not compete with Wilson and Gordon and it closed in 1881.[22]

Wilson reached its peak in 1900 with a school, church, hotel, general store, butcher, greengrocer, fruiterer, blacksmith, saddler, carpenter, and a chaff store that was used as a hall. The railway employed five men. Record yields were recorded in 1916–17, but the harvest was wiped out by a mice plague. There was a short resurgence when servicemen returned after World War I, and a substantial memorial hall was built. However, following a run of seasons with below-average rainfall, a disastrous drought in 1928–29 and the onset of the 1930s Depression, most landholders sold out. In 1942 the school and hotel were closed and the church dismantled. The last building to be occupied was the stationmaster's house, which had also been used as the post office.[23]

Simmonston was surveyed in anticipation of the railway line from Quorn passing to the west of the range. Two buildings, including a two-storey hotel and a general store, were commenced in 1880, but before building was completed word was received that the line would go to the east of the ranges and the town died before it had lived, becoming the 'town that never was'. Stephenston had a similar fate. It was surveyed in the 1876–79 period in the hope that the railway would pass through it. But the railway was located about six kilometres west. In 1880 the town had a blacksmith's shop, two general stores and a 'wine palace'. Later, a school and Methodist church were built. The school closed in 1912 and the church in 1920.[24]

Cradock was established at the request of local residents. By early 1879 the storekeeper had been appointed as postmaster, and in 1881 two hotels and a school had been constructed. Other businesses to develop included two black-smiths, a saddler and two drapers. In common with the rest of the north, the selectors at Cradock fared badly and by January 1883 many had hardly enough seed for the following year. They had been cropping for four years and every crop had failed. However, the residents had formed a progress committee and agitated for a bank and telegraph office, which they duly received. A Roman Catholic church was ready for its congregation in 1883 and the following year a Wesleyan church was opened.[25]

Both Cradock and Wilson appeared to take turns holding the annual Northern Areas Amalgamated Agricultural Society Show, the third and last of which was held in 1885. In that year crops were poor and, not for the first time, grasshoppers were eating the little wheat that had grown. However, a police station was built. A public institute and library and a Bank of Adelaide building were also constructed in these early years, and sports such as cricket, tennis and football were played. But the drought of the late 1890s caused many families to leave their properties and the town and district began to slide.[26]

For some towns the demise was much later. Michael Williams recalled that in 1955 Dawson had a post office, grocer and general storekeeper, a public hall, hotel, primary school and a shearing contractor. In 1970 it had lost every

Underground bakery, Farina

function except the post office and the public hall, which was used in that year as a church. Now even these functions have gone, the churches presumably having been closed many years before.[27] Gordon also appears to have lingered a little longer than some towns. In 1921 it had a hotel, two churches, a school, railway cottages, two stores, post office, racecourse, golf club and tennis courts. Prolonged drought caused many small selectors to sell out, and the buildings were gradually demolished during the 1950s.[28]

Perhaps the most amazing of these towns was Farina. The name was derived from the word 'farinaceous' and reflected hopes that it too would benefit from the great wheat drive of the 1870s, even though it was located on a gibber plain, not far from the commencement of the Birdsville and Oodnadatta tracks at Marree. Farina was established as a railway terminus, and for a while it was the northernmost town in South Australia. In 1882 a 20-million-litre reservoir, goods shed, cattle and sheep yards, stationmaster's residence and other buildings were erected. There was also a general store, brewery, saddlery, underground bakery, two hotels (the Transcontinental and the Exchange), and a school. Later, a post and telegraph office, police station, Anglican and Roman Catholic churches were established. For a while the town also had a doctor, Edward Hoche.[29]

The *Town and Country* correspondent, 'The Raven', visited Farina in 1884, but was less than impressed with what he saw. Both the hotels were crowded, but he and the other journalists were able to get beds in one of them. Although it was a hot night, it was impossible to keep the window open because of the stench from the back premises, which were strewn about with garbage and close to a pigsty. A piano was kept playing until nearly 4 am, while 'the hoarse and drunken voices of some dozen brawlers made sleep an impossibility'. During the small hours 'the remainder of the occupants of their room staggered in and behaved themselves in too disgusting a manner to particularise ... suffice to say we did not sleep a wink ...'[30]

Despite these excesses, Farina had a cosmopolitan touch. There was a Chinese camp on the outskirts of town, and an Afghan camp at Afghan Hill. The Chinese had been employed as labourers on the railway; some of them later worked on nearby stations and a few had vegetable gardens near the town. If the creek was ever in flood the vegetables were brought into town by boat. The Afghans had a number of camel teams, which were used to transport supplies from the railway to the stations and to transport wool back to the railway. Farina became an important service centre for livestock, wool and copper traffic, and in its heyday had a population of around 600. When Marree became the new railhead, Farina began to decline, and it was badly affected by the droughts of the late 1890s.[31] It lingered on for many more years, but with the closure of the railway to Oodnadatta, it too joined the pantheon of ghost towns that proliferate throughout the northern and mid-north regions of South Australia.

TASMANIA

A Place of Punishment

PORT ARTHUR WAS THE LEADING PENAL SETTLEMENT IN TASMANIA, IF NOT Australia. Today it is a well-known tourist destination, and possibly one of the country's most visited historic sites. Snuggled in around the low hills and slopes surrounding picturesque Mason Cove, the carefully manicured lawns, gardens and trees stand in sharp contrast to the misery that occurred so many years ago. From a distance, the buildings of the penal settlement are almost dwarfed by this scenery. The much-photographed penitentiary building, the turreted guard tower, the church and the hospital, are marvels of colonial architecture. As well, there are the less aesthetic, but still impressive remains of the model prison, the lunatic asylum and the paupers' mess. The neatly whitewashed cottages and gardens remind the visitor that this was the home of the free as well as the felon.

Port Arthur has long been considered picturesque. David Burn, writing in 1842 prior to the construction of many of the buildings that we see today, was generous in his praise: 'What lovely bays! What noble basins! What splendid anchorage!'[1] He, of course, did not have to live there. But, in establishing Port Arthur and a myriad of other convict stations and settlements on the Tasman Peninsula, the authorities did not have aesthetics in mind. As long as the English authorities kept on transporting convicts then the colonial administrations had to devise new ways of accommodating them.

Primarily because of their remoteness, the penal settlements at Sarah Island and Maria Island did not meet the colony's needs. The Tasman Peninsula, on the other hand, was admirably suited. It was much closer to Hobart, and the only access was by sea or Eaglehawk Neck, a narrow isthmus that would be relatively easy to secure. The ease of anchorage at Port Arthur and its access to large stands of timber were further determining factors. To secure Eaglehawk Neck, a chain of dogs (mainly deer-hounds and mastiffs) was established in a row of 18 kennels, and the isthmus was illuminated every

Port Arthur in 1847
(JW Beattie Collection; by permission
of National Library of Australia)

night by kerosene lamps and patrolled by guards. Many of the dogs, described as 'most ferocious', had not been off their chains for years. Separate detachments of guards were stationed at intervals along the banks of the narrow straits to apprehend any convicts attempting to swim across.[2]

Port Arthur started life as a penal settlement for second offenders. The first contingent of convicts arrived in 1830 and by the following year they had erected a number of huts for the guards and themselves, a cottage for the officers, a military barracks and a store large enough to hold supplies for six months. By 1833 all the convicts on Sarah Island and Maria Island had been transferred to Port Arthur, by which time there were 675 men present. This constituted five per cent of the total convict population of Van Diemen's Land, the remainder of whom were assigned to work for the free settlers.[3]

There was a large military and civil establishment at Port Arthur, with civilians in charge of stores, accounting, maintenance and engineering, the workshops and the hospital, school and church. For these people, and more particularly for their families, Port Arthur must have seemed like a prison. There were no shops or hotels, other amenities were limited, and there were irksome restrictions on movement into and out of the settlement, and on the amount of farming permitted. No civil officer or free person could leave the settlement without permission from the commandant, and they were not

172

permitted to keep livestock on the peninsula other than poultry and pigs at their own quarters. The officers were probably even more restricted in their movements, but were allotted ground for a garden ranging from one-fifth of a hectare for first class officers to one-tenth for others. There was a curfew at dusk, and all personnel needed a pass to be out at night.[4]

Families attempted to avoid the convicts, but some of the better behaved ones were employed as servants and tutors, and families frequently witnessed crime and punishment. Prisoners in chains were a common sight. Nevertheless, there were many agreeable distractions. Picnics, horseraces on the beach and parties were common, as were sports such as kangaroo hunting with guns and dogs, fishing, wombat hunting, cricket and boat racing. The settlement also eventually acquired a literary institute and library, and extra entertainments were sometimes arranged when ships came into port.[5]

Extensive lawns and gardens stretched downhill from the houses, but at every turn the civilian population could not but be reminded that they were in a penal settlement. Linus Miller, a political prisoner from Canada, described Port Arthur as a 'sink of sin and horrible iniquity ... hundreds of abominable crimes against nature ... are daily committed at this Sodom ...'[6] These sentiments would have been shared by most of the civilian population.

The convicts were classified according to the severity of their punishment and their level of education. They wore different types of clothing to

Part of the penitentiary and schoolhouse at the coal mines penal settlement, Plunkett Point

distinguish them from each other. There were seven classes of convicts, ranging from ticket-of-leave to the chain gang, and a convict could move up and down the scale depending on his behaviour. Most convicts were attached initially to labour gangs, and after one-third of their sentence had been served they were normally assigned to lighter work. Educated convicts were also employed in lighter work. Work in the gangs was intended to be 'of the most incessant and galling description', and the chain-gang men were often employed on stone breaking. The chains varied in width according to the convict's offence and hardihood, and in really bad cases logs were attached.[7]

In the early years of the settlement the most common form of punishment was the lash. It could be readily used and did not disrupt work to any great extent. By the 1840s, however, it had been largely abandoned and the main punishment was solitary confinement, work on the treadmill or in the coal mines. Absconders were harshly dealt with and received up to 100 lashes. If the prisoner should faint in the course of flogging, he was revived in a shallow salt bath. A doctor was always present and if he considered that the life of the convict was in danger he had the power to stop the flogging. Such events were normally held on Sunday mornings and inflicted in the presence of all prisoners and the standard rank and file of the military. After this workout it was off to church for 'prayer and solace'. The offenders, however, were normally given two days off and assigned to work in saltwater at the boat yard to help the healing process.[8]

Most historians agree that the convicts were adequately clothed and fed, although some of the meals, such as the morning gruel of course-ground flour and hot water, would have been hard to stomach. However, the quantity and quality of fresh food available was probably superior to that which many of them would have obtained as free men in England. Rations could be reduced if the convicts were engaged in light work, or in solitary confinement, but the settlements were designed to be productive work centres, and this could only occur if adequate food, clothing and medical treatment were provided. Over time there was a certain relaxation of discipline, and when Courtenay took over as commandant in 1848 he found that convicts were given tobacco and food for working for the officers and families.[9]

Initially, the convicts were housed in a large timber barracks, and as the number of prisoners increased, additional buildings were erected. By 1847 there were 16 huts each holding 30 convicts. A comfortable schoolroom for literate and illiterate convicts was also built; the contrast between it and the huts was intended to act as an incentive to reform. The large stone-built penitentiary was not used for this purpose until 1852. It was originally built in 1842 as a granary and corn mill, and was possibly the largest building in the colony at that time. In 1852 over 500 convicts were transferred from Norfolk Island to the Tasman Peninsula. One hundred of the worst of these were to be sent to Port Arthur and required special accommodation, and the granary was converted into a penitentiary for this purpose.[10]

Over time Port Arthur became an important industrial establishment,

The Port Arthur asylum is shameful evidence of a penal system that spawned a tragic harvest of prison-generated lunatics.

The burnt-out remains of the government cottage and church at Port Arthur, home of the felon and the free

The lime kilns on Maria Island were one of Diego Bernacchi's ambitious but ultimately unsuccessful business ventures.

The cold remains of the oven in the servants' quarters on Sarah Island

Perched atop a rocky outcrop, the penitentiary at Sarah Island was reputed to have such strict discipline that convicts dreaded the idea of being sent there.

The Iron Blow, near Linda and Gormanston, sits in a landscape that was once described as 'hell with the fire burnt out'.

based largely on the timber industry. Gangs of up to 70 men carried the heavy logs for long distances to the timberyard, and from there to the dockyard, with the gang looking to many observers like a large centipede. This was gruelling work, and if a convict fell down he risked being flogged, particularly if saddled with an unsympathetic overseer. Eventually tramroads were built to carry the logs to the sawpits. At the timberyard the logs were sawn for use in the settlement and for shipment to Hobart.

The main use of timber at the settlement was for shipbuilding. Inside the dockyard the prisoners considered the work to be almost as hard as that of the carrying gangs, as they sometimes had to work up to their shoulders in water. Supporting trades were sail making, cabinet making, coopering, wheelwrighting and smithing.[11] The shipyard was closed in 1849.

Carpenters' shops and a blacksmith's shop were also established, and a new blacksmith's shop was erected in the 1840s with a furnace capable of casting five tons of iron. This shop made all the iron work for the settlement, and later the probation stations on the peninsula. A tailor's shop and shoemaker's shop were also constructed, and later a tannery. Convicts who made clothes privately for the military were often paid in either contraband or money, and a cobbler could earn up to one shilling a week. As early as 1833 the settlement was also producing considerable numbers of bricks, and later, tiles and pottery were manufactured. Limekilns were also established.

The settlement also included a farm and dairy. On the farm the convicts were yoked up like human cattle, 14 to a team, to plough the fields. By the mid-1850s task work was more common, and included incentives such as partial remission of sentences, extra food or a small daily allowance of tobacco. In 1862 small weekly money payments were also made where appropriate. By the late 1860s and the 1870s the type of manufacture changed to a much lighter type of product, reflecting the increased number of frail and old convicts.[12]

The most controversial industry was coal mining, which took place at Plunkett Point, on the north of Tasman Peninsula. The coal mines were a punishment station and by all reports feared by the convicts, who had no previous experience in mining, and who had to work in cramped and dangerous conditions. An added touch was the construction of solitary confinement cells, at first located in the mine itself. These were subsequently abandoned when new cells — still visible today — were built near the surface. A report in 1837 stated that the underground cells were 'so much dreaded by the prisoner, being so awfully dark, and a species as it were of burying alive, that for the sake of humanity, they were seldom used'.[13]

In 1838 the wooden buildings were replaced by stone buildings. The complex included barracks for the troops and prisoners, a chapel, schoolroom, cookhouse, bakehouse and washhouse. A store and 16 solitary cells were located in the basement, which was above ground. There were also buildings for the soldiers, commanding officer, surgeon, constable and wharf staff.[14]

Theft and violence were constantly recurring problems, and there were continual concerns about homosexuality and the spread of venereal disease

Theft and violence were constantly recurring problems, and there were continual concerns about homosexuality and the spread of venereal disease. A report just prior to the closure of the mines as a convict station stated that some of the men were so sick with venereal disease that they were barely able to crawl about. The prevalence of homosexuality was greater at the mines than other stations, largely because of the nature of the employment, which was often unsupervised and afforded opportunities not available elsewhere. The separate cells in the basement were used to confine men suspected of such practices. In 1845 two convicts were found guilty of homosexual rape and executed for their efforts, and several years later the convict station was closed and the mines sold.[15] Today, the ruins of many of the buildings are still visible, including the basement cells. The misery, hardship and scandal associated with the mines sit incongruously with their physically attractive setting, the sparkling waters of Plunkett Bay.

Another aspect of life at Port Arthur that was shrouded in controversy and scandal was the convict powered tramway, which commenced at Norfolk Bay and ended up at Long Bay, a distance of six kilometres. From there the supplies were shipped to the quay at Port Arthur. Each carriage was pushed by six men, and could carry loads of half a ton, including passengers. Tramways also connected Port Arthur with the quarries and the forests.[16] A contemporary observer, David Burn, remarked that it

jars harshly against the feelings to behold man, as it were, lowered to the standard of the brute, to mark the unhappy, guilty creatures toiling and struggling along, the muscular power exerted to the utmost ...[17]

Another observer, Colonel George Mundy commented that 'our poor beasts of burthen at the end of the traject seemed terribly jaded, and I saw one of them continually trying to shift the irons from a galled spot on his ankle'. On their return the men were fed, having not eaten for 12 hours. He remarked that the work was sought after because many passengers, in breach of the regulations, gave some small reward to the convicts, allowing them to buy tobacco or other small luxuries.[18]

Another innovation was the establishment of a separate boys' prison at Point Puer, across the bay from the main Port Arthur settlement. The establishment of the settlement had been prompted by the considerable resistance of the free families of Van Diemen's Land to taking the boys on assignment because of theft and other misdemeanours. In 1834 the first group of boys arrived a little worse for wear, having broken into a wine supply which had been destined for the commandant. Point Puer became the destination for all young boys sentenced to transportation to Australia, and at its peak in 1843 there were about 800 there, ranging between 10 and 18 years of age.[19]

The boys were encouraged to take up trades in carpentry, shoe-making, tailoring, baking, gardening, bookbinding and turning, and the older boys were allowed to work at Port Arthur in stone cutting, brick making, and boat building along with blacksmith work and coopering. They were not allowed to leave the station until they were familiar with their chosen trade and their behaviour was good. The harshest form of punishment was flogging, the maximum being 36 lashes. Otherwise, the boys were kept in cells after working hours or placed in solitary confinement with only bread and water. Point Puer was criticised as too lax, and in 1849 it was abandoned.[20]

Possibly the most controversial aspect of Port Arthur was the establishment of the model prison, which was built to house the most incorrigible of the convicts. The key features of the prison were isolation and silence, and the prisoners would be punished if they were detected communicating

> or attempting to communicate with each other, either by words or signs, reading aloud, singing, dancing or making any other noise whatever, except such as may be unavoidable in the performance of their allotted work ...[21]

Three passages radiated off a central room, with cells on either side of each passage, and on the fourth side was the chapel. The exercise yards were located between each passage. Each prisoner exercised for one hour a day, and the yards were arranged so that they could not see each other. Outside their cells they always wore a cloth cap, with a hood which pulled down over the face permitting only the eyes to be seen. The prisoners and officers all walked in slippers and the officers did not speak to the prisoners. Each prisoner attended chapel three times a week. The chapel was arranged so that each prisoner could only see the minister and an officer in an adjoining seat. For punishment the men were put in a dark cell on a half ration of bread and water.[22]

A report in 1860 described the sight of the men in the prison as harrowing in the extreme. In some cells men were 'pacing up and down with an aspect of the most determined ferocity — in others they were walking and indulging in hideous grinning — some were standing in an air of mute despair'.[23] In the latter years of the settlement there was an increased number of deranged convicts, enough to warrant the building of the lunatic asylum in 1867. Alex Graeme-Evans has remarked on the inherent cruelty of this system, which in his words 'spawned a tragic harvest of prison generated lunatics'. He sheets much of the blame on Commandant Boyd, who had drafted the original rules for the model prison, and whose career was built around being a specialist in this type of imprisonment.[24] It is extremely unnerving to reflect on this cruelty. While the men were fed and clothed adequately and were not subject to corporal punishment, they were denied one of the most important human needs, the ability to communicate with another human being.

By 1853 the writing was on the wall for Port Arthur; transportation from England ceased in August. The gold rushes did not help either, as they drained thousands of young males to the mainland, and deprived Port Arthur of a fruitful source of second offenders. Now the emphasis was on welfare, not production, and this change was exemplified by the construction of a paupers' mess and a lunatic asylum, which housed those broken and beaten by the system. The asylum was the last major building to be constructed at Port Arthur. By the early 1870s it was considered that the cost of the settlement was excessive for the small number of men that were there, particularly as nearly all the buildings were dilapidated and in need of extensive repairs.

The closure of the penal settlement in 1877 was not the end of Port Arthur, merely the start of a new beginning under a different name: Carnarvon. Many of the other settlements on the peninsula also changed their names. By 1880 there were about 80 residents in the town, and by 1882 it had a post office, cricket club and lawn tennis club. On holidays and weekends visitors arrived in port by boat, but it took a few years before a hotel and boarding house were erected. Concerts were held regularly in aid of the piano fund, and the concert in October of that year featured for the first time the redoubtable Mohawk Minstrels. In December a rowing club was formed and over the Christmas period the annual sports and concert attracted a large crowd, many of whom travelled by boat from Hobart.[25] By about 1890 there were 200 people living in and around the town.

But fate was never far away, almost as if some malevolent presence was hovering above and attempting to expunge and cleanse the memories of the past. The settlement was visited by a number of fires, the first of which occurred in 1884, when the church was gutted. Another fire occurred in 1886 when four brick cottages, one of which was used as a general store, were burned down.[26] More serious was the fire of 1895. On this occasion a bushfire swept down on the town in the direction of the old church. Several houses, cottages and government buildings, including Government House, the lunatic asylum and the former model prison, were destroyed.

The wind carried sparks and flames in all directions, and soon the school was ablaze and fire had spread to Archbishop Murphy's building, which was the old hospital. It was a 'grand but awful sight, the blazing and smoking ruins forming in the town almost a semicircle of destruction'. There were several narrow escapes, including the Carnarvon Hotel, Rose Cottage, the police court and Trenville's private family hotel. The *Hobart Mercury*'s correspondent reflected that the smouldering ruins gave a 'grim and mournful appearance to the pretty surroundings', and it was hoped that 'this severe visitation, may prove the opening of a better future'.[27]

But these hopes were not realised, for in less than two years an even worse conflagration occurred, and what the fire of 1895 had not finished off, this one did. The correspondent for the *Mercury* saw it as divine intervention:

> [T]he destruction which visited Port Arthur was of a more intelligently merciful kind than that which visited another part of the colony, for the buildings destroyed were in most cases not homes, but places associated in the long ago with crime and human suffering ... There are many who will make no concealment of their satisfaction at the destruction of the Penitentiary. On holiday visits to Port Arthur in years gone by you always met the man who 'would like to put a limited quantity of dynamite or gunpowder' under the Model and the Penitentiary ... How some of the poor wretches who suffered and sorrowed in the port half a century ago would have rejoiced had they witnessed the place in flames on Friday night! Years of suffering would no doubt, to their minds have been at least partially avenged.

In town at the time were 600 passengers from the SS *Manapouri*, who were 'treated' to an unforgettable spectacle. The penitentiary, the police office and station, the Trenhams' boarding house, several cottages and the old hospital were destroyed. Mr Trenham, who had taken his wife to safety, returned to the building because he thought his daughter may have been inside, but he was unable to escape and was burnt to death. Following the 1895 fires the old hospital had been repaired, but now only the walls were left.[28] Remarkably, Carnarvon re-emerged from this carnage and continued to attract visitors for many years more.

With so much drama it is no wonder that stories of apparitions and ghostly encounters are ever present. Indeed, the nightly ghost tours at Port Arthur are one of its main attractions. The guides stress that they do not as a rule refer to such events unless there are multiple sightings by themselves or visitors, and in the office they have several large folders full of such stories. My favourite, if one can call it that, concerns a guide who went to lock up the model prison late at night, and chose to do so from the inside, walking down the dark corridors, locking the most distant door, then walking back to lock the other. She heard footsteps behind her and felt a chill sensation. Her pace quickened; so too did the footsteps. She started running; so too did the footsteps. Next she leapt down the steps into the alcove in front of the chapel; the footsteps landed on the floor just behind her. She raced to the door and shut it behind her, heaving a sigh of relief. Then she felt cold arms around her. Heart pounding and pulse racing, she sped to the visitor's centre to find the other guides enjoying a quiet coffee.[29]

Perdition and Paradise

THE MOST RENOWNED HISTORICAL FEATURE OF TASMANIA IS ITS remarkable array of convict settlements and towns. Of these, Port Arthur is the largest, the most diverse, and the most popular with visitors. However, it was not the first penal settlement in Tasmania (or as it was then known, Van Diemen's Land), nor was it the most notorious. This 'honour' goes to Sarah Island, located in Tasmania's Macquarie Harbour on the west coast. Van Diemen's Land was settled in 1803, and it was not long before Hobart as well as Sydney became the repository for England's convicts. By 1817 Van Diemen's Land had a population of about 5000 Europeans, of whom half were convicts, most of them transported from the mainland as second offenders. There was, however, no suitable court or penal settlement in Van Diemen's Land and all serious crimes had to be tried in Sydney, a costly and time-consuming exercise, and the guilty offenders sent to one of three penal settlements in New South Wales. Against this background it was proposed to establish a penal settlement at Macquarie Harbour on the west coast of Tasmania, because of its remoteness and its access to coal and stands of Huon pine.[1]

The principles on which the convicts were to be sent to Macquarie Harbour were made very clear. Banishment was to act as a deterrent as well as a punishment, such that it had to be 'considered by the whole class of convicts a place of such strict discipline that they may absolutely dread the very idea of being sent there'. They were to be found work and labour, even if it only 'consists of opening cavities and filling them up again'. To this Lieutenant-Governor Arthur subsequently added that:

> Unceasing labour, total deprivation of Spirits, Tobacco and comforts of every kind, the sameness of occupation, the dreariness of situation, must, if anything will, reform the vicious characters that are sent to you.[2]

The main settlement was on Sarah Island, which was opened in 1822, comprising at first of 110 persons, of whom there were 44 male convicts of 'bad character and incorrigible conduct', 11 who were 'tradesmen of good character', and 11 who were of 'useful avocations' and not under sentence. There were, in addition, eight female convicts, a military detachment of 17, with three wives and 11 children, and four officers. Further convicts arrived in subsequent years before reaching a peak of 320. It was not just a place of incarceration, for much of the work was hard and dangerous and the lash was used frequently as a punishment, especially in the early years. As many as 229 men were flogged in 1823.[3]

Thomas Lempriere, one of the superintendents, wrote that it was difficult to conceive why Sarah Island had been chosen. It was at the time thickly wooded and no part of it appeared capable of cultivation. Nor was there any water. He reflected that its overriding advantage must have been its isolation and difficulty of escape. The soil was gradually converted into arable land by the addition of soil from the mainland and the use of compost. He added that, but for the log fences built around the island as a protection against the wind and storms, 'not a cabbage could have been grown'. By the time that the penal colony had been established there were few trees left. The settlement included dockyards, lumberyards, a stone penitentiary, stores buildings, offices, a bake-house, gaol for solitary confinement, barracks, hospital and separate quarters for the officers, chaplain and doctor as well as the gardens and cemetery.[4]

Despite the isolation of Sarah Island there were many escape attempts, some of which were notorious. One of the most infamous was the escape of Alexander Pierce and seven other convicts in 1822. Within a few days the first of the party was killed with an axe, and his body butchered and divided equally amongst the survivors. Two of the party became apprehensive and returned to the penal settlement. The rest continued on their merry way, butchering each other when the opportunity presented itself, until only Pierce was left. He was later captured and returned to Sarah Island, but a year later he had escaped and again he killed his companion. He was later recaptured and in 1824 he was executed.[5]

In October 1827 nine convicts attempted escape. They had secretly built a raft, with which they intended to reach and then seize the *Prince Leopold*, which was then in port. However, the raft failed to float, and the escape attempt was transformed into a form of mass suicide, or escape by mass execution, for in despair and revenge they murdered Constable Rex in full view of four other men, whom they bound and gagged to ensure they witnessed the event. A marginally more successful attempt involved the seizure of a whale-boat by 14 convicts in 1824. Five of them were recaptured in less than a week and hanged. One of their number, Matthew Brady, became the leader of a gang of bushrangers, and remained at large for two years until he too suffered the same fate. Another boat seizure involved the brig *Cyprus* in 1827. The mutineers reached Japan and then China, after leaving a number of men behind in the Pacific Islands. Several of their number sailed to Mexico, but the others returned to England and were arrested on their arrival.[6]

Sarah Island was in some respects a prison for free and convict alike. It is a very small island, only three kilometres in circumference, and it would have been almost impossible for the women and children to have any privacy outside their homes. The children did not even have a school until 1829, and then it was only for a few hours a week. Neither was it a very comfortable island, for the harbour was subject to severe storms, some of which blew down small buildings and washed away logs and prepared timbers, and made it difficult to grow vegetables.[7] Lempriere commented that the most disagreeable feature of the weather was the rain, which could continue night and day without ceasing for weeks at a time. The remoteness of the settlement from any other town must have been particularly galling. The voyage from Hobart could take several weeks or longer and as a consequence serious food shortages occasionally occurred.[8]

Sarah Island was, however, not the only place of incarceration, for nearby Grummet Island, which is barely larger than a big rock, was used as a secondary detention centre. Each day the male convicts on the island had to row to Sarah Island, where they worked in chains, or to the logging areas. In bad weather the surf often broke over the island with great violence, leaving the jetty under water. The convicts had to wade to and from the boats, which meant that they were always wet on arrival. Initially female convicts were housed on the island, but they became the subject of attention from the soldiers, several of whom were court martialled for their efforts, and they were removed from the island to Hobart.[9] A small contingent of convicts resided on Phillip Island, which was used as a farm.

The main task for the convicts was timber-felling on the shores of Macquarie Harbour, although some were engaged in less arduous tasks such as lime-burning, charcoal-burning, brick-making, farming, general maintenance, as servants to the officers, or in the more skilled work of shipbuilding. Timber-felling was the most feared task, for each day the convicts had to row 16 to 22 kilometres to their place of work. They had to fell the trees, trim them, roll them to the water's edge and make them into rafts, which would be then towed to Sarah Island for use in shipbuilding or to be transported to Hobart. It was heavy, dangerous and uncomfortable work, for few of the men had any previous experience, and when making the rafts they had to work up to their chests in the water. According to Lempriere, the worst task was on their return to Sarah Island, for the convicts had to work in the water for hours at a time with hand spikes to roll the timber up.[10]

On Sarah Island itself the main form of work was shipbuilding, and for this purpose a dockyard area was built and later extended. It appears that the growth of this industry changed the character of the settlement, for skilled workers were in demand and as early as 1826, the commandant, against Governor Arthur's orders, had offered extra rations to the convict tradesmen. The growth of Sarah Island as a shipbuilding centre coincided with the arrival of master shipwright David Hoy.[11]

Macquarie Harbour,
Grummet Island; convicts
rafting pine logs, 1830
(JW Beattie Collection; by permission
of National Library of Australia)

Hoy was a man of wealth and ambition, who had been frustrated by the lack of opportunity in Hobart to build large vessels to his own design. On Sarah Island he built 96 ships and boats, making it the most prolific shipyard in Australia at that time. About a year after his arrival and the murder of Constable Rex, there was a marked change in the punishment regime consistent with the emphasis on shipbuilding. Late in 1828 the rate of flogging dropped dramatically from 8004 lashes to barely 800 in 1829, and solitary confinement in the brick gaol became relatively infrequent. There also appears to have been an increase in the incident of contraband trading and smuggling of tobacco, alcohol and other goods to the convicts at this time.[12]

The shipbuilding industry provided Sarah Island with its last and most legendary drama, the seizure of the *Frederick*. With the construction of the penal settlement at Port Arthur it was decided to abandon Sarah Island. Two officers, four soldiers, a seaman and 12 convicts were left behind to complete the fitting out of the *Frederick*. While two soldiers and a prisoner were fishing, the remaining prisoners rebelled, using two homemade pistols. All the soldiers, officers, the seamen and David Hoy were left behind with provisions and on 14 January 1834 the boat sailed out of the harbour. The escapees sailed to New Zealand, avoiding the main shipping lines, and arrived off the coast of Chile in South America in February, where they abandoned the *Frederick* and rowed the last 80 kilometres in the ship's whaleboat.

They settled in the town of Valdivia, where several of them married local women. With a change of governor in the region, they realised that their conditions may change for the worse. Three of them left on a ship to America in July 1834, three others offered to build a whaleboat for the governor and escaped in it, and the four remaining unfortunates were imprisoned and later handed over to the British navy. They were taken back to London, and then sent back to Hobart for trial in 1837. Found guilty of piracy they were sentenced to death, but as the ship had not been taken on the high seas the sentences were commuted to life imprisonment on Norfolk Island.[13]

Despite the passage of time on this rain and windswept island there are an amazing number of relics left, all of which have been subject to an ongoing restoration. The most notable ruin is the stone penitentiary perched upon a rocky outcrop, and reminiscent of an abandoned medieval castle. Other substantial ruins are the bakery oven and the gaol, which was used for solitary confinement. Elsewhere there are a number of stone chimneys from offices and cottages, and several forges. The base logs of the fence, wharves and jetties are visible at low tide, and the slipways for the shipyards are intact in places. By the early 1900s the island had become a favourite picnicking spot for residents of Strahan and Kelly Basin.

Maria Island is located about 18 kilometres from Triabunna on the east coast of Tasmania. It was established as a penal settlement in 1825, for a class of convict who had committed lesser crimes than those sent to Sarah Island. It is much larger than Sarah Island, with a decidedly more benign climate. The main settlement was at Darlington, where many buildings were constructed of bricks made on the island. The convicts worked as tradesmen in the tanning yards, lumberyards, brickyards, pottery, farm and hop fields, and in the cloth factory, which consisted of weaving, spinning, carding and pressing rooms.[14]

According to Lempriere, who was for a while second-in-charge, the convicts enjoyed privileges unknown at other settlements, such as tobacco, tea and sugar, and being allowed to cultivate gardens. The degree of discipline was well short of that at Macquarie Harbour, although infringements were almost always met with corporal punishment. As a consequence, in 1827 the commandant was directed to substitute solitary cells and chain gangs. Whatever privileges the convicts had, they were not enough to stop them from attempting to escape by raft or bark canoe, and in 1832 it was decided to close the settlement.[15]

In 1842 Darlington was resettled as a convict probation station under Superintendent Samuel Lapham, and by 1844 there were 627 convicts on the island. Separate brick apartments (single cells) were built at Darlington and Long Point. The stations were self supporting and crops of wheat, hops, flax, potatoes, turnips and other vegetables were grown. At Darlington a two-storey building was constructed with room for 205 convicts. The remainder were accommodated in huts with room for between three and 24 men, and in the penitentiary, which had been built in 1830. Originally, the penitentiary

had six rooms, five of which were dormitories, but at that time there were only about 140 convicts. In the second convict period 66 men slept in each of the six rooms until part of each dividing wall was removed in 1847 to make one large room with 282 beds guarded by a single officer.[16]

Colonel George Mundy, captain of the HMS *Havannah*, who visited Maria Island in late 1850 after it had been abandoned, was appalled:

> There was one feature of this defunct convict station that I viewed with disgust — a single dormitory for four hundred men! The bed places were built of wood in three tiers … The prisoner lies with his feet to the wall and his bed towards the centre of the apartment — like a bottle in its bin. This nocturnal aggregation of brutalised males is a feature of penal discipline that I was astonished to find had been so lately in operation.[17]

The new settlement was soon surrounded by controversy. James Boyd was appointed as an assistant superintendent in 1845 and published a report that was highly critical of the probation system and Darlington in particular. He listed a number of serious crimes, including the bludgeoning of an officer and conspiracies to attack, shoot or poison officials, but details of homosexual activities were cut from the printed Parliamentary Paper. In the following year an uproar was caused when the recently removed Assistant Superintendent Thomas Lafarelle, wrote to the Archbishop of Canterbury and other dignitaries charging that officials 'passed over lightly' various 'indecent crimes'.[18]

In 1847 Darlington was cleared of all convicts to receive 369 prisoners, almost direct from England. One of the more famous prisoners was William Smith O'Brien who, along with six other leaders of the Young Ireland rebellion, was transported to Van Diemen's Land in 1849. At Darlington he was imprisoned in a small cottage and isolated from all contact with others. He developed a friendship with the Lapham family, which ultimately led to the dismissal of Lapham, due to his liberal treatment of O'Brien, who attempted to escape, and, possibly because of scandal associated with Lapham's daughter. Darlington was closed in 1850, and the convicts transported to Port Arthur.[19]

Colonel Mundy described the abandoned settlement thus:

> Pity that, as in Norfolk Island, a paradise should have been converted into a pandemonium; and yet again it seems a pity that so extensive and expensive an establishment — hospital, stores, chapel, school, military and convict barracks, houses of the magistrate, surgeon, superintendent, etc. — should be abandoned to ruin. It would be more satisfactory to see them swept out of sight — obliterated from the soil — and this lovely isle allotted to a population worthy of its numerous advantages.[20]

But Maria Island was to have several new leases of life. In January 1884, Diego Bernacchi and his family arrived in Tasmania with the aim of establishing a silk and wine manufacturing industry. Bernacchi was from an illustrious Italian family and had represented silk firms in France and later opened branches in England for two companies. Not long after his arrival he chose Maria Island for his new venture, having obtained favourable leasing arrangements from the government. The Bernacchi family arrived on the island in April of that year and camped in a corner of the former religious instructor's quarters until a house could be fixed up for their use. By the following year about 20 vignerons were employed at Darlington preparing land for the vineyards.[21]

Bernacchi soon became known as 'King Diego'. Certainly his entertainments had regal connotations. In 1886 he invited members of parliament and the public for a weekend trip to inspect improvements. It was a lavish occasion. Bernacchi hired a boat and entertained the guests with music from an Italian band, the Crocci Brothers. At Darlington, 'rockets, blue lights, and roman candles were sent up, and the place was so illuminated with Chinese lanterns that it presented somewhat the appearance of an enchanted palace'. There were 100 employees with their families, and extensive plantings of grape vines and mulberry trees. Several months later the Bishop of Tasmania visited the island and held a baptismal service. At the time the old convict apartments were in the process of demolition, and the military buildings in use as accommodation, stores and a schoolroom.[22]

By 1888 Darlington had been re-named San Diego, and was a boom town with a population of more than 250. It had new terraces and cottages, including a row of twelve cottages, known as the 'Twelve Apostles', which were constructed for the vineyard workers. Other buildings included a post office and savings bank, school, general store, a shoemaker, butcher and baker, blacksmith, kitchen and a dining room for unmarried employees. The Federal Club provided foreign newspapers, books, a piano and sports equipment. Bernacchi had by then demolished the separate apartments and used the bricks for building cottages and paving the roads. The coffee palace was built on the foundations of the apartments, and provided a restaurant and accommodation. Bernacchi also built a licensed hotel, the Grand Hotel, with sweeping views of San Diego and the mainland. It was weatherboard and built in a Swiss-chalet style, with bedrooms for 30 or more guests and a four-terraced garden in front.[23]

At the opening in Easter 1888, Bernacchi entertained the Premier of Tasmania. Again it was a lavish affair, and on arrival the guests were regaled with a pyrotechnic display and Chinese lanterns. On Easter Monday an athletics sports carnival and concert were held. The columnist for the *Tasmanian Mail*, 'The Lynx', was quite beside himself, referring to the wonders of Diegoland, King Diego and the 'Fairyland of Australasia'. Several weeks later, on the occasion of the fourth anniversary of Bernacchi's arrival on the island, a banquet was held in the Federal Club for about 300 people, followed by a concert in the evening.[24]

By the late 1880s plans were under way for the exploitation of the island's limestone deposits for the making of cement. A steam tramway connected the

Empty silos, the cement mill and the commissariat at Darlington

Ruins of the Grand Hotel, hospital and the religious instructor's house, Darlington

jetty with the cement works and a large house for the works engineer, a two-storey cement works and 20 kilns were constructed. It was originally estimated that the industry would employ between 500 and 800 men; this was revised later to 200. But the end was nigh for Bernacchi's enterprises. The grape yields had not come up to expectations and all thoughts of profitable sericulture had vanished. Bernacchi found that financial support for the cement industry would not be forthcoming and, in November 1896, liquidators from the Van Diemen's Land Bank stepped in. With most of the assets sold, Bernacchi left almost immediately for Melbourne and later returned to England.

San Diego faded away rapidly and reverted to its original name of Darlington. The island was occupied by just a few families and visited only by holiday makers, who stayed either at Mrs Adkins' boarding house, or at Mrs McRae's house. Bernacchi did not forget the island where he had spent so many happy years. In 1914 his wife, Barbe, died, and he left England in 1919 with the intention of reviving the island's cement industry. A company was registered in 1920 and bought Mrs Brettingham Moore's 292-hectare property, on which the township and the limestone deposits were located.

In 1922 a new jetty was built and the old convict reservoir enlarged and cement pipes laid to carry water to Darlington. The population grew rapidly and within a few years reached a peak of 500 people. By early 1923 there were 170 men employed and comfortable rental houses available to families. Single men were accommodated in the old penitentiary and several stores were opened. The company's offices were located in the old Grand Hotel. Bernacchi attended the opening of the works in January 1924, but he fell ill not long after and died the following year. His daughter, who had travelled with him, married Hector McRae, who had lived on the island all his life, and they changed their names to Bernacchi-McRae.

Historian Margaret Weidenhofer has described Darlington in the 1920s as a lively place, with cricket, football and tennis clubs, a concert and glee club, progress association, medical association, school and activities such as surf bathing, campfire socials, movie pictures and dances. A large industrial complex was built overlooking the bay and jetty, and stone was taken from the cliffs at Fossil Bay and transported on a railway to the works. In 1924–25 output was about 30 000 tons, but by the following year it was obvious that the annual output needed to double that to be economic. By 1927 the company was in considerable debt and in 1930 it ceased business.[25]

The project had been doomed from the outset. Much of the limestone was useless for making cement, as it contained quartz and other impurities and between eight and ten tons of sandstone overburden had to be removed for every tonne of limestone. This time it really was the end. A number of buildings, including the 'Twelve Apostles', the former Grand Hotel and the school, were dismantled and moved to the mainland during the 1930s.

There are still many remains from all three periods of occupation on the island. Part of the jetty was the original one built in 1825 and later repaired by Bernacchi. Directly above the jetty is the silo for storing the finely ground cement prior to shipment, and further along, the clinker storage and cement mill. The raw mill was located behind these buildings, and further back again is a barn built in 1844 and a miller's cottage with a large stone circle where the windmill once stood. Further along the foreshore is the commissariat store, the oldest building on the island. There were storerooms both above and below and a bakery was attached. Up the hill behind the store are the ruins of the religious instructor's house, and the fireplaces and terraces of Bernacchi's Grand Hotel.

The penitentiary, mess room, Smith O'Brien's cottage, officials' cottages, cookhouse and bread store, chapel and the coffee palace are part of the main complex. The foundations of the apartments can still be seen. Across the road are the schoolmaster's house and superintendent's quarters, and nearby are six terraced cottages built in 1887 and two houses dating from 1890. Walking away from the town towards Bernacchi's first cement complex are the footings for the 'Twelve Apostles', a two-storeyed cement works and, behind that, lime kilns built into a hill. The remains of a cottage and manager's house can also be seen. In 1971 Maria Island was declared a national park, and it has become an important tourist attraction. At last the island has found peace and rest after so much misery, courage and broken dreams.

When Copper was King

THE COPPER-MINING INDUSTRY ON TASMANIA'S WEST COAST SPAWNED A number of mining towns in the late 1800s. Two of the towns, Pillinger and Crotty, have long since gone, whilst Linda and Gormanston are almost abandoned. These towns were associated with the copper mines at Mount Lyell, and more particularly the flamboyant and long-since departed North Mount Lyell Copper Mining Company. Only Queenstown, in the Queen Valley, survives and indeed thrives today as a viable town.

At Linda the few buildings in the town, such as the remains of the concrete-built Royal Hotel, a coffee shop and several cottages, are strung out along the main west coast highway. There are only four permanent residents, ably assisted by 'Bill the sheep', who attentively follows Kelvin Bradshaw and his son Doug around the town. In his quieter moments Bill enjoys a drink of beer and chews cigarette butts.[1] Across the road is the cemetery, gaunt and barren upon a rocky, windswept hill. It is a forbidding landscape, perhaps the Australian answer to Tolkien's 'Land of Mordor'. The valley floor is strewn with water-washed boulders, and the bare rocky hills are devoid of vegetation except for the small, scraggy and blackened shrubs, burnt by countless fires.

Further up the hill towards Queenstown is Gormanston, its wide, well-paved and now largely empty streets proclaiming a busier and more prosperous past. My introduction to the town was facilitated by a dog called Cecil, who led me to one of the few remaining inhabitants, Noelene Bradshaw. Noelene's father, Cliff, was renowned throughout Tasmania for his outstanding bushmanship.[2] Gormanston still has a scatter of buildings, but the main evidence of life appears to be rabbits (though there are only a few game ones about when Cecil does his rounds). Gormanston once rivalled Queenstown; it certainly doesn't now.

The original Mount Lyell mine was discovered by Mick and Bill McDonough and Steve Karlson in 1883. One spot to attract their attention

Gormanston still has a handful of buildings, but the main population seems to be rabbits.

The scant remains of the jetty at East Pillinger, once a busy port for James Crotty's North Lyell mine

The dilapidated jetty at West Pillinger is slowly being reclaimed by the bush.

This blacksmith's cottage at Steiglitz was in use up until the 1940s.

One of the many Cornish miners'
huts at Herons Reef near Fryerstown

The Duke of Cornwall engine house,
near Fryerstown, was part of an
ambitious but unsuccessful mining
venture.

was a massive outcrop of weathered and broken iron boulders known as the 'Iron Blow'. Bill McDonough sold his share in the Iron Blow on the condition that the buyer pay off his debt at Henry's Store, which was located on the pack trail from Strahan. A Linda digger, James Crotty, bought out Mick McDonough's alluvial claim and obtained his share in the Iron Blow by paying out his debt at Henry's Store. In 13 years time this share was to be worth about £1.5 million.[3]

The following year several men were employed blasting and excavating the Iron Blow in search of gold. They were not aware of, or at that stage interested in looking for, copper.[4] To finance the work the partners sold equal shares to Henry and to Peter and Karl Karlson, and formed the Mount Lyell Prospecting Association. However, the mine was not profitable, and the Karlsons were also forced to sell their shares. A few days later a despondent Steve Karlson was told that the association had struck it rich. Crotty was ecstatic, and soon there were several hundred miners in the valley. But the Karlsons were in no mood for celebrations and litigation, which was ultimately unsuccessful, soon followed.

Rough justice prevailed, however, for the association in turn was unsuccessful and Crotty found himself working as a miner in the underground sewers in Sydney. In the meantime, a new company was formed, but it too failed. And there matters may have rested, but for the rise of the Zeehan silver mines to the north. Silver prices were booming at this time, and by the middle of 1891 there were 159 companies and syndicates on the Zeehan field, and their shares were soaring. Zeehan acquired a stock exchange with 60 members.

Before long several Broken Hill investors arrived on the scene. Two of these men, William Orr and Bowes Kelly, visited the Iron Blow with Crotty, who was now the mine caretaker. The company offered Kelly and Orr a controlling interest in the mine, which they accepted, but only after the asking price had been bargained down by about two-thirds. Tests indicated that the ore was very rich in copper and a new company, the Mount Lyell Mining Company, was formed. In 1894 the company struck several rich silver lodes, and bolstered by the boom in West Australian goldmining, obtained the necessary capital amidst soaring share prices.[5]

It was proposed to construct a railway from the mines to the port of Strahan and construct smelters in the nearby Queen Valley. The railway was at the time Tasmania's largest construction job. New towns, Penghana and later Queenstown, were built, and by June 1896 the two large furnaces were ready. They were an instant success. The following month the first train arrived at Queenstown, and by the following year shares in the new company had risen over eightfold on their value of two years earlier. Shares in other copper mining companies followed suit, and the stage was set for what historian Geoffrey Blainey has described as the 'last great mining boom of the century'.[6]

Over the ridge from Queenstown were a number of other mines, notably Crotty's North Lyell mine, and the towns of Linda, Gormanston and North Lyell. A report in 1894 described Gormanston as 'progressing steadily'.

Linda, early 1900s; a landscape evoking images of Tolkien's 'Land of Mordor'

Gaffney's two-storey Mount Lyell Hotel was the largest and most conspicuous building. Next was the single-storey Exchange Hotel. There were three stores, one owned by Gaffney and another by Henry, two butcher shops, a post office and a police officer.[7] By 1896 a correspondent for the *Tasmanian Mail* described Gormanston as 'very prettily situated', and although scattered it had a 'substantial and permanent appearance'. The Mount Lyell Hotel was still the most prominent building. In addition, there was Cannon's Hotel, a post and telegraph office, bank, three or four stores, a bakery, barber, butcher and a cordial manufacturer, but no blacksmith or churches. Ministers of different denominations visited Gormanston and held services in the billiard room or boarding room of one of the hotels. There were about 300 residents.[8]

Rivalry between Queenstown and the Linda Valley towns was intense. James Crotty had become very wealthy because of his shareholding in the Mount Lyell Mining Company, but he had quarrelled with Bowes Kelly over the price that Kelly had paid for a controlling interest in the Iron Blow, and a number of other matters. Crotty was determined to construct his own railway and erect smelters to treat ore from his North Lyell mine, and formed the North Mount Lyell Copper Company for this purpose. He did not, however, live to see the outcome, for he was taken suddenly ill and, after lingering for a few days, died in April 1898. He bequeathed most of his money to the Roman Catholic Church and left his widow a £300 legacy, £100 a year for life and another £500 a year if she entered a convent. Understandably, she contested the will, was successful, and received an income of £1000 a year for the rest of her life.[9]

The key to Crotty's plans was the new town of Kelly's Basin or Pillinger, which was to be the port from which all materials would be transported and all copper exported. By early 1898 there were 120 residents at Kelly's Basin. By the end of the year there were hundreds of men at work on the railway line and elsewhere, such as the brickworks and sawmill. Two separate towns were built at Kelly's Basin. On the east side there were workers' huts, a dining hall, a band and billiard hall, a company-run store, and the slightly larger homes of the company officials. The government town of Macquarie was on the west side. There was a ferry service between the two settlements, but almost all of the 300 residents of Kelly's Basin were living illegally on the east side.

It was inevitable that East Pillinger would be the favoured site, for that was where most men worked. The results, however, were less than ideal. Camps were crowded together in unhealthy swamps and before long an estimated 50 per cent of the population was afflicted with typhoid, and there were several deaths. There was, however, time for amusements and cultural activities. Amenities included an athletics club and a library, which was established in the band hall, and two hotels, the Macquarie and the Shamrock, which was eventually let out to a Percy Waxman, who renamed it the Sorrento. By late 1899 a progress committee had been formed to take responsibility for sanitary conditions. It had a fair bit of work to do, for fetid piggeries were located in the centre of the town, kitchen garbage was strewn everywhere, there was no provision for the disposal of night soil, and there were very few outhouses.[10]

By early 1900 there were further businesses, such as another hotel, butcher's shop, ironmongers and a hall built by Percy Waxman next to his hotel. The hall, which could seat 300, was the social focus of the community, with events ranging from weekly church services to balls and concerts, including those by travelling companies. By April the new school was ready to commence classes. But the main excitement was yet to come, for the government was determined to evict those living as squatters. In defence of the residents, a Homestead Protection League was formed, but to no avail, for within a week of a heated debate in the State Parliament, the buildings were pulled down.[11]

By September 1900, the first train load of ore from the company's North Lyell mine arrived at Pillinger, and passenger traffic soon followed. A Roman Catholic church had also been built, with seating for about 200, and the Federal Coffee Palace, providing board and lodging, now graced the town. New Year's Day 1901 was a lively affair. The newly formed aquatic club had its first annual regatta, and an excursion train from Gormanston arrived, bringing 200 passengers, including the band. A steamship brought another 100 from Strahan. Sarah Island was on the steamship's itinerary. New Year's Day 1902 was held in a similar style, and included an aquatic club meeting and a grand ball at Waxman's Hall in the evening. A cricket club was formed in February and work commenced soon after on preparing a ground and pitch.[12]

The Linda Valley towns were also booming, and it seemed for a while that Gormanston would become a serious rival to Queenstown, for by 1898 it had four large hotels, a miners' hall, band hall, churches, two brass bands and a wide main street that was filled with shops. At North Lyell, the miners had built dwellings on the mining leases and near their places of work, and a hotel, stores and a boarding house were soon established. By 1900 Linda had 600 people, two hotels and billiard saloons, and it began to rival Gormanston. The three mining towns had over 2000 people and were growing daily. They were not, however, in the easiest of physical environments. Gormanston was very exposed to snow, wind and rain (it rarely received less than 2500 millimetres per year). And in the summer the threat of bushfires and the potential loss of lives, homes and other property hung over the community.[13]

All this growth and development masked serious problems with the management of the North Mount Lyell Copper Company, for there were numerous engineering blunders at the mine, tramway, sawmill and brickworks. The sawmill was described as awkward and antiquated and the railway engineer and chief assayer were unreliable, often indulging in long drunken sprees during working hours. Recruitment practices were unsatisfactory, ore reserves were overestimated, and the railway cost three times more than the estimates. At the port the crossings and switches were so defective that the train ran off the rails a dozen times in five months. At Linda construction work commenced on a branch line from the railway station to the mines, but the cost became so great that it was abandoned. An aerial tramway was built, but it also proved unsatisfactory.

Worse still were the smelters, which were located at Crotty, well south of the Linda Valley. Construction did not begin until a year after the railway had been built, and even then they were sluggish and inefficient, and almost half of the copper was lost in the slag. A further problem was the lack of fuel and iron ore for fluxes, both of which had to be transported at great expense. To overcome these difficulties blast furnaces similar to those at Queenstown were erected, but at the opening ceremony the overhead flue of one of them became so hot that the rafters caught fire. It was not a promising start and worse was to follow, for a lightning strike flattened the chimneystack, which was rebuilt without letting the mortar set, and became tilted on a precarious angle.

Rumours about an amalgamation of the two companies abounded. Mount Lyell had by far the better smelters, the largest town and best links with other west coast towns, while North Lyell had the best railway. But the creditors had the final say, and in May 1903 North Lyell yielded. For Crotty, and to a lesser degree, Pillinger, it was the end of the line. Many families were destitute. Crotty only existed for the smelters, and now they were to be disbanded. Villas, shops, a church, school and a 30-room hotel had only been completed that very month, and now, along with all the miners' homes, they were worthless. Some were chopped down for firewood or auctioned at mock prices, and the hotel was abandoned before it had even sold a pint of beer.[14] A relief committee was formed to assist families that needed immediate support, particularly as many of the men had been working on half wages for some time. Almost all the shops closed, though food was donated liberally by the citizens of Linda, Gormanston and, in particular, Zeehan. The first train load of people left within a week of the amalgamation announcement, and a few weeks later Crotty was almost deserted.[15]

The once bustling main street of Gormanston, early 1900s

At Pillinger there were similar scenes of destitution. Some business people stayed on, as there was still some trade from the ships and trains that called at the town. But the new amalgamated company was to use the Queenstown to Strahan line for its main business — the carting of copper, materials and equipment. Most of the townsfolk left and their houses were dismantled. By 1920 there were only 22 residents, including the ferryman, the owners of the Shamrock Hotel, a storekeeper and the postmistress, who also served as a teacher. There were probably no more than about a dozen occupied buildings. The train service continued until 1925, carrying mainly firewood and mine timber and occasionally some copper concentrates or picnic excursions from Linda and Gormanston.[16]

Pillinger is now totally deserted, though there are relics of the past. At East Pillinger these include the remains of a jetty, the oven chimney for the mess room, the remains of two brick kilns, a large boiler, and a steam engine from the last train. At West Pillinger there are two jetties and the Reindeer Lodge, which was built around the remains of a railway carriage. Today, as in the past, the best access is by boat from Strahan. Crotty is gone completely, drowned beneath the floodwaters of a dam.

Linda and Gormanston survived, for they were dependent upon the mines and benefited from the new management, and probably received a fillip from the influx of Crotty and Pillinger residents. 1903 was an active year for both towns. Boxing contests, football matches and other sporting contests including pigeon racing were held regularly. Gormanston had several lodges, such as the Oddfellows, a branch of the Australian Natives' Association, the Amalgamated Miners' Association, United Irishmen's League and the Political

Labor League, all of which, along with the churches and other organisations, held regular meetings and social functions. High copper prices in 1905 saw a return to prosperity. Eventually, Linda and North Lyell had between them over 20 businesses, six boarding houses, four hotels and two halls, one of which was Waxman's.[17]

Geoffrey Blainey has remarked that Linda was regarded as far livelier and wilder than Gormanston. Both towns were famous for their tough boxers and footballers and their skilled axemen. According to local historian Edward Wedd, the district had six football teams: three at Queenstown, two at Gormanston and one from Linda. Because it was so wet, grass would not grow on the ovals and they were surfaced with fine gravel and sand, which led to more than a few gravel rashes. Socials were also popular and were held in each of the towns. The big balls were the main events, especially St Patrick's Ball, and the Easter athletics carnival was particularly well attended, drawing competitors from all three towns. According to Geoffrey Blainey the carnival attracted between 1500 and 2000 people. By 1907 there were more than 2200 people living in the Linda Valley towns.[18]

At Linda there was a large number of businesses, but no churches. There had been a Presbyterian church, but it was dismantled owing to the lack of a congregation. All the churches were in Gormanston. The hills and mountains were denuded of all trees and foliage, for the trees had been used for timber and firewood, and the scrub had been killed by the sulphur from the smelters in the adjoining valley. One visitor described the valley as 'hell with the fire burnt out'. Many locals used Pillinger as a fishing spot and an embarkation point for trips to the Gordon River and Sarah Island, especially when the berries and fruits were in season. Once a year the unions organised a picnic and athletic carnival to Pillinger. A brass band was in attendance and there were races and novelty events. The courting couples and the men usually came home on the last train, the latter having spent most of the day at the Pillinger hotel.

Wedd was a child at the time of the 1911 strike and the 1912 Mt Lyell mine disaster, but remembered vividly the effects of both events on the community. At the time of the strikes he recalled that the miners' families were living on coupons and everyone nearly starved. He recounted that there were plenty of fights at school among the boys caused by some of them calling the bosses' sons scabs. Even some of the girls were fighting because they were hungry, while the bosses' daughters were not. His memory of the mine disaster was particularly vivid, because his uncle was one of the men trapped in the mine.[19]

The disaster was one of the defining events in the valley. There was no emergency warning system in the mine because nobody believed that the mine could catch fire, and there was no rescue plan or rescue equipment. To warn the miners below, men had to descend the main shaft and run along a maze of drives and cross-cuts, but the extensive smoke hampered rescue efforts. Suitable breathing apparatus had to be shipped from Melbourne and taken by train to Queenstown, and it was another five days before the last of the

… it was another five days before the last of the miners could be brought to the surface. Forty-two men did not make it out alive.

miners could be brought to the surface. Forty-two men did not make it out alive. In these small, tightly knit communities, the losses must have been keenly felt.[20]

After World War I the mining company embarked on a number of initiatives to make all the mining towns more attractive and to improve facilities for the miners and their families. The company's welfare program had an immediate effect on industrial relations, and there were to be no more general strikes. Another important element of this program was the cheap food campaign, which involved initially the buying out of several businesses and the introduction of grocery deliveries, which in turn led to the closure of the smaller stores.[21]

The death knell for Linda was the company's decision to build new homes in Gormanston, offering very cheap rentals and single men's accommodation. Gormanston already had the best shopping centre, better streets, churches, some professional services, a courthouse, miners' hall, bank, mining office, police and the shire council office. Linda was not entirely neglected, for in both towns the company built pastime clubs, with a large range of recreational facilities. But the clubs and boarding houses drew much of the business from the hotels, and before long the local bakery and the hotel were closed. Eventually the pastime club was closed.[22]

Despite these traumas the townsfolk did not lose their sense of humour. Both towns held their 'back to' days. On the occasion of the 1922 function the good folk of Gormanston had this to say:

> The population of Gormanston is 1590, and of Queenstown 3209. Why is it, then, that Gormanston can with easy complacency await the onslaught of sportsmen from a community with twice its numbers, and match their champions man for man? It is because Gormanston is superior in intellect, although Queenstown claims predominance in morality; if the contest were of a religious character, Gormanston would not enter. The highlanders of Gormanston have the virtues and defects that are associated with dwellers in rugged and picturesque surrounding. They are brave, intelligent, enterprising and honest; but, on the other hand, they have large feet, rough manners, and are not beautiful.[23]

Not to be outdone, the citizenry of Linda proclaimed the following year that:

> The women of Linda are all beautiful, the men are brave, the children intolerably virtuous, and the hens lay pure-bred eggs when they feel inclined to. The climate is salubrious and bracing, inducing a high birth-rate; deaths are rare … Cows do not love Linda, neither do horses, goats, sheep, deer, buffaloes, elephants, nor elks: but dogs, cats and other domestic animals attain a high degree of beauty and fertility.[24]

Gormanston's day of reckoning was still some time away. The first blow was the company's decision in 1927 to drive a tunnel from the Queenstown

The Royal Hotel at Linda with the mines of Mount Lyell in the distance

side of the hill into the North Lyell mine, reducing substantially the handling costs of extracting the ore, which could then be dispatched directly to the smelters. Combined with the increased use of motor vehicles, it was now no further for the miners to travel to the mines from Queenstown than from Gormanston. By 1950 the Linda Valley towns had only a quarter of the population they had held in 1910, and the town of North Lyell had ceased to exist. The ravages of fire had also added to Gormanston's woes. There were only a few shops, a hotel, miners' hall, post office, school and about 500 residents.[25]

The closure of the big West Lyell mine in the 1970s was the final blow. It lay just inside Gormanston's municipal boundaries and deprived the town of its main source of revenue. There was also a glut of houses in Queenstown, and many locals abandoned their homes to settle there. One by one the general store, post office, school, church and the hotel were closed, and the Shire Council Chamber was burned down. The council eventually amalgamated with Queenstown.[26] Noelene Bradshaw, a long-time resident and a member of the council, was saddened by the town's closure. She estimates that there are no more than about two dozen people left in Gormanston now.[27] The deserted streets and vacant allotments stand as a monument to the west coast's wild and vibrant past.

VICTORIA

From Steiglitz to Fryerstown

VICTORIA HAS MANY OLD GOLDFIELDS AND FORMER GOLDMINING TOWNS, but it is rare to see grand buildings left derelict or deserted streetscapes from that era, as most of this state's gold towns have survived. There are exceptions, however. Steiglitz, for example, has a few scattered buildings and wide-open spaces. Yet the graceful brick courthouse recalls a much more prosperous past, as does the footpath paving and gutters evident along Molesworth and other streets. The Church of England building, the 'new' post office (now a residence), Scott's Hotel (also a residence), and some old homes along Clow Street are further signs of the old town. Steiglitz is the only town in Victoria without electricity. Until three years ago it shared this distinction with Walhalla; now it alone has the honour.

The town's only business today is Phil and Gillian Dickson's Peppercorn Place, a cedar weatherboard building located on the site of a former cottage of the same name. Phil and Gillian came to Steiglitz in 1980 and lived in the old cottage until a fire destroyed it. They rebuilt and opened for business in 1993, providing meals and guided tours. I shared a pleasant few hours with Phil. He told me that relatively recently he had learnt that his great-grandmother had run a boarding house in old Steiglitz.

Steiglitz derived its name from Charles von Steiglitz, who settled in the area in 1842. By March 1855 there were nearly 300 alluvial miners on the field, most of them making good wages with easy work. Not long after, reef gold was discovered and soon 500 miners had rushed to the field, making Steiglitz one of the first quartz goldfields in Australia. One of the first quartz miners was a squatter, Andrew Love, who established a crushing plant and became chairman of the local miners' committee. He later became a parliamentarian. Not all miners had Love's credentials. One claim was owned by two Russians who had a propensity for drinking lamp oil and eating candles, including those owned by others.[1]

Steiglitz courthouse is a touch of grandeur in an otherwise deserted landscape.

By the end of 1855 the population had risen to 2000, and the inevitable concerns about law and order were heightened by the absence of the constabulary. A public meeting was held, following which a letter was sent to the Chief Secretary. It stated that while the population was generally sober and industrious, the neighbourhood was infested by a 'number of bad characters' who were robbing stores and people on the road going to and from the diggings, physically assaulting them in the process. Early the following year a sergeant and two troopers were sent to the town, and there were no further complaints. The most serious offence over the next few years was sly-grog selling, and after that was controlled the offences became even more trivial.[2]

A reorganisation of the mining claims on the field led to a sustained burst of productivity and prosperity. By 1856 there were seven crushing machines on the field, but the small claims had become unprofitable at depth, and a number of them were amalgamated for working on a larger and more economical scale. By 1859 production was dominated by two large companies and the yields were high. Over the next few years a number of other companies were established, many with their own crushing plants, and previously deemed unprofitable claims were reopened and worked at depth.[3]

The Steiglitz boom was reflected in the establishment of the churches and denominational schools. A Wesleyan church was established in 1856, followed by a school later that year. By 1859 all four denominations had churches, and two of them had schools. The boom was reflected in other ways as well. Coaches met the train at Meredith twice daily, the sale of allotments in the town was booming and two banks had established branches. In 1862 a Philharmonic Society was formed and in 1864 the Oddfellows opened a branch. One Easter Monday they marched in a procession led by a brass band to a picnic in Dennis' paddock, followed by an anniversary supper in their hall. The Alfred Hall was also used for balls and other social functions, and the churches held their anniversaries and tea meetings.[4]

A town council was formed in 1866, but at about the same time gold production slumped and many miners left the field. There had been the usual wave of speculation, poor management and over-investment in incidentals that plagued so many early reef mines in Australia. In addition, the payment of wages was often in arrears, with many miners becoming destitute. Nevertheless, the field did recover and a period of steady prosperity lasted until 1873. During this time a mechanics' institute opened, which included a new public library, and became a popular community meeting place. However, by the following year the mining population had halved, and over the next 20 years there was a steady decline. By the late 1870s there were only 100 miners on the field. The current substantial courthouse was built in 1875, but a mere four years later the court sittings were discontinued.[5]

The second boom commenced in 1893. At this time a local newspaper, *The Steiglitz Miner*, commenced business and proudly proclaimed that a doctor's brass plate had been erected and that visitors continued to arrive daily, with 25 having to be turned away from one boarding house in one night. There were now 40 reef mines at work and by the following year the population had risen from 275 to 2000. Steiglitz was by far the largest town in the shire, with 90 per cent of the population, but the council was located in Meredith. Subsequently, it was agreed that the council meet alternatively or at least quarterly at Steiglitz. The impact of the boom on school attendance was dramatic, and many children were obliged to sit on the floor or borrow chairs.[6]

Business was brisk. Hotels, barbers, dressmakers, a chemist, watchmaker and jeweller, stationer and bookseller, undertaker, timberyard, billiard rooms, a boot and shoemaker, wheelwright, saddlery, tailors, dressmakers, butchers and numerous general stores flanked the streets. Leisure, pleasure and social improvement were all on the agenda. Societies and associations included a progress committee, mutual improvement society, amateur dramatic club, the Bluebell Minstrel Troupe, the Iolanthe Quadrille Club, a brass band, juvenile brass band, and branches of the Rechabites, Engine Drivers' Association, Masonic Lodge, United Ancient Order of the Druids, Australian Natives' Association, and two branches of the Band of Hope. Outdoor concerts were popular, and occasional banquets were held when a battery was christened or a visiting dignitary arrived. Sport clubs included football, racing, rifle, field sports, sparrow clubs and two tennis clubs.[7]

With such a plethora of outlets and potential amusements Steiglitz was a lively town. An entertaining description of a Saturday night in August 1894 is recounted by Ray Sumner in *Steiglitz: Memories of Gold*:

At the Coffee Palace the lights are bright and the bar is well filled. For the Coffee Palace is also a wine saloon ... From the interior come the sounds of music and sing-song and merry-making ... The shops on either side as we come down are little oases of light ... Hairdressers, with hotel keepers are busy to-night; in both streets the knights of the razor are hard at work ... Having had a shave the next thing to be done of course, is to go and have a drink. First at one hotel and then at the other. These are where the life of Steiglitz centres ... Clow Street, being the principal business thoroughfare of the township, makes a really good appearance, with its bright and well-dressed shop-windows, and there are married couples shopping there — but not many ... After inspecting the billiard rooms ... we ... find our way to the free-and-easy in Alfred Hall ... It would be hard to believe, did we not hear it, that there could be so much genuine talent amid the rough surroundings of a goldfield ... Good singing, good music and an intelligent, well-dressed audience form the chief feature of this weekly entertainment ...[8]

Despite these signs of prosperity and merrymaking, the day of reckoning was drawing near. Some of the mines were struggling and on tribute, and while the correspondents constantly predicted that something great was around the corner, it never eventuated. Steiglitz was a very active community, however, and the first warning signs were to a degree masked by this activity. For instance, in February 1895 there was a miners' anniversary sports day, and the first public performance of the Steiglitz Beebirds minstrels was held in the Australian Natives' Association Hall to a 'thronged house'. A race meeting and a variety entertainment featuring the local brass band were also proposed. Over the next few months a literary and debating club, gun club, draught and chess club and a formal football competition with neighbouring towns were established.[9]

At the same time, however, the local brass band was suffering from a lack of funds and the departure of its more prominent members from the district. The Wesleyan denomination had also withdrawn its minister from the district as there was insufficient revenue to support him. By 1896 gold production had fallen, and by 1900 the population was only 500, by which time the local newspaper had many advertisements for the sale of houses and shops at bargain prices. In 1904 the population had fallen to a mere 150 and many families, houses and other buildings were removed. There was some revival during the 1930s Depression, based largely on alluvial mining, but by 1935 the government battery, Oddfellows' Hall and the Roman Catholic church had been relocated elsewhere, and by 1941 all reef mining had ceased.[10] Steiglitz's golden days were over.

North of Steiglitz, in the Castlemaine area, are Vaughan, Fryerstown and Welsh village. Fryerstown once had a population of many thousands; now there are only a small number of residents, and no shops or stores of any description. A number of buildings from the 1850s and 1860s has, however, survived. Still visible and intact are the Burke and Wills Mechanics' Institute, post office, courthouse, several churches, old cottages and stores, all of which are now privately owned and mostly restored. Out of town on the Chewton road are the splendid remains of the Duke of Cornwall enginehouse.

The crowning glory is the Herons Reef area, which is one of the Victorian goldfields' gems. It is privately owned by Les and Madge Simmons. Les, a Kokoda Trail veteran, originally bought the land at Herons Reef for recreational purposes, but when he discovered the history of the area he decided to take it a step further. The property is now listed by the National Trust and is on the State Heritage Register, and is open to visitors. One of the amazing features of Herons Reef is that it experienced every type of goldmining over an 80-year period, and includes the ruins of the Anglo-Australian enginehouse, the remains of Cornish and Chinese miners' huts and a ceremonial pig oven.[11]

Fryers Creek was among the very richest of the early Victorian goldfields. One of the biggest gold nuggets in Victoria, the Heron nugget, weighing 1022 ounces, was found there in April 1855. It was named after the popular gold commissioner, Thomas Heron. Nuggets of up to a hundred ounces were common in Golden Gully, and at Horseshoe Bend in 1856 one party found £24,000 of gold in three weeks.[12]

With finds such as these it is little wonder that in the early days the goldfield had a reputation for lawlessness. The gold commissioner reported in late 1852 that there were daily cases of robbery and shooting, and sly-grog selling was extensive. During one week in August 1855 one gang was involved in seven armed robberies and other pillages, actual or intended. They were later apprehended by a group of miners in a sly-grog shop. One correspondent remarked that while Ballarat was peaceful, at Fryers Creek 'quarrels, dissension, bloodshed and danger of the direst description reigned supreme'. Two of the more notorious bushrangers were a one-eyed ex-convict named Tom

The Burke and Wills Mechanics' Institute, Fryerstown

She remembered one Chinese pedlar who sold tea, cotton, needles, socks, pillowcases and novelties, and who always had a cup of tea at their home when passing by.

Wilson and Black Douglas, both of whom had a gang of accomplices. These men preyed on lonely diggers or travellers. There was little about them that was honourable or noble.[13]

There was a very large Chinese population on the field, one observer recording in June 1855 that 'judging from recent appearances, if the Chinese are to inundate this place much more, we shall have very few English left'. A short while later that month there were further large increases in the number of Chinese on the field, who by then represented about half of the total population. In some quarters they were not warmly received. For instance, in 1857 there was a series of meetings condemning them. The grounds of discontent were spurious and obviously racially motivated, covering such matters as lack of morality, stealing, dragging down the European 'to their own level', living too cheaply and hoarding their money and sending it back to China, or in other words, not contributing to the colonial economy.[14]

However mean-spirited some of the diggers were, the Chinese did at least have official protection. In one incident in late 1857 the chairman of the local court remarked that:

[T]he European miners of New Year's Flat displayed a bad spirit towards the Chinese, and he was sorry to say that Mr McMillan had been charged with pelting stones at and setting dogs on them.

The chairman promised to visit the field together with the interpreter and inquire into the matter.[15]

Many of the Chinese were engaged in professions and trades other than mining. When the gold declined most left, but some stayed on and worked in other activities such as market gardening. Some Chinese were also employed by the reef-mining companies to help recover the gold after the stone had been processed by the crushing plants. Large market gardens were developed along the Loddon River between Glen Luce and Vaughan. Ruth Rowe, in her reminiscences, recalled sitting and watching the Chinese water their vegetables with water pots, tins and buckets. The produce was brought to town in baskets carried on shoulder yokes. She remembered one Chinese pedlar who sold tea, cotton, needles, socks, pillowcases and novelties, and who always had a cup of tea at their home when passing by.[16]

One of the more famous mines on the field was the Duke of Cornwall, not because it was a great goldmine, for indeed it was a failure, but for the impressive Cornish enginehouse. The mine and plant were commissioned in 1869, with the owners continually comparing their mine to the Mosquito mine of their neighbours, the Rowes. They assumed that as the Mosquito improved with depth so should theirs. But the bonanza never materialised and very heavy debts were incurred. In 1875 the plant and mine were bought by the Rowes for a bargain price, and worked in conjunction with their mine.[17]

Another important part of the goldfield was Spring Gully. Gold was found there in 1852 and a self-supporting town quickly sprang up, with the usual

The Welsh village on the Mount Alexander goldfield; there are no grand buildings, but many stone ruins.

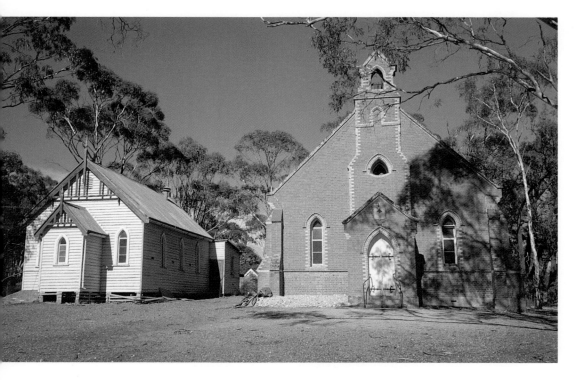

The former Presbyterian church is one of Tarnagulla's many impressive buildings.

The humble miners' huts are a distinct contrast to Tarnagulla's many grand public and commercial buildings.

Very little traffic now passes through the once busy goldmining town of Moliagul.

An abandoned boarding house at Merino; a town that prospered on the strength of its wheat and dairy industries

Killick's store at Galong; the pre-1930 buildings along the main street have an air of 'genteel decline'.

An empty bank building at Merino

Merino's well-kept main street looks healthy enough, but almost all of the shops are now closed.

array of stores, hotels and churches. Prominent buildings were Hoskin's Emu Store and Hotel and the Spring Flat Hotel. There was also a hotel and store at nearby Cornishtown. The main form of mining was alluvial, though there was one very rich reef mine known originally as Emu Reef, and later as the Spring Gully goldmine. Today at Spring Creek there are the remains of several miners' huts, and the substantial foundations of the Spring Gully Junction and Spring Gully Company mines. Pennyweight Hill also flourished briefly. By the end of 1857 boarding houses and refreshment tents were 'going up in any number' and grog sellers were making their piles.[18]

Fryerstown reputedly had a population as high as 15 000, although these numbers probably relate to the goldfield rather than the town. As an indication of size, there were at least 25 licensed hotels in the district in the early years, as well as a thriving trade in sly grog. This situation changed with the introduction of the Licensing Act in 1853, for the licence fees were high enough to discourage the less well-appointed establishments. The first licensed hotel was the Digger's Rest in 1854, followed by the Fryerstown Hotel. Another early hotel was the Cumberland, which was the centre of the town's social life until the building of the mechanics' institute. In 1885 there were still 22 licensed hotels. In that year legislation was introduced to reduce the number of public houses in Victorian mining towns, and Fryerstown's quota was set at 12.[19]

A number of breweries supported the hotels. Benjamin Edhouse built the first in 1856 and the demand was so great that he extended the building and renamed it the Loddon Brewery. Further extensions were carried out in 1864. The largest brewery was the Belle Vue, which was constructed in 1861. It was sold in 1870 and converted into an entertainment hall, which was used for many years by the lodges and other organisations. There were two other smaller breweries as well.[20]

The establishment of the churches followed hard on the heels of the hotels; indeed, according to a local historian, the late George Brown, the first church built on the Mount Alexander goldfields, which included Chewton and Castlemaine, was built in Fryerstown. Open-air services were also held in the very early years. The Methodists were very active. They had a large congregation of Cornish miners and built one church in 1855 and another a year later. The Episcopal church was the next to be built. Presbyterian and Anglican churches were opened in 1861, and the Roman Catholic church in 1865, although all three churches would have held meetings, open-air or otherwise, well before then. A church was also built by the Bible Christians.[21]

The late Ruth Rowe, a former resident, recalled that community life in Fryerstown centred a great deal around church activities. Her uncle was a Methodist preacher, who owned the first Edison phonograph in the district. He would record concerts and church services and visit homes, taking his recordings to the ill or the aged who had missed the service. Church attendances were very good, and during the week there were cottage meetings, prayer meetings and other activities, and the Band of Hope, the Home Mission and the bible class met regularly. She recalled that the Fryerstown Methodist choir was one of the best on the circuit. A temperance choir was formed in the early 1900s. The church anniversary was an important event each year, but the highlights were the Sunday school anniversary and picnic. At the latter event, teachers and pupils, with banners flying, would assemble in front of the church and march up to the cricket ground, singing as they went.[22]

Ruth remarked that there were many occasions when the children took part in concerts, and sometimes they travelled to Chewton or Castlemaine to hold performances. She remembered that there were many special celebrations and ceremonial occasions, some of which had a distinct 'Empire, King, Queen and Country' flavour. On the occasion of Queen Victoria's death in January 1901 the shops were dressed in mauve and black mourning, and on the coronation of King Edward in 1902 there was a procession with people dressed as guards and lancers, followed by a sports afternoon and concert. The end of the Boer War was celebrated by a procession headed by the Fryerstown brass band, then the Lodges and the school children, after which there was a picnic and concert. Pioneers' Day was held in February of each year. This occasion involved a train trip to Melbourne (from Chewton) and a steamer trip to Port Phillip Bay, to the accompaniment of the Castlemaine Foundry Band.[23]

Perhaps the town's most famous building is the Burke and Wills Mechanics' Institute, which was built in 1863. Until then Fryerstown did not have a public meeting place and most local functions were held in the hotels, which usually had a large room set aside for such purposes. The laying of the foundation stone was a grand occasion. It commenced with divine service at All Saints' church, then a procession led by the newly formed Fryerstown brass band, followed by the school children and the various Masonic lodges of the district, and ended with a luncheon at the Cumberland Hotel. At the official opening several months later a banquet catered for 163 people.[24]

By the time that Ruth was attending school in the 1890s the goldmining boom had long since subsided. But Fryerstown still had a post office, court-house, five churches, two schools and a mechanics' institute. There was a busy market square and a large number of businesses, including seven hotels, a brewery, doctor's office, Carter's boot factory, a blacksmith, carpenter, wheelwright, two drapers, two butchers, a bakery, several general stores, grocers and bank agencies and a branch of the Bank of Victoria. Wood-cutting was also an important industry. There was a twice-daily mail service and a daily coach service with Castlemaine, except on Saturdays when there were three. Both Fryerstown and Castlemaine had Saturday shopping.[25]

Vaughan was a similarly bustling town in its heyday, and at one stage was reputed to have had a population of 13 000. A correspondent wrote that:

> It [Vaughan] has always been a kind of little sequestered hamlet, but now it has the appearance of a busy little town, with its hotels and ball and concert rooms unequalled in size on the Mount Alexander diggings, and erected at great expense by Messrs Bond Brothers and other substantial buildings. The Messrs Bond

Cornish miner's hut, Herons Reef

opened their splendid concert room last Thursday with a select ball ... The supper was of the most recherche luxury which the colony and the season could afford ... It will be a long time before the ball at the Union Hotel, Junction, will be forgotten.[26]

One of the prominent businesses at Vaughan in the 1850s was the firm of Ball & Welch, which established a drapery store that attracted women from all over the district. Today, there are a few buildings on the main road hailing from the past, and a small, though very interesting Chinese cemetery, but little else. According to a former local resident, Jeannie Lister, roadworks and the sealing of the main road in the 1960s obliterated many buildings, including the old Chinese quarter and Roger's cordial factory. Now there are only a few original buildings along the side of the road.[27]

Well to the north of Fryerstown is Welsh village or The Welshmans, so called because almost all the miners there were of Welsh extraction. It has no grand edifices, but is unique for the relatively large number of old stone building remains, most of them dating from the main phase of mining activity in the late 1850s. The remains of the buildings, the majority of which were used as stores, pantries or kitchens, were located on a series of raised terraces and were probably abandoned in the 1870s.[28] The village is isolated and can only be reached on foot, which is no doubt why so much of it still exists. Together with much of Steiglitz, Fryerstown and Vaughan, it offers a different view of the past — the modest buildings in stark contrast to the grand edifices and stately buildings so often associated with Victoria's gold-boom days.

Tarnagulla and Beyond

A VISIT TO TARNAGULLA IN THE CENTRAL GOLDFIELDS AREA OF VICTORIA is a journey back in time. The main street is not deserted, for there are many buildings, but few are open for business. Most of them, such as the former Colonial Bank, and the even older Union Bank building, 'The Lochcarron', have become private homes, and the attractively restored Victoria Hotel and Theatre now serves as a community hall. One block back is the former courthouse, now a private residence, and the Uniting church, formerly the Presbyterian, and one block further back again, the primary school, Roman Catholic and Anglican churches. All of these buildings date back to the 1860s or before, when Tarnagulla was a booming goldfield town, humming with the sound of several thousand residents.

At first Tarnagulla was known as Sandy Creek and like many other Victorian goldfield towns it had its beginnings in the first gold rushes in the early 1850s. Most of the mining was alluvial, but there was one area of reef gold which went under the unimposing name of Poverty Reef. Apparently it was so named because of its association with one of the early miners on the reef, Captain David Hatt, whose vessel was wrecked at Poverty Bay in New Zealand. While the sailors were struggling to reach shore, a young Maori woman swam out and rescued Hatt. Subsequently they married and settled in Australia at Sandy Creek.[1] Poverty Reef was, however, anything but poor and by the late 1850s it had become the focal point of the field.

Prior to the wholesale working of the reef mines, the field was worked predominantly by Chinese alluvial miners. Although there were no incidents of violence on the field, relationships with some of the Europeans were often strained. In September 1857, for example, a meeting was held at which the miners complained about the Chinese. The correspondent estimated that the Chinese were eight times as numerous as the Europeans, and asserted that because of this superiority of numbers they had assumed an 'overbearing demeanour'. Within a few weeks the Chinese had left the diggings and their camps were burnt. It was noted that the Chinese had not been forced off the field, but had left of their own accord. Local historian Lynne Douthat has commented that their departure was related to large gold finds at Jones Creek or, as it was later called, Waanyarra.[2]

By the following month a rush had set in around some of the reef claims at Tarnagulla, and the population was stated to be increasing every day. The yields were good and several stores had opened, others were about to be erected and a number of substantial cottages had been built. A new reef, known as the 'Sabbath reef' was regarded as the richest on the field. Within a few months the field was hailed as one of the richest reef-mining areas in Victoria. Money was plentiful and the miners seemed prosperous indeed. Mr Foos of Dunolly had erected a hotel, and over £200 had been subscribed for a race meeting.[3]

A letter to the editor some weeks later commented that all the reefs were payable and some were 'exceeding rich', in particular Poverty Reef. Another writer remarked that Sandy Creek was 'becoming the leading place in the surrounding district'. Most of the storekeepers and hotel owners had either erected new premises or were enlarging them. The quartz reefs were still self supporting, with little or no capital brought in from other diggings, and the miners were described as of a 'more sensible practical working class than those generally met with on alluvial sinking'. This, it was felt, was due to the steady nature of reef mining and the great expenses associated with it.

This growth continued unabated at Sandy Creek and other nearby diggings, the first signs of social organisation emerging with a reefers' ball at Foos' Hotel in May 1858 and a tea meeting several months later when the schoolhouse was opened. At the latter function there were between 200 and 300 persons present. But the function did not end on a cheery note, for the Church of England representatives assumed that the building would be handed over to them. At a subsequent meeting several days later a crowd of 300 residents were present, one of the crowd forgetting himself to the extent of pushing one church representative's hat over his eyes. On a more positive note, however, a progress committee had been formed.[4]

It was soon remarked that everything seemed to have been forgotten in the search for gold, for the town had not been regularly laid out nor the land sold. The town had a population of about 3000, whereas a year before it had only 300. There were 176 claims on the reefs and four crushing machines, with another four under construction. Several good hotels and stores besides other businesses served the growing community. Before long the town had a hunt club boasting 30 members and a chapel had been constructed for the Primitive Methodists. The latter had been erected at the instigation of four women, who had 'scoured the hills and gullies' looking for subscriptions. Three hundred people attended the opening. As an indication of the wealth of the community, in January 1859 a quoits match was held for a purse of £200, believed at the time to be the largest amount ever played for in Victoria.[5]

The elegant frontage of the
Colonial Bank, Tarnagulla

By August another rush had started, this time at the Half Way diggings, between Tarnagulla and Newbridge, and numbers were pouring in from other goldfields. The rush impacted quickly on Tarnagulla, for a few weeks later the Bank of Australasia had commenced business and was erecting permanent premises, and a branch of the Union Bank had opened up for regular business. Additional accommodation had been built at Foos' Golden Age Hotel to cater for the increasing number of visitors, and the hall had been converted into a theatre. Tarnagulla also had a library and reading room, which was occasionally used for lectures, and tenders had been called for the erection of a telegraph office and the establishment of a daily mail service.

In September the floating of the Sandy Creek Poverty Reef Mining, Quartz-crushing and Washing Company caused much excitement. The success of a number of the claims on the reef was well known locally and led to a rush for share applications. A correspondent commented that the number of shares available was not even enough to satisfy local demand. Storekeepers, tradesmen and miners who had worked for wages on the reef, flocked to apply for the shares. 'Some of them, cash in hand, offered to pay down the whole amount of deposits and calls at once ...'

By the following month it was remarked that the 'building mania' still continued, with all surveyed allotments on the southern end of the proposed

The Victoria Hotel and Theatre, Tarnagulla, was the scene of many a lively social event.

town occupied, a brick building for the Union Bank nearly complete, and work commencing on a two-storey brick-built hotel. Tenders had also been called for a warden's office. Within a few days of these comments another rush started at Hard Hills to the south, where there were soon 500 men on the ground. A month later it was remarked that the town had changed markedly over the last three months and that the demand for sites was so great 'that every available portion of Main Street is built upon and high prices are realised for frontages in this street'. The rush to Inglewood some months later also had an impact, for the town was now the centre of extensive traffic to that field, and there were daily coaches to many other fields. The boom was felt in other ways as well, for there were nightly theatrical performances at several of the hotels, including the Lyceum Theatre.[6]

While expressing some disappointment in the great expectations held of the town some three years before, a correspondent in June 1862 made the following complimentary remarks:

> Brick buildings are taking the place of the old canvas tenements. The Union Bank, a structure that would do credit even to the metropolis and the Company's Hotel ... is equally entitled to notice. Another brick hotel, adjoining the new building of Mr Barlows, which is also of brick, is going up, and will be a splendid structure. The store lately belonging to Mr Brown is now being metamorphosed into a Baptist Chapel ... it is also said that some other permanent buildings are about to be erected immediately.[7]

In August of that year the first annual meeting of the Tarnagulla Benevolent Society was held. The society had been formed to provide relief on a nonsectarian basis to widows, orphans, and the sick and destitute in the town. In that year the funds went to 28 adults and 47 children.[8]

The inauguration of a new institution such as a church was always a major event in the life of any goldfields town and Tarnagulla was no exception to this. Such events were celebrated vigorously. Thus, in March 1863 more than 400 people attended a ceremony in the Victoria Theatre, which was held to celebrate the induction of a Presbyterian minister into the district. Church leaders and members from other congregations also attended, to the melodious strains of the Philharmonic Society. The society was one of the town's major institutions and was present at all important functions, in addition to holding its own concerts. The Victoria Theatre, owned by a Mr Barlow, was at that time the largest theatre in the district.[9]

The correspondent for the *Dunolly and Burnt Creek Express* reporting on the event stated that:

> For years Tarnagulla has been the hotbed of scism [sic] and religious cliques have held tyrannical sway — practising severe asceticism they strongly censure those who do not follow their example or adopt their views. It has also become a very School for Scandal. Let us hope that the cordial reception given to Mr Hamilton by all denominations, may be the means of disseminating a better feeling, and, that in time, Christian charity may be known, even at Tarnagulla.[10]

The lodges also had an important role to play. One of the first to be established was the Loyal Garibaldi Lodge. Every year it held an anniversary to which members of the district's other lodges were invited. At the third anniversary in 1863, the occasion was marked by a procession that paraded from the lodge through the main streets of the town to the Victoria Theatre.[11]

Some civic celebrations, such as the marriage of the Prince of Wales to Princess Alexandra, created a celebratory fervour. On that occasion, a committee of residents was formed to make arrangements.

> Processions, public dinners, bonfires, illuminations, banqueting and dancing were all decided on, all of which, illuminations excepted, were thoroughly successful ... On Tuesday morning, every house, from the Exchange as far as the eye could see, was festooned, and decorated with evergreens ... At 11 o'clock a procession was formed ... consisting of Odd Fellows, engineers, artizans [sic], reefers, and others, numbering about 250, who, with flags floating and band playing, in defiance of the rain that poured down, marched steadily on, cheering lustily — encouraged by the smiles and waving of handkerchiefs of the ladies, who mustered in strong numbers, and whose good looks constituted the only sunshine enjoyed that day.

Obviously not all sectarian animosities had been laid to rest, for the non-attendance of the children of one denomination was noted and regretted.[12]

Three hundred children attended the first anniversary of the Band of Hope in October 1863. The annual school picnic in November was a monster occasion, with nearly a thousand adults and children joining in the event. This occasion was followed up by picnics and sports on the banks of the Loddon River. In January 1864 there was a Band of Hope temperance meeting and a lecture in the Victoria Theatre, as well as a benefit reading in the theatre in aid of the Benevolent Society. As a further sign of growth in the town, in April of that year a branch of the Colonial Bank of Australasia was opened. Both miners and storekeepers welcomed the new bank, as the Union Bank had often objected to buying small parcels of gold and had frequently paid less than could be obtained elsewhere, for instance in Dunolly.[13]

The following month there were further signs of progress. A Presbyterian bazaar, held over five days at the Victoria Theatre, attracted people from all over the district and raised a large sum of money. In June the cornerstone of the Church of England building was laid and the new Presbyterian church was opened. A meeting of the Wesleyans was also held for the purpose of raising funds for the construction of a church, and the town's first newspaper, the *Tarnagulla Courier*, opened for business. The Wesleyan church — the town's largest yet with seating for 300 — was opened in April 1865. In August the mechanics' institute, which included a public library and other facilities, was opened amid considerable fanfare with a variety evening in the Victoria Theatre. By this time two other lodges had also been established, the Independent Order of Rechabites and the Foresters of Court Tarnagulla. The court convened for the first time at the new courthouse in September 1865.[14]

As numbers swelled, business boomed. Those advertising in the *Tarnagulla Courier* in November 1864 included two fancy repository stores (which sold stationery, books, music and musical instruments), two chemists, three drapers, four bakers, two butchers, three blacksmiths, two bootmakers, a fruiterer, six storekeepers and four hotels. Other establishments included a stockbroker, a cordial and soft drink manufacturer, a gold buyer and assayer, two builders and carpenters, a painter, ironmonger, sawmiller, wheelwright, watchmaker, timber merchants, two builders and carpenters, a surgeon, photographer, painter, theatre owner and a botanical gardens and tea rooms.[15]

One of the most elaborate celebrations held in Tarnagulla was on the occasion of the visit of the Duke of Edinburgh to Melbourne in 1867. A large bonfire with fireworks was stacked on Mount Alfred, though it was set alight by some miscreants in advance of the official proceedings. It lit the town so brightly that the smallest print could be read in the streets. The following day the town presented a 'lively appearance', and all down the street were flags of 'every device and colour'. More bonfires were lit and later in the evening a mock 'battle' with fireworks was conducted from the balcony of the Colonial Bank building.

The main celebrations occurred several days later. The procession was led by the town band, and included the lodges, clergy, tradespeople, children and anyone else who cared to join. It was estimated that at least 2000 people were

Anglican church, Moliagul, one of several original nineteenth-century buildings

present at a picnic held at the cricket ground. The *Tarnagulla Courier*'s correspondent commented that it was one of the prettiest sights ever witnessed at Tarnagulla, 'the band playing, the children singing, and everybody hurahing [sic] … every face bore a happy and contented look, whilst there were none of the squalor and misery, such as always attend any public entertainments in Melbourne and other large cities'.[16]

One of Tarnagulla's features, both then and now, is the recreation reserve. For a number of years the Christmas–New Year period had, as in most country towns, been celebrated by picnics and sports days. In 1870 the community decided that, in the future, such functions would be held in the town, and the first steps towards beautifying the reserve area were taken. The following year work commenced on the construction of swimming baths. Soon, the reserve became the social focus of the community. In 1873 a monster fete was held to raise funds for the building of a new state school, which included the usual procession and brass band. By the early 1880s plans were afoot to erect a pavilion, which still stands today.[17]

The 1860s and early 1870s were the boom years for Tarnagulla, but like so many other goldfield towns, the main mines did not last. In its day the Poverty Reef was fabulously rich, but by 1874 operations had ceased, and in 1879 it was wound up. Nevertheless, mining on the other lodes continued and the town remained a sizeable community for many years. In 1887 the *Town and Country Journal* reported that the town's main street was 'well lined with trees, and possesses numerous stores, business houses, and public buildings. Chief among the last mentioned is a commodious structure used as a council chamber, and a mechanics' institute'. There were also two banks and a large steam flourmill. The correspondent was also impressed with the various places of worship and the state school. However, by the following year there was only one bank, the Colonial having ceased trading and sold the building to the Union Bank.[18]

By the early part of the century the town's fortunes had declined further. In 1915 the last meeting of the Tarnagulla Borough was held, after which the borough was incorporated with Bet Bet Shire. According to local authors Ken and Edna Arnold, by 1920 the main businesses left in town were a solicitor, one bank, a chaff-cutting works, the flour mill, a bootmaker, blacksmith, cycle agent, garage, post office, hotel and one wood merchant.[19] Now there is a population of about 140 people plus a tavern, post office and caravan park and occasionally a store.

Other towns in the district shared a similar fate, blossoming briefly before fading away. One such town was Moliagul to the west. Gold was first found in 1855, and the field became the scene of numerous rushes, one of which took place in 1858 when there was a population of about 1800. There was a

Llanelly public hall, formerly the school, is another splendid edifice in the bush.

renewed burst of activity in the early 1860s. For instance, in January 1863 a Temperance Society and Band of Hope were formed, the latter of which soon had some 120 members. New Year's Day was celebrated with a picnic and sports day, followed by a tea and lecture at the Primitive Methodist chapel. The newly formed progress committee was to the fore in requesting improved mail services, a police station and a site for a mechanics' institute.[20]

There were, however, constant concerns about proposals to sell off some of the gold-bearing land near the town, one correspondent referring to the encroaching farmers as the 'Magpie-ocracy'. In August 1863 White's Commercial Hotel had been opened and a ball held in the evening to mark the occasion. Like all other goldfield towns in the district Moliagul shared in the usual ceremonies and celebrations. In May 1863 a holiday was declared on the occasion of the marriage of the Prince of Wales to Princess Alexandra, and a large bonfire was erected on the hill and a grand ball held in the evening at Morris' Hotel. By October a Primitive Methodist chapel had been erected and a few weeks later the cricket club's first meeting was held. The Christmas and Boxing Day festivities were elaborate. A picnic and concert were held first at Morris' Hotel, and subsequently a sports day was organised by the Commercial and Moliagul hotels. By that time a new store and a daily mail service had been established.[21]

Entertainments followed thick and fast in the New Year. In February the local choristers serenaded the fruiterer on the occasion of his marriage. Other more formal soirees were a performance at Morris' Hotel by a couple of strolling players, and a marionette entertainment, both of which played to crowded houses. Early in March a temperance lecturer spoke in the Primitive Methodist chapel and a tea meeting was held in the new Wesleyan chapel. Later that month there was a concert in Morris' Hotel in aid of the Dunolly District hospital and a concert by a Church of England choir at the school-room. In April a 46-ounce nugget was found and a small rush took place opposite one of the hotels. The latest additions to the town were a new store, shoe mart and a blacksmith's shop.[22]

Moliagul's main claim to fame, however, is the Welcome Stranger nugget, the largest in the world. In February 1869 John Deason and Richard Oates were digging around the roots of a tree looking for wash dirt when Deason's pick hit a nugget, which was later weighed at 2316 ounces, almost all of which was gold. Today, a pleasant discovery walk has been constructed at the site of the diggings at Black Gully, about two kilometres west of the town.[23] Moliagul itself is now a small village with just a handful of residents and only one business, the hotel. However, the splendid old church and state school buildings remain, and on the main street, apart from the hotel, are several old shopfronts, an abandoned garage and a few homes.

Llanelly, formerly known as New Chum and Maiden Town, is located to the north of Tarnagulla. Gold was found in this area in 1860, but it was not until after the rush at nearby Hard Hills that a township began to form. In October 1863 it was remarked that 'we are great in tea meetings and day schools'. A new chapel was opened, and a tea meeting was held to celebrate that occasion and the establishment of a new day school. An amateur dramatic club, formed in 1866, gave its second performance in a new concert hall attached to Marrow's Hotel. Llanelly too, joined in the Victoria-wide celebrations for the visit of the Duke of Edinburgh. In this task they were assisted by coaches and other vehicles from Tarnagulla, and by the Tarnagulla brass band. There were about 1200 people in attendance.[24]

By the mid-1870s, although it still had many businesses, the town was in decline. Most businesses had closed by 1920 and were later demolished. One of the few buildings to escape destruction was the post office and general store, which operated until 1960. The post office building still remains today, along with the former school building.[25]

South of Tarnagulla lies Waanyarra, formerly known as Jones Creek. The first gold finds were in 1853 and at one time there were over 1000 miners on the field. By 1858 there were about 300 European miners. Subsequent interest in the field depended upon whether a large nugget had been found recently. For instance, 145-ounce and 140-ounce nuggets were found in 1855, and the following year 281 ounces was found in a shallow hole. In 1857 Henry Davey found a nugget weighing 538 ounces only about a metre underground, and in 1863 a nugget weighing 406 ounces gross was found.[26]

One infamous incident in the late 1850s concerned the murder of two men. Charles Dunbeer confessed to taking part in the murder, implicating three others, including Mary Ann Dodd. At his trial he denied taking part in the murder. Dunbeer's resentment for Dodd was such, however, that on her release from gaol he bit her nose off, for which he received a three-year sentence.[27]

Mining was notoriously thirsty work, and there were eight hotels or inns in the town. In 1868 there were six stores, an inkmaker, gunsmith, tailor, two wheelwrights, a saddler, two carpenters, a baker, two tobacco growers, two blacksmiths, four dairymen, a butcher, shoemaker, brickmaker and four gardeners. By 1879 the population had fallen to 300. There was a short-lived rush in 1903 to Waanyarra Rush. More promising was the Poseidon rush in 1906, which followed the discovery of a massive 953-ounce (gross) nugget only about 25 centimetres underground. The Poseidon rush was the last one in the Tarnagulla area.[28]

The next round of mining activity took place in the 1930s when unemployed men were encouraged to work on the goldfields. A canvas township sprang up at Waanyarra Rush, where there were about a hundred men, many of whom were dependent upon food supplied by the farmers' wives.[29] Now only the cemetery is left. Waanyarra is typical of many former bustling gold-mining towns that have all but faded into oblivion. It provides a sharp contrast to the more extensive and elaborate remains of larger, and perhaps more evocative, towns such as Tarnagulla. Both have, however, their place in the history of abandoned or partly abandoned towns in regional Australia.

Epilogue: A Tale Too Often Told

IN THE COURSE OF MY TRAVELS AROUND AUSTRALIA, SEVERAL QUESTIONS kept provoking me, in particular, what is a ghost town? In the case of totally abandoned towns the answer is obvious. In partly abandoned towns, the answer is addressed with more difficulty — it all depends on the circumstances. Towns, like human beings, are living entities. They may not breathe, but they contain people who do. And just as a patient can get a second life, so can a town; and so too can it die.

The process of decline can be fast, as it was with many mining towns, or it can be slow as in some rural areas and run for generations. The critical question is to what extent is this process occurring today? Is what I have described in this book merely of historical curiosity, or are there other implications? In the case of the mining communities, such abandonment will continue. For the most part it will be immediate, as the larger mining concerns are run on a fly-in, fly-out basis, and often there are no families to consider.

But what of rural Australia? Is the decline in South Australia's mid and far north likely to be repeated? The farm population continues to decline for both environmental and technological reasons. Banks, schools and churches are closing, with the garages and shops not far behind them. The pattern in the past was that the older people stayed on, for they had little alternative. Who would buy their homes, and if they sold them where could they afford to go? The younger ones, for the most part, left.

In this chapter, the towns included demonstrate the modern phenomenon of rural change and decline. There were many possible examples. In the end I chose three towns — Merino in the Western District of Victoria, and Stockinbingal and Galong on the south-west slopes of New South Wales. In my judgement these towns are on the edge. I make no predictions as to their future, but simply observe how each of the communities is addressing the process of change.

Having all but travelled the length and breadth of Australia in search of abandoned towns, I was incredulous when my brother Chris suggested that I should have a look at Merino. I am a frequent traveller through the Western District of Victoria to my home town of Mount Gambier across the border, and even though Merino was less than an hours' drive away I had not heard of it. The possibility that a nearly abandoned town could exist in an area as fertile as the Western District had never occurred to me. But there it was.

At first glance Merino certainly did not appear deserted, for the well-kept main street looked healthy enough, and there were plenty of shops and a large bank building. But on closer inspection it was obvious that almost all the shops were closed apart from the hotel and garage-store at the other end of town, and this process had clearly happened not all that long ago. It was an amazing sight. Just as I was taking all this in and fumbling with my cameras, I was met by Bob Luehman, who invited me into the Merino Public Hall, where an astonishing collection of well-documented photographs was on display. Bob was one of a small band of people who had renovated the hall and improved the town.

When John Egan built his house at present day Merino in 1854 there were only two other houses, and the main form of farming was wheat growing. The following year Thomas Clarke arrived and two years later he built the first hotel.[1] Obviously a healthy future for the town was anticipated, for the main street was 60 metres wide and the cross streets 30 metres. The streets were wide enough to incorporate the first racecourse, which started in front of one of the hotels, circumnavigated the town and finished up at the rear of the hotel.[2]

By 1857 Merino had two dozen houses, a hotel, private school and a three-

High Street, Merino, c.1900
(Courtesy Merino Public Hall Committee)

storey brick-built steam flourmill. A public school was built the following year and in 1859 the town acquired a post office, Church of England school and a second store. A Masonic lodge was built in 1861, by which time the population was 394, and two years later a coach-building factory was built and a cricket club formed. A Roman Catholic church was built in 1864, followed by Church of England and Methodist churches. The late 1860s and early 1870s were boom years. The population had risen to 604 in 1871, but only three years later it was 2000. Merino benefited from its location on the track between Casterton and Portland, which was the main port for the Western District. Incredible as it may seem today, Merino was a much more populous town than Casterton and Coleraine, and probably at that time was on a par with Hamilton and Warrnambool.[3]

In addition to those establishments already mentioned above, in 1874 Merino had a Good Templars lodge, police barracks, an athletics sport association, agricultural society, rifle club, Wesleyan and Presbyterian churches, a mechanics' institute and a courthouse, which had been removed from Digby. The businesses included three hotels, a flourmill, a branch of the Bank of Victoria, two coachbuilders, two shoemakers, a cordial manufacturer and a chemist. Although the population was in decline by the late nineteenth century, a branch of the Australian Natives' Association was formed in 1898, and in 1915 a branch of the Red Cross was opened. The following year a butter factory was established.[4]

Today the population is about 200. According to Bob Leuhman there was no single reason for Merino's decline. After the world wars large grazing properties were subdivided for soldier settlement on farms of about 80 hectares. But over time these farms were not economical, and some farmers could only support themselves by off-farm work such as shearing. The children were not paid for their work, and as it was not possible to put all of them on the land, they left the town. By the 1960s the farmers were selling their properties, a development which coincided with a trend towards farm consolidation. There were fewer people in the district and town.

Another important factor was the cessation of rail services. The railway had originally linked Merino with Casterton and Hamilton, but its closure increased Merino's isolation and terminally affected its stock and agent and saleyard businesses. This situation was not helped by the failure of the stock agents to combine or cooperate to improve business. After World War II road transport largely replaced droving and stock could be trucked to the larger yards at Hamilton.

A further serious blow to the town was the closure in 1966 of the butter factory, one of the largest businesses in Merino. This substantial edifice still stands on the outskirts of town. A declining and now aging population, combined with improvements in roads and the greater accessibility to motor vehicles, set off a downward spiral of events. The town's small shops could no longer compete with the big stores in the larger towns, and one by one they closed.[5] Merino is no longer on a main linking road, but on a secondary road,

Opening of the butter factory
in Merino, November 1931;
490 people attended the function in
the Mechanics' Hall.
(Courtesy Merino Public Hall
Committee)

and a visit to the town has become a detour rather than a destination. While it is still a functioning town, perhaps its main importance in the future will be as a well-preserved monument to the past.

Stockinbingal, located between Harden and Temora in New South Wales, was never as large as Merino, but was certainly much more populous than it is today. The main street bears witness to this, for it is replete with closed shops, bar two small general stores, and the bank is closed (is there any other form of bank in rural Australia?) Stockinbingal was proclaimed as a town in 1885. The main impetus for the town was the opening of the railway between Cootamundra and Temora in 1893. Soon after, Stockinbingal became an important rural centre for the surrounding farming district, and a second wave of prosperity followed the commencement of work on a branch line to Forbes in 1912.

There were many businesses. Starting from the western end of Martin Street there was a barber, drapers, blacksmith, Commercial Bank and residence, a newsagency and general store, fruit shop, bakery, and several other businesses. Along Ellwood Street there was a doctor, dentist, barber, two butchers, a post office, saleyards, a hiring agency for horses and sulkies, a produce store and Ellwood's Hall. Other businesses in the town included two hotels, a bicycle repair shop, stock and station agents, a fancy leather goods store and a taxi service. There was also an orchard and a market garden, the latter of which was owned by a Chinese gardener, Ah Kay.[6]

The period up until the late 1920s was the most prosperous, and almost all the town's businesses and amenities were established during this period. A correspondent of the *Cootamundra Herald* offered his assessment in 1911:

It is safe to say that no place in the locality of Cootamundra has advanced so rapidly in the last few years as our neighbouring little village of Stockinbingal ... New buildings are going up in several directions, new hotels, new stores, new private residences, while a new public school is to be completed in the next few months. The Roman Catholics are contemplating building a new church and convent ... The erection of a School of Arts is being discussed and a sum of 50 pounds is already subscribed. A Court House and Clerk of Petty Sessions Office will soon be an established fact, so that in the event of so many churches missing any one on a Sunday, the man in charge will be able to pick them up and deal with them during the week.

He reserved special praise for the Commercial Hotel, which featured 17 new rooms

all beautifully finished in fine pink plaster walls and ornamental Wunderlich ceilings ... The floors are all lined with lino of a pretty design, the finishing throughout is of a high quality, everything being absolutely new even to the linen and bedding ... The artistic taste of the owner is displayed in the beautiful pictures ready for hanging on the walls, consisting of superior oil paintings of landscape and other scenes, pictures rarely displayed on hotel premises.[7]

A new wing to the hotel was officially opened in 1913, in front of a crowd of 500. It included a spacious billiard room on the ground floor and on the second floor, additional bedrooms.[8]

Ellwood's Hall was built in 1912–13 and in 1936 supper rooms were added. Over the years most of the social functions and entertainments were held in the hall. The council purchased the hall in 1968 and handed over control of it to the Stockinbingal Advancement Association. A new St James' Church of England building with a seating capacity of 170 was erected in 1911, completely free of debt, and a new Methodist church was opened in 1928. This church was damaged extensively in 1972 and the Methodist and Presbyterian congregations, who had shared the church, were invited to use St James, and a fellowship of the three churches was formed. A new Catholic church and convent school were opened in 1913, and some years later this became a full-time boarding school.[9]

Behind Stockinbingal's progress in the early years was the Farmers and Settlers' Association, which was formed in 1893. It had a major role in seeking improvements to roads, drainage, railway facilities, and in establishing a bank branch, school of arts, stone post office, telephone links and a public school. Local branches of the Country Women's Association and the Red Cross Society were also set up. A hospital was built in 1927, and a new police station and a courthouse were opened in 1940.[10]

According to several local residents, the town began to decline visibly with the sealing of the main road to Cootamundra and Temora in the 1960s, and the greater availability of consumer goods and improvements in motor vehicles, which led many residents to transfer their custom to the larger towns. The availability of cheaper petrol in the larger towns was another significant factor. But the decline probably began well before then and was almost certainly a result of the Great Depression of the 1930s, the foreclosing of farms, and their sale and amalgamation into larger holdings. Almost overnight there was less money to be spent and before long, fewer people to spend it.

The population fell from 650 in 1928 to 354 in 1940. In 1941 the Commercial Bank branch closed and in 1957 St Ita's boarding school closed, followed by the Catholic school a few years later. There were positive changes and improvements in these years, but not enough to stem the tide of change. In 1974 the Bank of New South Wales closed, and almost all the remaining stores have since followed. There have been more foreclosures of farms in recent years.[11]

There have been some positives, such as the substantial investment in the wheat silos and plans to make Stockinbingal a major wheat distribution centre. According to the publican, Pat Shiels, the cheaper price of land and the ease of commuting with the larger towns have encouraged several new families to build in the town and there has been an increase in the number of school-age children. Rae Webber, a local resident who has done much to promote and restore the town, has spoken enthusiastically about the need to preserve the historic main street architecture. The railway station and surrounding grounds have, for instance, been renovated, and while some buildings are at present neglected, there are residents who are aware of their significance and the need to retain them for future generations.[12]

Galong, near Harden in southern New South Wales, owes its existence to the establishment of the Melbourne-to-Sydney railway, and much of its fame to the former monastery at nearby Galong Castle. The castle was the home of Ned Ryan, and later his son John, who bequeathed it to the Cistercian and Redemptorist Fathers.[13] Galong was not only a rural and rail centre, but was renowned for its castellated monastery and became something of an educational centre in the district.

An application was made for a school in 1881, but by the following year the railway construction gangs and their families had moved on. A school was, however, established in 1890 with 20 pupils. In 1913 there were 37 children at the school. The convent of St Lawrence had also been established and children of the Roman Catholic faith attended that school. The convent, school and a church were conceived originally by Anastasia Ryan, who lived at Galong Castle, in return for the establishment of a community of sisters at Galong.[14]

It soon became apparent that there were not enough children to support the convent sisters and a small-scale boarding school for junior boys, known as St Lawrence's College for Boys, was opened in 1917. The opening was a grand affair and drew visitors from all parts of the local district. The college was up-to-date in every respect, including hot and cold water and electric light, and accommodated 50 boarders and 40 day pupils.[15]

Galong Castle (St Clement's), Galong

About five months later St Clement's Redemptorist College, which was located at Galong Castle, was officially opened. This function surpassed all others held at Galong, for there were in excess of 2000 visitors, who arrived by car, sulky, horse, bicycle and on foot. It was attended by a large number of clergy, including the Archbishop of Brisbane. The editor of the *Harden Express* gushed:

As the vast congregation knelt beneath the cloud-flecked empyrean with the golden sunshine, tempered with cool breeze, reflected on heads bowed in reverential devotion, it required no great feat of imagination to picture the hosts of heaven joining in the chanting which rose in mellow volume — a celestial anthem of thanksgiving for the earthly monument to God.[16]

However, the proximity of these ecclesiastical edifices did not prevent the usual spiritous excesses. In his book, *Galong Cemetery*, Max Barrett recalled that because of the lack of a lock-up the local constable had to handcuff the more inebriated residents to fence rails until such time as they dried out or could be taken into Binalong.[17]

Galong experienced its most prosperous years between 1910 and 1930, commencing with the rerouting of the railway line a short distance away from the existing line. The old town had been built around the old railway line, and included a hotel and several stores, some of which were in time relocated closer to the new railway station. One of the largest stores was owned by Killick and Sons. They employed about 20 people and ran wagonettes and several spring carts continuously to McMahon's Reef, taking the shearing orders out to the sheds as far south as Bookham. The store was relocated in 1922. There were also two stock and station agents, saleyards, post office, a bank, bootmaker, blacksmith, baker and butcher and a police station. In addition to the farms and shearing sheds the stores also supplied produce to St Lawrence's.[18]

At about the time that the new railway station was built a new hotel, the Royal, was also constructed, and the town businesses were gradually relocated closer to the hotel and the station. The hotel benefited initially from the presence of the large railway construction gangs. There were about 24 men employed permanently at the railway station, including the staff and three maintenance gangs. In addition, there was a butter factory and a freezing works used for rabbits. Dairying was the main form of farming and quarrying for road gravel and stone was also undertaken.

Four cricket teams, a race track, rifle range, golf course and sports ground ensured there was plenty of scope for social activities in the town's early days. During World War I there were fund-raising activities, such as a War Chest, Frances Day Fund, Patriotic Wheat Fund Scheme, and various balls and concerts in aid of the convent and Randwick Hospital. One of the less successful fund-raising events occurred in November 1917 when the police took action against the organisers of a coursing function on the grounds of cruelty to the rabbits. The proceeds went in fines.[19]

Despite the depressed economic conditions of the 1930s Galong maintained a lively community and sporting life. Organisations in the town included the Oddfellows, Red Cross, a branch of the Australian Labor Party and a progress association. Concerts, balls, sports days and show days were also held. For instance, at the Oddfellows annual ball in July 1931 there were 55 couples present. The golf links were officially opened in April 1932.[20]

Despite all these portents for prosperity the town gradually declined. The closure of the railway station was a major blow, for it employed a large number of men. Equally traumatic was the closure of St Lawrence's College, for it was a substantial purchaser of foodstuffs and other produce. During the 1930s depressed prices for farm produce, combined with dry weather conditions, impacted on the dairy farms. According to Athol Luke, a long-term resident of the town, once there were 40 dairy farms in the neighbourhood; now there are none. The eventual closure of the quarry, freezing works and butter factory also had an effect. Improved motor transport and roads had their impact here, as in almost every other small rural town in Australia.[21]

Today the main street of Galong has an appearance of genteel decline. Almost all the buildings date from the period prior to the 1930s. Killick's store, the two stock and station agent buildings, old post office and bank and several other buildings are abandoned or used as private residences. In the older part of town the old hotel and a store are used as private residences. On the plus side, however, St Lawrence's is now an attractive retirement home, and the garage, hotel and a small post office-cum-store are still in business. The Luke family own the garage and hotel, and have been to the forefront in developing the retirement home and expanding the hotel. They are confident of the town's future, and provide a fine example of what can be achieved with a little drive and imagination.

The three towns discussed in this chapter differ little in their circumstances from many others in rural Australia that have also passed through a long period of decline. For many towns time is running out. The future is, however, not altogether without hope. Most towns have some features that can be exploited to advantage; for instance location, natural surroundings, history or architecture. Old buildings in a state of advanced decay can, with some attention, be attractive and eye-catching assets. The growth of large regional centres provides opportunities for developing a feeder or dormitory role, especially where the cost of housing is significantly lower.

There are enough success stories to suggest that over time the process of decline can be halted, if not reversed. Most state governments have some form of regional development program that can be tapped into, but this form of assistance cannot always be relied on. Ultimately the key to survival lies within. Towns are composed of people and it is their enthusiasm, initiative and sheer doggedness that will win the day. The qualities that saw the growth of so many settlements over a century and a half ago differ little from those needed now.

Glossary

Afghans — Vernacular for camel drivers and camel team owners from Afghanistan and from what is now known as Pakistan.

Alluvial mining — The washing of mineral-bearing sands, gravels or clays, which have been removed from their parent rock by erosion and incorporated in water deposited alluvium. Washing was by *cradle*, *panning*, *sluicing*, *puddling*, or a combination of each. The wash dirt was located in current streambeds or in old streambeds, which are elevated above the former. In old streambeds the use of water races was essential. Alluvial gold and tin were recovered by these processes.

Amalgamated claims — Adjoining mining claims that have been combined to allow more economical workings.

Assay/assayer — The process of analysing an ore to determine the metal content. Usually applied to gold and silver. It often involved crushing a small sample and smelting it in a small furnace.

Auriferous — Containing gold.

Battery — A machine with sets of vertical stampers or rods that rise and fall onto ore placed on the floor of a mortar box. They can have any number of stampers (or heads), from one to 60. They were usually steam- or petrol-powered.

Blast furnaces — A furnace in which a mixed charge of ore, flux and fuel (usually coke) is blown with a continuous blast of hot air to stimulate the chemical reduction of metals to its metallic state. They were used for the treatment of iron, silver, lead and copper. The most common form was the steel-built water jacket furnace, which eventually replaced the *reverberatory furnace*.

Chlorination — Method of retrieving gold from refractory (heavily mineralised) ore by roasting it in a *reverberatory furnace*, then dissolving the material in a chlorine solution in wooden vats. The gold is then precipitated from the solution with ferrous sulphate. This process was used in the 1880 and 1890s and eventually replaced with *cyanidation*.

Coke oven — beehive-shaped masonry oven, usually in banks of multiple ovens for producing coke from coal.

Concentration — elimination of the non-valuable lighter portions of crushed ore and collection of the valuable heavy components. Plant included such items as Wilfley tables, Prue Vanners, jigs and buddles, which were often referred to broadly as 'tables'. The Wilfley was a slightly sloping table, which was shaken while water and crushed ore were poured down it, the gold being caught between ripples on the surface.

Cradle — A device for retrieving alluvial gold. It was a timber box open at one end and resting on curved rockers. Wash dirt was placed in a removable hopper on top of the cradle, and the earth washed through the hopper's perforated base with water. Gold was caught behind the riffles in the box. The process was called cradling.

Cradling — *see* **Cradle**

Crushing or reduction plant — Used to break the ore into finer components to allow further processing. It may include jaw breakers, Cornish rolls (with opposing steel rollers), *batteries*, or mills such as the Huntington. The latter crushed the ore with steel rollers rotating against the side of a cylindrical iron pan. Reduction plants usually incorporated a *concentration* plant.

Cyanidation — A process of extracting gold by treating the finely crushed ore with a solution of cyanide in large tanks, then recovering the gold by filtration and precipitation with zinc. It was introduced in 1892 and replaced *chlorination*.

Dollying — A primitive process for extracting gold, whereby the ore was crushed in a mortar and pestle, called a dolly pot, before panning.

Dredge — A large-scale tin and gold recovery plant mounted on a floating pontoon and equipped with digging, washing and concentrating apparatus. The wash material is raised from the stream floor by a chain of continuous buckets or by a suction pipe, and after processing it is deposited behind the dredge.

Dry blowing — A means of alluvial gold extraction in arid regions where no water was available. Methods ranged from simple winnowing in the wind to the use of a machine with a bellows, which blew air through the wash dirt.

Fluxes — Substances added to ore in the smelting processes to induce a chemical reaction. Common fluxes were ironstone and limestone.

Horse whim — *see* **Whim**

Inclined tramway — A tramway linking a mine and/or mill located on the bottom of a valley with the top, or linking a mine on a slope with a mill at a lower level. Could be self-acting if the descending loaded trucks were used to pull up an empty truck at the other end of the cable, or could be operated by a winding engine on the top.

Joss house — Vernacular for Chinese temple. Could be a very substantial size or only a small hut. Found on goldfields and in towns and cities.

Lode — A mineral deposit in solid rock.

Longwall mining — Method of extracting coal on a continual working face. The roof was allowed to collapse behind the working area, which was held up by steel beams and hydraulic rams.

Open cut — An excavation rather like a quarry.

Panning — A method of extracting gold by washing the alluvium in a dish and allowing it to accumulate in the rim.

Pig oven — a circular stone-built ceremonial oven for roasting pigs. They were built by the Chinese, and often found in their villages on the goldfields.

Poppet head — An iron, steel or timber structure of legs built over a shaft. It is equipped with pulleys over which the ropes or cables run that raise and lower the cages in the shaft.

Puddlers/puddling machine — A circular trench in which wash dirt and water were mixed and broken up by a plough attached to a long pole in the centre of the circle, which was pulled around by a horse walking around the outside of the puddle. Used where the mineral was embedded in heavy clay. Commonly used on goldfields.

Race — An open channel for conveying water to alluvial workings. A race for supplying water was a head race, and one for removing water a tail race. The head race could be many kilometres long.

Reef mining — The mining of gold-bearing rock, sometimes referred to as hard rock or quartz mining. Such mining is characterised by adits or tunnels and shafts, and invariably involves the construction of a reduction and *concentration plant*.

Retorts — A series of furnaces for processing oil shale rock. The oil shale was crushed and then heated at a low temperature inside metal cylinders enclosed in brickwork. The oil shale would then be extracted for further processing.

Reverberatory furnace — A brick-built furnace used for smelting ore. Timber was commonly used for fuel. Once molten, the metallic component became separated from the lighter slag and were both drawn off separately.

Sluicing, sluice boxes — A commonly used method for extracting alluvial gold or tin. In common sluicing, the ground to be treated was first dug out or loosened and washed by water conveyed over the top of the excavation by a *race*. The washed material was then either run through sluice boxes or a ground sluice constructed of rocks. A sluice was a wooden box that contained ripples. The gold or heavy material was collected behind the ripples in the box or behind the rocks. In hydraulic sluicing a hose was used to wash the material from the excavation into the boxes.

Tailings — Rock, earth, gravel or sand that is the residue from the separation (or other treatment) of wash dirt or ore by water and chemicals, for example by *sluicing*, *chlorination* or *cyanidation*. Applies to residue from both reef mining and alluvial mining.

Tribute/tributers — A contract under which a party of miners working on their own account (tributers) gave the mine owners a proportion of their earnings. Often found in mines where the owners have ceased operations, but where ore can still be won. It often represents, therefore, the last phase of mining.

Whim (or horse whim) — A structure of strong timber supporting a large horizontal drum around which ropes are wrapped, and attached via a *poppet head* to buckets in a shaft. The drum is attached to a long beam with a horse harness at its end. As the horse walks around the drum it turns and raises one end of the rope while lowering the other.

Imperial and metric measurements

Imperial measurements (£) are used for currency. As a guide to standards of living then and now, an ounce of gold in the nineteenth century was valued at about £3 10s. A yield of one ounce a week was, therefore, the equivalent of at least good wages, often more. Current (June 2002) A$ prices for gold suggest that it has held its purchasing value reasonably well over the last 100 years, but more in line with minimum wages. Most measurements have been cited in metric.

one acre = 0.40 hectares
one gallon = 4.5 litres
one ounce = 28.3 grams
one pound = 0.45 kilograms
one ton = 1016 kilograms

Notes

GHOSTS OF THE MURCHISON

1 H.H. Wilson, *Gateways to Gold*, Rigby, Adelaide, 1969, p. 35.

2 Vera Whittington, *Gold and Typhoid. Two Fevers. A Social History of Western Australia, 1891–1900*, University of Western Australia Press, 1988, p. 243; P.R. Heydon, *Just a Century Ago*, Hesperian Press, Perth, 1987, p. 23.

3 Whittington, *op cit*, p. 244.

4 Julius M. Price, *The Land of Gold*, Sampson Low, Marston and Company, London, 1896, p. 174.

5 Heydon, *op cit*, pp. 10–30; Whittington, op cit, pp. 250–251; West Australian Department of Mines, *Annual Report*, Brisbane, 1896, p. 54.

6 P.R. Heydon, *Gold on the Murchison*, Hesperian Press, Perth, 1986, pp. 22–24. The first account of gold in the area was by a surveyor, Robert Austin, in his exploration of the Murchison hinterland in 1854. He described the area near present-day Cue as one of the finest goldfields in the world, but no notice was taken of this advice.

7 George Hope, *The Murchison Goldfields: Supplement to the Geraldton Express*, 1897, p. 38.

8 *ibid*, p. 35.

9 *ibid*, p. 55.

10 Hope, *op cit*, pp. 36, 42–43; Heydon, *Gold on the Murchison*, *op cit*, pp. 35–37. One such rough and ready character in those early days was Russian Jack, who was well known on the Murchison and Kimberley goldfields. He was reputed to have been chained by the police to an upright log set in the ground, but on the policeman's return the next day Jack and the log were gone. Both were later found in one of the hotels, Jack at the bar, and the log on the counter. I have come across this tale on other mining fields in Australia, and suspect that it is a 'generic' story; one of Australia's enduring bush legends.

11 Hope, *op cit*, p. 42.

12 *ibid*, pp. 46–58.

13 Vivienne May, *Travels in Western Australia*, Hesperian Press, Victoria Park, 1993 (first published 1901), pp. 185–186. She stated that there seemed to be a great many women in Cue, although it had been 'only a few years since the arrival of a fair lady in Cue was an event of importance, in which almost the entire population showed their interest by crowding around the coach'.

14 Hope, *op cit*, pp. 69–74.

15 *Murchison Times and Day Dawn Gazette*, 28 July, 2 August 1900.

16 Hope, *op cit*, pp. 87–96.

17 *Murchison Times and Day Dawn Gazette*, 7 April, 19 November 1898.

18 *ibid*, 24 December 1898, 7 February, 26 May 1900.

19 Heydon, *Gold on the Murchison*, *op cit*, pp. 84, 98; *Murchison Times and Day Dawn Gazette*, 12 March, 25 May 1912.

20 *ibid*, 6, 20 June, 28 November 1912.

21 *ibid*, 20 June, 23 July, 26 November 1912.

22 *ibid*, 12 April 1918; Heydon, *Gold on the Murchison, op cit*, pp. 107–120.

23 *ibid*, pp. 102, 107–120; *Murchison Times and Day Dawn Gazette*, 12 April 1918; *Murchison Times*, 21 March, 10 April 1936.

24 *ibid*, 18, 25 September, 9 October 1937.

25 Heydon, *Gold on the Murchison*, *op cit*, pp. 127–133; *Murchison Times*, 9 October, 1 December 1937.

26 Heydon, *Gold on the Murchison*, *op cit*, p. 133; *Countryman*, 21 July 1955; Normandy Mining Ltd and Hampton Goldfields Ltd, *Big Bell 1936–1955. A Goldfields Ghost Town*, Adelaide (undated pamphlet).

27 Heydon, *Gold on the Murchison*, pp. 144–146. Cue derives some benefits from the Harmony Company's operations at Big Bell. There are about 30 employees who live in town, but the vast majority live on the mine site on a fly-in, fly-out basis. Simon Hawkins, Shire of Cue.

AN AMERICAN DREAM

1 *Murchison Times and Day Dawn Gazette*, 5 April, 5 May 1898.

2 Gwalia Historical Museum, *Gwalia Leonora*, pamphlet, undated.

3 George H. Nash, *The Life of Herbert Hoover. The Engineer 1874–1914*, W.W. Morton and Company, New York, pp. 57–59.

4 *ibid*, pp. 60–61.

5 *ibid*, pp. 64–65.

6 Geoffrey Blainey, 'Herbert Hoover's Forgotten Years', *Business Archives and History*, February 1963, vol. 111, no. 1, pp. 56–57.

7 Nash, *op cit*, pp. 64–69.

8 *ibid*, pp. 71–73; P. Bell, J. Connell, J. McCarthy, *Gwalia Conservation Study*, July 1985, p. 56.

9 *ibid*, p. 64.

10 *ibid*, pp. 56–57; Nash, *op cit*, pp. 74–75; Bell, Connell, McCarthy, *op cit*, p. 64; W.A. Heritage Committee, Historic Gwalia Heritage Trail, pamphlet, p. 8, undated.

11 Nash, *op cit*, p. 83.

12 Bell, Connell, McCarthy, *op cit*, p. 57; C.W.F. Turnbull, *Looking Back. Leonora…Gwalia…1895–1963*, Leonora Tourist Committee, Leonora, 1990, p. 28.

13 *ibid*, pp. 32, 40, 50, 66.

14 *ibid*, pp. 16–17, 28–31, 41–45.

15 *ibid*, pp. 52–63, 74.

16 *ibid*, pp. 39, 42, 46–47, 54, 87.

17 *ibid*, pp. 78–80; Bell, Connell, McCarthy, *op cit*, p. 65.

18 *ibid*, p. 65; Turnbull, *op cit*, pp. 78–81, 85, 88–98.

19 Bell, Connell, McCarthy, *op cit*, pp. 69–70; Turnbull, *op cit*, p. 127.

20 Discussions with Ian McKay, November 2001; discussions with Eric Omodei, December, 2001; Turnbull, *op cit*, pp. 140–142; Bill Bunbury, 'Golden Opportunities'?: Immigrant Workers on

Western Australia's Eastern Goldfields, 1900–1965', in Iain McCalman, Alexander Cook and Andrew Reeves (eds), *Gold. Forgotten Histories and Lost Objects of Australia*, Cambridge University Press, Cambridge, 2001, pp. 144–146.

21 Bell, Connell, McCarthy, *op cit*, p. 71; Turnbull, *op cit*, pp. 162–173, 188–189.

22 Bell, Connell, McCarthy, *op cit*, pp. 75–76.

23 *Kalgoorlie Miner*, 14, 16, 19, 21, 24 December 1963.

24 Turnbull, *op cit*, pp. 195–196.

25 Bell, Connell, McCarthy, *op cit*, pp. 76–77.

TOMBSTONES AND TUMBLEWEED

1 By 1895 the business sector of Menzies consisted of 'orderly and comparatively substantial buildings', for instance, 12 stores, a mechanics' institute, and a branch of the West Australian Bank. Vera Whittington, *Gold and Typhoid. Two Fevers. A Social History of Western Australia, 1891–1900*, University of Western Australia Press, 1988, p. 277.

2 *ibid*, pp. 278–295.

3 Michael R. Best, *A Lost Glitter. Letters between South Australia and the West Australian Goldfields, 1895–1897*, Wakefield Press, Adelaide, 1986, pp. 145, 149.

4 Vivienne May, *Travels in Western Australia*, Hesperian Press, Victoria Park, 1993 (first published 1901), pp. 145–147.

5 Warden W. Lambden Owen, 'Early Days of Menzies — North Coolgardie Goldfield', PR 282, Battye Library, Perth, in Pat & Brenda Rodgers, *No Sign of the Time. A Collection of Stories of the Menzies District*, Hesperian Press and Shire of Menzies, Perth, 1992, pp. 9–12.

6 West Australian Department of Mines, *Annual Report*, Perth, 1897, p. 47.

7 *Western Mail*, Christmas Number, 1901, p. 41.

8 *ibid*, 1902, p. 56.

9 Norma King, *Ghost Towns of the North Country*, Norma King, 1974, pp. 12–13.

10 West Australian Department of Mines, *op cit*, 1897, p. 71.

11 *Western Mail*, Christmas Number, 1902, p. 56.

12 Ivan Elliott, *From Kookynie to Keysbrook*, Access Press, Perth, 1988, pp. 15–16.

13 Rodgers, *op cit*, pp. 117–120.

14 *Western Mail*, Christmas Number, 1901, pp. 41–42.

15 *ibid*, 1902, p. 57.

16 *ibid*, 1902, p. 57; 1903, p. 55; Elliott, *op cit*, p. 13.

17 C.W.F. Turnbull, *Looking Back. Leonora…Gwalia…1895–1963*, Leonora Tourist Committee, Leonora, 1990, p. 58.

18 West Australian Department of Mines, *Annual Report*, Perth, 1917.

19 The *Morning Herald* series of *West Australian Guide Books No. 2, North Eastern Goldfields from Kookynie to Laverton*, undated, but probably 1904. Also the photographic collection at the Eastern Goldfields Society, Kalgoorlie.

20 Discussion with Shyeema Peebles, December 2001.

21 May, *op cit*, p. 157.

22 *ibid*, pp. 156–157; West Australian Department of Mines, *op cit*, 1899, p. 57.

23 *Western Mail*, Christmas Number, 1901, p. 48.

24 May, *op cit*, p. 149.

25 Turnbull, *op cit*, pp. 3–4, 21, 30, 37.

26 Rodgers, *op cit*, pp. 178–179.

27 Margaret Bull, *White Feather, The Story of Kanowna*, Community Publishing Project Publication, Fremantle Art Centre Press, Fremantle, 1981, pp. 28–32.

28 Delta Gold N.L. and the Heritage Council of Western Australia, The Kanowna Heritage Trail, undated pamphlet, pp. 4–5.

29 *ibid*, pp. 14–47; Bull, *op cit*, pp. 41–43, 61–66; *Western Mail*, Christmas Number, 1898, pp. 76–77; 1900, p. 55.

30 Bull, *op cit*, pp. 48–50; John Marshall, *Battling for Gold*, E.W. Cole, Melbourne 1903, pp. 171–176.

31 *ibid*, pp. 152–162; W.G. Manners, *"So I Headed West"*, W.G. Manners & Co., Hesperian Press, Victoria Park, 1992, pp. 97–99; Bull, *op cit*, pp. 82–93.

THE WINDS OF CHANGE

1 Onslow is located 320 km south of Karratha and about 500 km north of Carnarvon.

2 Martyn and Audrey Webb, *End of Empire*, Artlook Books, Perth, 1983, pp. 78–79.

3 Webb, *op cit*, pp. 107–110; Onslow Tourist Committee, pamphlet, Old Onslow Heritage Trail, undated, p. 9.

4 Webb, *op cit*, pp. 110–115.

5 *West Australian*, 30 December 1897; Webb, *op cit*, pp. 92–94.

6 *ibid*, p. 102; discussion with Laura Shannon, January 2002.

7 *West Australian*, 12, 14 April 1909.

8 Webb, *op cit*, pp. 118–119.

9 Onslow Tourist Committee, *op cit*, p. 13, Webb, *op cit*, pp. 151–152.

10 Kathy De La Rue, *Pearl Shell and Pastures*, Cossack Project Committee (Inc.), 1979, pp. 49–57.

11 *ibid*, pp. 69–77.

12 Kay Forrest, *The Challenge and the Chance. The Colonisation and Settlement of North West Australia 1861–1914*, Hesperian Press, Victoria Park, 1996, pp. 77–80, 165–181.

13 *ibid*, pp. 169–170.

14 Arthur C.V. Bligh, *The Golden Quest*, Publicity Press, Sydney, 1955, pp. 35–37.

15 De La Rue, *op cit*, pp. 76–82; Forrest, *op cit*, pp. 109–115.

16 De La Rue, *op cit*, p. 106.

17 *ibid*, pp. 57–58.

18 *ibid*, pp. 107–109.

19 Susan Janice Hunt, *Spinifex and Hessian. Women in North-West Australia, 1860–1890*. West Australian Experience Series, University of Western Australia Press, Nedlands, 1986, pp. 123–135.

20 William Lambden Owen, *Cossack Gold: the Chronicles of an Early Goldfields Warden*, Sydney, 1933, pp. 23–27.

21 *West Australian*, 5 April 1898.

22 *ibid*, 5, 6 April 1898.

23 Brain Hoey, *Cossack, Land of the Silver Sea*, B. Hoey, Perth, 1996, pp. 17–19.

24 Hoey, *op cit*, pp. 19–23, 27–29.

25 *Cossack Historic Walk*, pamphlet, undated.

26 Discussion with Ellen DeHayr, October 2001.

27 In the Japanese section one grave belongs to a diver who died of paralysis while on the schooner *Willie* in 1890. Other Japanese buried at the cemetery are Kaichi Nakada, who died in 1891, Sakutaro Murumatsu, who died in 1898, Tetsukichi Fukumoto, who died in 1914, and Seigoro Nabiki, who died in 1929.

UNDER NORTHERN SKIES

1 *Town and Country Journal*, 8, 22 May, 19 June 1886, 31 July, 15 October 1887.

2 Harriet W. Daly, *Digging, Squatting and Pioneering. Life in the Northern Territory of South Australia*, facsimile edition, Hesperian Press, Perth, 1984, pp. 298–299.

3 *Tasmanian Mail*, 6 November 1886. G.H. Lamond, *Tales of the Overland. Queensland to Kimberley in 1885*, Hesperian Press, Perth, 1986, pp. 51–52.

4 Cathie Clement, *Old Halls Creek: A Town Remembered*, National Heritage, Mt Lawley, 2000, pp. 9–12; *Town and Country Journal*, 22 May 1886.

5 Lamond, *op cit*, pp. 49–51.

6 Fred D. Burdett, *The Odyssey of a Digger*, Herbert Jenkins Ltd, London, 1936; Clement, *op cit*, pp. 6–7. Kimberley Language Resource Centre, *Moola Bulla. In the Shadow of the Mountain*, Magabala Books, Broome, 1996, pp. 36–39, 41–42, 44–46, 101–108.

7 Clement, *op cit*, p. 13

8 *ibid*, pp. 14, 22–27; Burdett, *op cit*, pp. 259–261.

9 The Hon. David Carnegie, *Spinifex and Sand*, C. Arthur Pearson, London, 1898, pp. 322–329.

10 Clement, *op cit*, p. 33; Kimberley Language Resource Centre, *op cit*, pp. 121–122.

11 Clement, *op cit*, pp. 34–42.

12 Ion L. Idriess, *The Nor'-Westers*, Angus & Robertson, Sydney, 1954, p. 196. According to some accounts Aboriginals were also very adept at prospecting for gold, which they sold to the Europeans. Kimberley Language Resource Centre, *op cit*, pp. 51–52; W.E. Harney, *North of 23°, Ramblings in Northern Australia*, Australasian Publishing Company, Sydney, 1946, pp. 202–203.

13 Clement, *op cit*, pp. 53–57.

14 *ibid*, pp. 58–61.

15 Access to the mine and town sites requires the approval of the mining company. At the time of my visit the mine was owned by Anglo Gold Brocks Creek. I was accompanied on site by the caretaker, Josef Bollmann. Discussion with Stan Haeusler, June 2002.

16 Department of Lands, Planning and Environment, Northern Territory, *Northern Goldfields Loop pamphlet*, undated; M.H. Tamblyn, *Mines, Money and Men: Top End Mining, 1895–1921*, Historical Society of the Northern Territory, 1990, pp. 51–57.

17 Timothy G. Jones, *The Chinese in the Northern Territory*, Northern Territory University Press, Darwin, 1990, p. 72; Department of Lands, Planning and Environment, *op cit*; Tamblyn, *op cit*, p. 27.

18 Department of Lands, Planning and Environment, *op cit*.

19 Timothy Jones, *Pegging the Northern Territory. A History of Mining in the Northern Territory 1870–1946*, Northern

20 *ibid*, pp. 48–49, 61.

21 *ibid*, pp. 50–54. Jones, *The Chinese in the Northern Territory*, *op cit*, pp. 49, 55. The railway was built almost entirely by Chinese labourers, of whom there were as many as 3000.

22 Jones, *Pegging the Northern Territory*, *op cit*, pp. 53–63; Jones, *The Chinese in the Northern Territory*, *op cit*, pp. 50, 85. With talk of Federation the Administration came under increasing pressure to impose restrictive immigration and goldfields legislation. By 1889 the Chinese population in the Territory began to fall. However, even as late as 1891 most goldmining was still done by Chinese miners.

23 Department of Lands, Planning and Environment, *op cit*.

24 Jones, *Pegging out the Northern Territory*, *op cit*, p. 74; Department of Lands, Planning and Environment, *op cit*.; D.E. Kelsey, *The Shackle*, Ira Nesdale (ed), Lynton Publications, Blackwood, 1975, pp. 95–96.

25 Department of Lands, Planning and Environment, *op cit*.

26 Sue Harlow, *Tin Gods. A social history of the men and women of Maranboy 1913–1962*, Historical Society of the Northern Territory, Darwin, 1997, pp. 6–9.

27 *ibid*, pp. 9–12.

28 *ibid*, pp. 15–17, 21–23, 26–33.

29 *ibid*, pp. 3, 61–62.

30 *ibid*, pp. 63–68. Relationships between Europeans and Aboriginals were not always harmonious, but some long-term miners developed a closer understanding of the Aboriginal people, and in some cases married Aboriginal women. These associations were often frowned upon in official circles. Peter and Jay Read, *Long Time, Olden Time. Aboriginal accounts of Northern Territory History*, Institute for Aboriginal Development publications, Alice Springs, 1991, p. 109.

31 M.J. O'Reilly, *Bowyangs and Boomerangs*, Hesperian Press, Perth, 1984, pp. 71–73, 78–83.

32 Harlow, *op cit*, pp. 36–41; O'Reilly, *op cit*, p. 77.

33 Harlow, *op cit*, pp. 49–50, 56; Hugh Clarke, *The Long Arm*, Australian Large Print, Melbourne, 1990, p. 119; Harney, *op cit*, facing p. 99; O'Reilly, *op cit*, p. 82.

34 Harlow, *op cit*, pp. 45–48, 52–53.

35 Vanda Marshall, *We Helped to Blaze the Track*, Vanda Marshall, Townsville, 1980, pp. 68–69.

36 Discussion with Ron Miller, November 2000.

37 Discussion with Rosemary Steele, December 2000.

EAST OF ALICE

1 Peter Forrest, *Report on a study of historic sites and materials at Arltunga*, Community Services Division, Department of Community Development, March 1981, pp. 85–88.

2 *ibid*, pp. 90–91.

3 *ibid*, pp. 25–26; *Adelaide Observer*, 11 February, 28 July, 15 September 1888.

4 Forrest, *op cit*, pp. 35–40.

5 Kate Holmes, *The White Range Settlement Area, Arltunga Goldfield*, N.T., March 1980, pp. 5, 29–30.

6 Forrest, *op cit*, pp. 27, 41, 72.

7 Holmes, *op cit*, pp. 8–10, 32, 50–51.

8 *ibid*, pp. 12–13; *Town and Country Journal*, 27 May 1903.

9 Doris Blackwell and Douglas Lockwood, *Alice on the Line*, Landsdowne Publishing, Sydney, reprinted 1997, pp. 167–172.

10 Robert Frearson, *Guide and Handbook to the Arltunga and Winnecke's Depot Goldfields*, 1903.

11 Holmes, *op cit*, pp. 13–19, 42–43, 50–52.

12 R.G. Kimber, *Man From Arltunga*, Hesperian Press, Victoria Park, 1986, pp. 1–4, 8–32.

13 R.B. Plowman, *The Man From Oodnadatta*, Angus & Robertson, Sydney, 1940, pp. 170–181.

14 P.S. Hossfeld, *The Ciccone Mine, Winnecke Goldfield*, Aerial Geological and Geophysical Survey of Northern Australia, Report no. 22, September 1936.

15 Coralie and Leslie Rees, *Spinifex Walkabout*, Australasian Publishing Company in association with George G. Harrap & Co., London, 1953, pp. 251–253.

ARCHIBALD WILSON'S LAMENT

1 Diane Menghetti, *Ravenswood. Five Heritage Trails*, Department of History and Politics, James Cook University of North Queensland, 1992, p. 18.

2 D.C. Roderick, 'Ravenswood 1868–1917', *Lectures in North Queensland History*, Second Series, James Cook University, 1975, pp. 147–151; Menghetti, *op cit*, 1992, pp. 5–6.

3 Roderick, *op cit*, pp. 153–155, 163; Peter Bell, *Ravenswood Conservation Management Plan*, report to Ravenswood Restoration and Preservation Association Inc, June 2000, pp. 13–14.

4 Roderick, *op cit*, pp. 156–163; Menghetti, *op cit*, pp. 5–8. The variety of sulphides in the ore meant that no one method of treatment was by itself suitable.

5 Bell, *op cit*, p. 15, Queensland Department of Mines, *Annual Report*, Brisbane, 1880, p. 230.

6 Roderick, *op cit*, pp. 156–163.

7 Menghetti, *op cit*, p. 8.

8 Bell, *op cit*, pp. 26–27.

9 *ibid*, p. 27; Doug Hunt, 'The Ravenswood strike', *Lectures in North Queensland History*, no. 4, James Cook University, 1975, pp. 161.

10 *Town and Country Journal*, 9 September 1903.

11 Bell, *op cit*, p. 27.

12 *ibid*, p. 27; Doug Hunt, 'The Ravenswood Strike', *Lectures in North Queensland History*, no. 4, James Cook University, 1975, p. 161.

13 Ian Black and Company, *Ravenswood*, produced for the Ravenswood Church Restoration Committee, 1977, p. 5.

14 *Brisbane Courier*, 11 December 1912; Hunt, *op cit*, pp. 164–166. Doug Hunt has postulated that the strike was part of a wider union strategy to secure the loyalty of its local members and other Queensland workers.

15 *Brisbane Courier*, 10, 15 January 1913.

16 Hunt, *op cit*, pp. 167–169; Queensland Department of Mines, Annual Report, Brisbane, 1917, p. 123; 1918, p. 119.

17 Bell, *op cit*, p. 39.

18 May Crow, *Ravenswood Remembered*, Ravenswood Restoration and Preservation Association Inc, 1997, Decline of Ravenswood, Community Life, Lifestyle, Miners as I Remember Them sections.

19 *ibid*, Community Life section; *Townsville Catholic News*, February 1962, p. 6; March 1962, p. 8.

20 Discussions with Woody Pigram, October 2001; Senex, 'Did things go boom in the night', *Townsville Catholic News*, December 1961, pp. 9–10.

21 Discussions with Dianne and Gina Schluter, October, December 2001.

22 Jill Mather and Jim Cox, *Ravenswood*, Darymple Shire Council, undated, p. 9.

FROM THE ETHERIDGE TO IRVINEBANK

1 Janice Wegner, *The Etheridge*, Studies in North Queensland History no. 13, Department of History and Politics, James Cook University, Townsville, 1990, p. 30.

2 *ibid*, p. 26; G.C. Bolton, *A Thousand Miles Away. A History of North Queensland to 1920*, Jacaranda Press in association with the Australian National University, Brisbane, 1963, p. 46; William Henry Corfield, *Reminiscences of Queensland, 1862–1899*, A.H. Frater, Brisbane, 1921, pp. 36–38; *Town and Country Journal*, 25 June 1870.

3 R.B. Brown, 'Chinese on the Gilbert River Gold-field', in K.H. Kennedy (ed), *Readings in North Queensland Mining History*, History Department, James Cook University of North Queensland, Townsville, vol. 11, 1981, pp. 169–171, 176–178.

4 Wegner, *op cit*, pp. 30–33.

5 *ibid*, p. 34; also *Brisbane Courier*, 19 June 1878; discussions and correspondence with Lyn French, December 2001 and Jan Wegner, July 2002; *Town and Country Journal*, 16 August 1884.

6 Wegner, *op cit*, pp. 56–57, 97–98, 104–105, 130–132.

7 *ibid*, pp. 91–95, 109, 126. At first the copper deposits were exploited by Einasleigh Freehold Copper Mines, which constructed a smelting works on the edge of Copperfield Gorge in 1901.

8 *Town and Country Journal*, 30 December 1908.

9 Wegner, *op cit*, pp. 107–109, 121–126.

10 *Town and Country Journal*, 23 December 1908; Wegner, *op cit*, pp. 111–113. The fall in population was largely a result of water shortages. The claims were worked mainly by dry blowing.

11 Colin Hooper, *Kidston*, Colin Hooper, Townsville, undated, p. 4, 18; Wegner, *op cit*, pp. 115–117, 126–130.

12 Hooper, *op cit*, pp. 7–8; Wegner, *op cit*, pp. 132–135. Information and photographs supplied by Allyn and Natasha Zabel, January 2002.

13 Ruth S. Kerr, *John Moffat of Irvinebank*, J.D. & R.S. Kerr, Brisbane, 2000, p. 66.

14 *ibid*, pp. 72, 222; Ruth S. Kerr, *Irvinebank: Mining Community and Centre of an Empire*, J.D. & R.S. Kerr, Brisbane, 1984, p. 1.

15 Bolton, *op cit*, p. 291; Kerr, *John Moffat of Irvinebank*, *op cit*, pp. 74–75; Kerr, *Irvinebank: Mining Community and Centre of an Empire*, *op cit*, p. 4.

16 Kerr, *John Moffat of Irvinebank*, *op cit*, p. 128; *Irvinebank: Mining Community and Centre of an Empire*, *op cit*, pp. 5–8.

17 *ibid*, pp. 12–14; *Wild River Times*, 29 March, 14 June,

21 December 1898, 15 November 1899.

18 *Town and Country Journal*, 7 October 1903; Kerr, *Irvinebank: Mining Community and Centre of an Empire*, op cit, p. 16.

19 Kerr, *John Moffat of Irvinebank*, op cit, pp. 221–232, 240–241; *Irvinebank: Mining Community and Centre of an Empire*, op cit, pp. 17–19.

20 The original concentration tables are also still in place and the whole complex is housed under a roof, which is one of the reasons it is so well preserved.

21 Discussions with 'Lappa Liz', October 2001.

22 G.K. Bolton & Ruth S. Kerr, *Chillagoe*, G.K. Bolton, Cairns, 1998, p. 2; *John Moffat of Irvinebank*, op cit, pp. 155–161, 166–167.

23 Bolton & Kerr, op cit, pp. 14, 19–20, 22–24, 30–31.

A BROODING MOUNTAIN

1 P.J. Trezise, *Quinkan Country*, A.H. & A.W. Reed, Sydney, 1969, pp. 66–67.

2 Peter Bell, *'If Anything, Too Safe'. The Mount Mulligan Coalmine Disaster of 1921*, Department of History and Politics, James Cook University, Townsville, 1996, pp. 5–22. Chillagoe Limited's mines, smelters and railways were purchased by the newly elected Labor Government in 1918, but the coal mines remained the property of the Company. Monies were made available by the government under the purchase arrangements to allow for improvements in the mining plant.

3 *ibid*, pp. 22–24.

4 *ibid*, pp. 25–27. This was, in any event, checked out before work commenced.

5 *ibid*, pp. 28–30.

6 *ibid*, pp. 33–39. Bell has commented that if the disaster had occurred in later years a mine rescue would not have been attempted, and the mine would have been permanently sealed with the bodies still below.

7 *ibid*, p. 41; *Brisbane Courier*, 22 September 1921.

8 Bell, op cit, p. 44; *Brisbane Courier*, 21 September 1921.

9 *ibid*, 21 September 1921; Bell, op cit, pp. 43–47.

10 *ibid*, pp. 49–86, 92–104. In addition, the first day of a new cavil could be confusing as the men had to become accustomed to a new workplace and often a new working partner.

11 *ibid*, pp. 112–120, 122–124, 132–135, 142.

12 Alan Foskett, 'Mount Mulligan', *Walkabout*, vol. 20, 1954, p. 37

13 *The Cairns Post*, 31 October 1957.

14 *ibid*, 31 October, 12, 19 November 1957.

15 Bell, op cit, pp. 144–146.

16 *Town and Country Journal*, 29 April 1876. Also quoted in Glenville Pike, *On the Trail of Gold*, Glenville Pike, Mareeba, 1998, p. 46.

17 *ibid*, p. 51.

18 *Town and Country Journal*, 29 April 1876.

19 Pike, op cit, pp. 59–60.

20 *Town and Country Journal*, 3, 17 June 1876.

21 *Brisbane Courier*, 17 March 1877.

22 *ibid*, 9 May, 11 August 1877.

23 *ibid*, 29 September 1877.

24 *ibid*, 29 December 1877; Queensland Department of Mines, *Annual Report*, Brisbane, 1877, p. 12; Noreen Kirkman, 'Mining on the Hodgkinson', in K.H. Kennedy (ed) *Readings in North Queensland Mining History*, vol. II, History Department, James Cook University of North Queensland, Townsville, 1982, p. 178.

25 Queensland Department of Mines, op cit, 1881, p. 18; Kirkman, op cit, p. 182.

26 Queensland Department of Mines, op cit, 1883; p. 24; 1886, p. 31.

27 Kirkman, op cit, pp. 188–189; Frank Dempsey, *Old Mining Towns of North Queensland*, Rigby, Adelaide, 1980, pp. 64–65.

28 Peter Bell, 'Legends from the Mount Mulligan coal mine Disaster', *Royal Historical Society of Queensland. Historical Papers*, X1, 1979–80, pp. 89–102.

THE ROAD TO PALMER

1 P.J. Trezise, *Quinkan Country*, A.H. & A.W. Reed, Sydney, 1969, pp. 15–29.

2 Department of Resource Industries and Queensland National Parks and Wildlife Service, *Golden Palmer Heritage Map*, 1990.

3 Department of Resource Industries and Queensland National Parks and Wildlife Service, op cit.

4 Etheridge correspondent for the *Cleveland Bay Express*, writing from Georgetown on 15 September 1873 and quoted by Noreen Kirkman, 'The Palmer River Goldfield', *North Queensland Mining History*, K.H. Kennedy (ed), History Department, James Cook University, Townsville, 1980, p. 114.

5 Kirkman, op cit, p. 115; *Town and Country Journal*, 27 December 1873.

6 Kirkman, op cit, pp. 116–118; *Town and Country Journal*, 14 March, 9 May, 29 August, 5 December 1874.

7 *ibid*, 14 February, 9, 23 May 1874.

8 *ibid*, 22, 29 August 1874.

9 *ibid*, 24 October, 12, 19 December 1874.

10 *ibid*, 12, 19 June, 6 November 1875.

11 *ibid*, 28 October 1876; Anne Smith & B.J. Dalton, *The Bowly Papers. Letters 1873–78, Reminiscences & Photographs of C.W. Bowly in North Queensland*, Department of History & Politics, James Cook University, Townsville, 1995, p. 116.

12 *Town and Country Journal*, 30 December 1876; Kirkman, op cit, pp. 118–120.

13 *Cooktown Courier*, 17 April 1878, quoted in Kirkman, op cit, p. 119.

14 *The Brisbane Courier*, 16 March 1877.

15 Kirkman, op cit, pp. 132–135.

16 *ibid*, p. 126; John Hay, 'Remnants of a golden era — Palmer River Goldfield 1986', *Journal of the Royal Historical Society of Queensland*, vol. xiii, no. 2, May 1987, p. 65; Peter Bell, *History of the Chinese in Australia*, March 1997, unpublished paper, pp. 13–14; *Town and Country Journal*, 5 August 1876.

17 Kirkman, op cit, p. 127.

18 W.R.O. Hill, *Forty–five Years' Experiences in North Queensland 1861 to 1905*, H. Pole and Co., Brisbane, 1907, pp. 68, 77.

19 Kirkman, op cit, p. 127.

20 Bell, op cit, p. 13; William Henry Corfield, *Reminiscences of*

Queensland, 1862–1899, A.H. Frater, Brisbane, 1921, p. 53; Kirkman, *op cit*, pp. 127–128.

21 Anne Smith & B.J. Dalton, *op cit*, p. 115.

22 J.H. Binnie, *My Life on a Tropic Goldfield*, Bread and Cheese Club, Melbourne, 1944, p. 18.

23 *ibid*, pp. 28–29.

24 *ibid*, p. 36.

25 Bell, *op cit*, p. 15; Noreen Kirkman, 'Chinese miners on the Palmer', *Journal of the Royal Historical Society of Queensland*, vol. xiii, no. 2, May 1987, pp. 58–59.

26 Noel Loos, *Invasion and Resistance: Aboriginal–European relations on the North Queensland frontier, 1861–1897*, Australian National University Press, Canberra, 1982, pp. 71–75.

27 *ibid*, pp. 79–80.

28 Corfield, *op cit*, pp. 63–64.

29 Loos, *op cit*, pp. 83–85; Bell, *op cit*, p. 14; Eric Rolls, *Sojourners*, University of Queensland Press, St Lucia, 1992, pp. 204–204; Hector Holthouse, *River of Gold*, Angus & Robertson, Sydney 1967, pp. 86–97.

30 Bell, *op cit*, p. 14; Bell, 'What happened to the Macquarie Brothers?' Bulletins 276 and 277, December 1982, January 1983, Cairns Historical Society; 'Pauline Hanson and the Cannibalism myth', notes for a paper presented at the Australian Historical Association Conference, Newcastle, 28 September 1997.

31 Taam Sze Pui, *My Life and Work*, Innisfail, 1925, p. 12, quoted in Shen Yuanfang, *Dragon Seed in the Antipodes. Chinese–Australian Autobiographies*, Melbourne University Press, Carlton, 2001, p. 51.

32 Kirkman, 'The Palmer River Goldfield', *op cit*, pp. 135–142.

33 Queensland Department of Mines, *Annual Report*, Brisbane, 1902.

A STOCKBROKER'S PARADISE

1 I am indebted to the staff of Newcrest, who showed me around some of the old mining plant.

2 Discussions with Cassandra van Nooten and Stan Dunwoody, October 2001 and Fred Brophy, January 2002.

3 Discussions with Tommy Mulhall, December 2001.

4 *Morning Bulletin, Rockhampton*, 15 July 1931.

5 A.K. Denmead, 'The Golden Plateau — 1931 to 1976', *Queensland Government Mining Journal*, April 1976, p. 136.

6 *ibid*, pp. 136–137.

7 *Morning Bulletin, Rockhampton*, 15 July 1931.

8 A.K. Denmead, *op cit*, p. 137.

9 *Morning Bulletin, Rockhampton*, 2 April 1932.

10 A.K. Denmead, *op cit*, pp. 137–138.

11 *Morning Bulletin, Rockhampton*, 14–15 July 1932.

12 A.K. Denmead, *op cit*, pp. 137–138.

13 *Morning Bulletin, Rockhampton*, 8, 15, 26 September 1932.

14 *ibid*, 6, 21, 27 October 1932.

15 A.K. Denmead, *op cit*, p. 138.

16 E.S. Watson, *Pioneer Pictures of Cracow Goldfield 1932*, E.S. Watson, 1932.

17 Noela Denmead, 'A Woman's View of the Crackow Rush', *Queensland Government Mining Journal*, April 1976, p. 142.

18 *ibid*, pp. 142–144.

19 *Morning Bulletin, Rockhampton*, 17 January, 12, 27 May, 7 July, 24 November 1933.

20 Queensland Department of Mines, *Annual Report*, Brisbane, 1934, p. 66.

21 A.K. Denmead, *op cit*, p. 138.

22 Queensland Department of Mines, *op cit*, 1937, p. 72.

23 *ibid*, 1938, p. 68; A.K. Denmead, *op cit*, p. 140.

24 *ibid*, p. 140.

25 *Morning Bulletin, Rockhampton*, 20, 30 June, 27 July, 26 August 1938.

26 *ibid*, 20, 30 June, 27 July, 31 August, 14 November, 8 December 1938.

27 Queensland Department of Mines, *op cit*, 1943, p. 78.

28 A.K. Denmead, *op cit*, p .140.

29 *Sunday Mail*, 8 February 1976; *Morning Bulletin*, 9 February, 2 March 1976.

VALLEYS OF OIL

1 R. Ian Jack, 'Joadja, New South Wales; The paragon of early oil-shale communities', *Australasian Historical Archaeology*, 13, 1995, p. 31.

2 *ibid*, pp. 31–32; A.S. Luchetti, 'The oil shale industry: its growth, development and demise', in *The Oil Shale Industry*, A.S. Luchetti (ed), Lithgow District Historical Society, Lithgow, 1979, pp. 12–13; Iris Pariddeus, 'Hartley Vale' in Luchetti, *op cit*, pp. 31–33; *Town and Country Journal*, 21 March 1874. At Hartley Vale there were two companies, one of which had a refining plant in Sydney. Seven years later the two companies merged, and an inclined railway was built to connect the mines with the main Western railway. Most of the shale was sent to the refinery at Sydney.

3 G.H. Eardley, E.M. Stephens, *The Shale Railways of New South Wales*, Australian Railway Historical Society, Sydney, 1974, pp. 88–93, 99–105, 113–115; *Lithgow Mercury*, 4 July 1913. In the 1890s the company's property was acquired by the New South Wales Shale and Oil Company, which was operating at Hartley Vale. In 1906 the New South Wales Shale and Oil Company's properties were purchased by the Commonwealth Oil Corporation, which was about to commence operations at Newnes in the Wolgan Valley.

4 Allan Cargill, 'Glen Davis', in Luchetti, *op cit*, pp. 39–54. It was partly owned by a US company, Gelantine Davis, one quarter by the State Government and one half by the Commonwealth Government.

5 *Sydney Morning Herald*, 9 January, 17 June 1951; Cargill, *op cit*, pp. 47–48. The reports in the *Herald* are based on official government statements, where the blame for falling production was sheeted home directly to the miners. However, according to Allan Cargill, the miners had quite legitimate safety fears.

6 *Sydney Morning Herald*, 29 July 1951.

7 *ibid*, 27 June 1952. They failed by only five days to break the record stay-in strike created by French miners at Auschel.

8 I have seen the video clip at Leonie's and Greg's house at Mittagong. A shadowy figure dressed in a long black frock with

a cassock on the head, unmistakably a priest, can be seen near the retorts. At the end of the clip another figure can be seen to the right of the priest. At least one corroborative story has since come to light. It is still being verified.

9   Heather Burke, Newnes *Shale Oil Complex Archaeological Report*, Report to the Australian Heritage Commission and the NSW Department of Planning, vol. 1, Sydney, 1991, pp. 27–31; Luchetti, *op cit*, p. 18. Prior to 1911 the shale was sent to Torbane for retorting and to Hartley Vale for refining.

10 Lawrence Salter, *The Commonwealth Oil Company at Newnes: A History of the Township and Railway*, Lithgow District Historical Society, Occasional papers, 1982, pp. 10–11.

11 Luchetti, *op cit*, pp. 15–21. His family moved to Newnes from Hartley Vale in 1907, and he was eventually employed on the railway.

12 Salter, *op cit*, pp. 11–16.

13 Burke, *op cit*, pp. 25–27; Luchetti, *op cit*, pp. 16–18; *Lithgow Mercury*, 19 March, 4 July 1913, 16 February 1914.

14 Salter, *op cit*, p. 12; *Lithgow Mercury*, 25 May 1924, 1 June 1927.

15 *ibid*, 5 September 1927.

16 Salter, *op cit*, p. 13.

17 *Lithgow Mercury*, 16 February 1931.

18 Burke, *op cit*, pp. 26–27; *Salter*, *op cit*, p. 13.

19 Leonie Knapman, *Joadja Creek*, Hale & Iremonger, Sydney, 1988, pp. 20–30.

20 *Town and Country Journal*, 4 October 1879.

21 *Sydney Morning Herald*, 30 June 1880.

22 *Knapman*, *op cit*, pp. 40–42, 48–53.

23 *ibid*, pp. 48–50; Leonie Knapman, Adrian Hutton, *Joadja Creek*, Oil Shale Ghost Towns, Mittagong, 1997, p. 9.

24 Knapman, *op cit*, 1988, pp. 60–62, 75–83, 94–96, 98–104.

25 Jack, *op cit*, pp. 38–39.

ALONG THE KIDMAN WAY

1   *Town and Country Journal*, 10 July 1875.

2   NSW Department of Mines, *Annual Report*, Sydney, 1882, p. 117; Neville Burgess, *The Great Cobar*, Neville Burgess, 1995, p. 92, 101; William. J. Bennett, *A Contribution to the History of Mount Hope. The William Clark Story*, privately published monograph, undated, p. 9.

3   NSW Department of Mines, *op cit*, 1885, p. 104.

4   *Town and Country Journal*, 12 May 1888.

5   NSW Department of Mines, *op cit*, 1890, p. 131; 1894, p. 53; 1895, p. 61; 1896, p. 48; 1897, pp. 65, 93; 1902, p. 46; 1906, p. 45, 1909, p. 46; 1914, p. 52. In 1897 the Great Central was also worked on tribute. This method of mining, however, had its disadvantages, for the tendency was to extract only the richest ore and neglect the need for longer-term development.

6   *ibid*, 1894, p. 32; 1895, pp. 29–30; 1896, p. 36; 1902, p. 46.

7   Leila Alderdyce, *Gilgunnia, A Special Place*, Leila Alderdyce, Young, 1994, pp. 24–25, 28–29. The only supply available initially was from nearby Wirchilleba station. A teacher's lot in nineteenth-century gold mining towns was often not a happy one, for officialdom was well aware of the ephemeral nature of many of them and was reluctant to over commit financially. I

retell accounts of some of these tensions in south-east NSW in *Lost Mines Revisited*, Barry McGowan, Canberra, 1996.

8   *ibid*, pp. 26–32; discussions with Norm MacMillan, February 2002.

9   Burgess, *op cit*, pp. 79–80.

10 NSW Department of Mines, *op cit*, 1882, p. 117.

11 *Town and Country Journal*, 19 May 1888.

12 Nymagee Centenary Committee, *Nymagee Centenary 1879–1979*, place of publication unknown, 1979.

13 NSW Department of Mines, *op cit*, 1896, p. 48; 1901, p. 48; 1902, p. 46; 1903, p. 44.

14 *Cobar Leader*, 6 September 1901, 28 March, 4 April 1902; NSW Department of Mines, *op cit*, 1904, p. 44; Burgess, *op cit*, p. 141. By 1904 the small blast furnaces at Nymagee were replaced by one large one.

15 NSW Department of Mines, *op cit*, 1907, p. 50.

16 Nymagee Centenary Committee, *op cit*, p. 10.

17 NSW Department of Mines, *op cit*, 1909, p. 46; 1913, p. 51; Nymagee Centenary Committee, *op cit*, p. 8; *Western Age*, 2 February, 22 June 1917.

18 *ibid*, 15 March, 23 April, 7 June, 27 September 1918.

19 NSW Department of Mines, *op cit*, various years; E.C. Andrew, *The Canbelego, Budgery, and Budgerygar Mines, Part II of the Cobar Copper and Gold-Field*, Geological Survey of New South Wales, Mineral Resources no. 18, Sydney, 1915, pp. 4–8.

20 *Town and Country Journal*, 1 June 1904.

21 Burgess, *op cit*, pp. 164, 195–197.

22 *ibid*, pp. 119–120; NSW Department of Mines, *op cit*, 1894, p. 32; *Town and Country Journal*, 3 November, 29 December 1894.

23 NSW Department of Mines, *op cit*, 1895, p. 29; Burgess, *op cit*, pp. 219–120; *Town and Country Journal*, 30 May 1896; *Cobar Leader*, 25 October, 1901, 3 January 1902.

24 Information provided by Michael and Shirley Mitchell, February 2002.

25 Conversation with Michael and Shirley Mitchell, January 2002; Sheridan Burke, *Bush Lives: Bush Futures*, Historic Houses Trust, Sydney, 1998, p. 63.

BOOM AND BUST ON THE BARRIER

1   NSW Department of Mines, *Annual Report*, Sydney, 1883, p. 113; *Town and Country Journal*, 25 August 1883.

2   *Adelaide Observer*, 22 March, 17 May, 14 June 1884.

3   *ibid*, 14 June 1884.

4   *ibid*, 14 June 1884; *Town and Country Journal*, 25 August, 15 September 1883.

5   A.G. Hales, *The Wanderings of a Simple Child: Sketches of Australian Life*, Runge & Co., Sydney, 1891, pp. 34–35.

6   *Town and Country Journal*, 24 September 1887.

7   *ibid*, 28 June 1884.

8   *Adelaide Observer*, 14, 21 June, 12 July 1884.

9   *Town and Country Journal*, 28 June, 12 July 1884. The Apollyon mine at Day Dream was described as the 'mine par excellence'. The ore was sent to Germany for smelting. A smelter was built in 1885.

10 *ibid*, 26 July 1884; *Adelaide Observer*, 9 August 1884.

11 *ibid*, 23 August 1884.

12 *Town and Country Journal*, 30 August, 6 September 1884; *Adelaide Observer*, 23 August, 27 December 1884.

13 NSW Department of Mines, *op cit*, 1884, pp. 107–108; H.B. Kearns, *Silverton*, Broken Hill Historical Society, Adelaide, 1992, p. 9.

14 *Adelaide Observer*, 27 December 1884; Percy Meggy, *Sydney to Silverton*, H. Solomon, Sydney, 1885, pp. 65–66.

15 *Adelaide Observer*, 17 January, 4, 11, 18 April, 30 May 1885.

16 Kearns, *op cit*, p. 16.

17 *ibid*, pp. 18, 30.

18 *Adelaide Observer*, 29 August 1885.

19 *ibid*, pp. 46–50.

20 *ibid*, pp. 35–37. One of the owners of the railway and BHP was John Reid. He also owned the *Silver Age*.

21 NSW Department of Mines, *op cit*, 1886, p. 101; 1887, p. 104.

22 *Town and Country Journal*, 17 September 1887.

23 Special correspondent of the *Adelaide Observer*, *The Barrier Silver and Tin Fields in 1888*, Adelaide, 1888, pp. 51–52.

24 Kearns, *op cit*, p. 51; Special correspondent of the *Adelaide Observer*, *op cit*, pp. 49–50.

25 *ibid*, pp. 53–54.

26 *Adelaide Observer*, 13 April 1889.

27 NSW Department of Mines, *op cit*, 1886, p. 110.

28 *Town and Country Journal*, 19 November 1887.

29 Special correspondent of the *Adelaide Observer*, *op cit*, pp. 55–58; Barrier Miner Business Directory, 1891.

30 *Town and Country Journal*, 20 August, 3 September, 19 November 1887.

31 NSW Department of Mines, *op cit*, 1887, p. 104; Special correspondent of the *Adelaide Observer*, *op cit*, p. 75.

32 *ibid*, pp. 71–73.

33 Barry McGowan, 'Dust and Dreams. A regional history of mining and community in south-east New South Wales, 1850–1914', Ph.D., ANU, 2001, p. 72; Kearns, *op cit*, p. 51.

34 *Adelaide Observer*, 21 March 1891.

35 *ibid*, 9 May, 13 June 1891; Cyril H. Henshaw, *The Tarrawingee Tramway*, Railmac Publications, Elizabeth, 1984, pp. 11–21.

36 *ibid*, p. 36.

CORNER COUNTRY

1 The first gold on the diggings was found near Depot Glen, but the area was soon abandoned in favour of Mount Browne. *Adelaide Observer*, 26 March 1881.

2 Charles Sturt, *Journal of the Central Australian Expedition 1844–45*, Jill Waterhouse (ed), Caliban Books, London, 1984, p. 20. The party included James Poole and Dr John Brown as officers and young John McDouall Stuart as a draughtsman.

3 Charles Sturt, *Narrative of an Expedition into Central Australia*, T. and W. Boone, 1849, reprinted, Corkwood Press, North Adelaide, 2001, pp. 135–170; Sturt, *Journal, op cit*, pp. 44–48.

4 *ibid*, p. 47; Sturt, *Narrative, op cit*, p. 198, pp. 207–208.

5 *ibid*, p. 175; Daniel George Brock, *To the Desert with Sturt*, Royal Geographical Society of Australia, South Australian Branch, Inc., Adelaide, 1975, pp. 114–116. Brock states that the underground dwelling was about five metres by four metres, and about two metres deep.

6 Sturt, *Journal, op cit*, p. 52; *Narrative, op cit*, p. 204.

7 *ibid*, p. 212.

8 *ibid*, pp. 214–217.

9 Sturt, *Journal, op cit*, pp. 57, 96; *Narrative, op cit*, pp. 218–333; Brock, *op cit*, pp. 177–202.

10 Sturt, *Narrative, op cit*, pp. 333–349; Brock, *op cit*, pp. 203–222.

11 *Adelaide Observer*, 26 March 1881.

12 *ibid*, 4 June 1881.

13 E.F. Murphy, *They Struck Opal!* Associated General Publication, Sydney, reprinted, David & Julie Pawsey, Belair, in association with the White Cliffs History Group Inc, pp. 60–63. According to Murphy the first gold on the field had been found by a man called Evans and his Aboriginal partner, who had found nuggets by digging up the surface with a yam stick. Geoffrey Svenson has commented that there is sufficient corroborating information to lend considerable credence to Murphy's account. Geoffrey Svenson, *Marginal People. The Archaeology and History of the Chinese at Milparinka*. MA. University of Sydney, 1994, p. 38.

14 *ibid*, pp. 63–64. The incident concerning the threatened pulling down of the store was reported in the *Town and Country Journal*, 4 June 1881.

15 *ibid*, 29 October 1881. He discounted the accounts of rowdiness connected with the flour shortages, however, Murphy's account and that of other reporters indicates otherwise.

16 J.C.F. Johnson, *To Mount Browne and Back*, Advertiser Print, Adelaide, 1881, pp. 17–22.

17 *ibid*, pp. 22–23, 30.

18 *Town and Country Journal*, 25 March 1882; *Adelaide Observer*, 25 March 1882.

19 *Town and Country Journal*, 1 April 1882; *Adelaide Observer*, 1, 22, 29 April 1882.

20 Murphy, *op cit*, pp. 71–73.

21 *Town and Country Journal*, 29 April, 13 May 1882; NSW Department of Mines, *Annual Report*, Sydney, 1882, p. 99.

22 *Town and Country Journal*, 25 August, 23 September 1882.

23 *ibid*, 23 September, 7 October 1882.

24 NSW Department of Mines, *op cit*, 1882, pp. 98–99.

25 *Town and Country Journal*, 25 August 1883; NSW Department of Mines, *op cit*, 1883, pp. 115–116.

26 *Town and Country Journal*, 9 August 1884.

27 NSW Department of Mines, *op cit*, 1884, pp. 108–109, 1885, pp. 103–104; 1888, pp. 120–121; 1889, pp. 124–125.

28 *ibid*, 1888, p. 121; 1891, pp. 138–139; 1892, p. 21; 1893, p. 24; 1896, p. 37; 1897, p. 51; 1898, p. 55; 1899, p. 48; 1900, p. 34; 1901, p. 24; 1902, p. 13.

29 Svenson, *op cit*, pp. 47–48, 61, 76–85.

30 John Gerritsen, *Tibooburra. Corner Country*, Tibooburra Press, Tibooburra, 1981, p. 63.

31 *ibid*, pp. 68–69; Svenson, *op cit*, p. 164; Geoffrey Svenson,

What was at Milparinka, Milparinka Archaeology, February 1995, pp. 6–7.

32 Discussions with Phillip Young, January 2002; *Stock Journal*, 1 November 2001, p. 31.

FROM WAUKARINGA TO YUDNAMUTANA

1 *Adelaide Observer*, 12 May 1894.

2 *Adelaide Register*, 11 August 1873, 30 July 1874; C.M. Horn and W.P. Fradd, 'Gold mining in South Australia. The first fifty years', in Jonathon Selby (ed), *South Australia's Mining Heritage*, Special publication no. 7, Department of Mines and Energy and the Australasian Institute of Mining and Metallurgy, Adelaide, 1987, p. 78.

3 Horn and Fradd, *op cit*, p. 82; *Adelaide Observer*, 24 June 1882.

4 *ibid*, 12 May 1894; Horn and Fradd, *op cit*, p. 82.

5 *Adelaide Observer*, 3 March 1888, 22 February, 19 July 1890, 10 January 1891; Horn and Fradd, *op cit*, p. 82.

6 *Adelaide Observer*, 12 May 1894 ; George Farwell, *Ghost Towns Of Australia*, Rigby Limited, Adelaide 1965, pp. 1–16.

7 For instance, the mines were closed in 1874, 1885 and 1889; J.B. Austin, *The Mines of South Australia*, C. Platts, E.S. Wigg, F. Dehane, J. Howell, W.C. Rigby, G. Mullett, 1863, Adelaide, Facsimile edition, 1968; Hans Mincham, *The Story of the Flinders Ranges*, Rigby, Adelaide, 1983, pp. 128–30.

8 Nic Klaassen, *The Northern Flinders Ranges: Mountains, Minerals and Mines*, N. Klaassen, Eden Hills, 1991, pp. 130–131.

9 *ibid*, pp. 171–172; *Adelaide Observer*, 15 September 1888.

10 Klaassen, *op cit*, pp. 171–177; Vivienne May, *Sunny South Australia*, Hussey & Gillingham, Adelaide, 1908, p. 308.

11 *ibid*, pp. 119–122; Geoffrey Blainey, *The Rush That Never Ended*, Melbourne University Press, Carlton, 1981, pp. 114–115; Klaassen, *op cit*, pp. 53–55.

12 *ibid*, p. 53.

13 *Adelaide Register*, 12 September 1861.

14 Austin, *op cit*, p. 68; Klaassen, *op cit*, pp. 59–61.

15 *ibid*, pp. 62–65; Mincham, *op cit*, p. 126.

16 Graham Aird and Nic Klaassen, *Beltana. The Town That Will Not Die*, Lutheran Publishing House, Adelaide, pp. 9–11.

17 Rebecca Parkes, 'Of Camels and Cameleers. The archaeology of Afghan settlements in Australia', BA (hons), ANU, Canberra, 1997, pp. 9–11. Parkes has remarked that most of the cameleers came from Afghanistan, Pakistan and Baluchistan, but others also came from Turkey, Egypt and Iran.

18 *ibid*, pp. 12–15.

19 Aird and Klaassen, *op cit*, pp. 14–15.

20 *ibid*, pp. 15–17.

21 Klaasen, *op cit*, pp. 183–199.

22 *ibid*, pp. 199–200; Nic Klaassen, *Sliding Rock*, Nic Klaassen, Eden Hills, 1988, pp. 169–173.

23 *ibid*, pp. 187–188; Klaassen, *The Northern Flinders Ranges*, *op cit*, pp. 201–204.

24 Austin, *op cit*, p. 48.

25 Reg C. Sprigg, *Arkaroola–Mount Painter in the Northern Flinders Ranges, S.A. The Last Billion Years*, Arkaroola Pty. Ltd., Adelaide, 1984, p. 243; Mincham, *op cit*, p. 136; Trevor Gibbons,

Tracks in a Wilderness, Rostrevor College, Adelaide, 1975, p. 50.

26 Austin, *op cit*, pp. 47–48.

27 Sprigg, *op cit*, pp. 239–242.

28 *ibid*, pp. 135–136.

LEAVING THE LAND

1 D.W. Meinig, *On the Margins of the Good Earth*, Rigby Limited, Adelaide, 1972, pp. 22–24.

2 *ibid*, pp. 26–28, 166–175.

3 Surveyor-General's Report on Demarcation of Northern Rainfall, South Australia, *Parliamentary Papers*, 1865–66, vol. 2, p. 78; Report of Surveyor-General on Northern Runs, South Australia, *Parliamentary Papers*, 1865–66, vol. 2, p. 82.

4 Meinig, *op cit*, pp. 45–46; Minutes of Evidence on State of Northern Runs, South Australia, *Parliamentary Papers*, 1870–71, vol. 2, P.N. 23, paras 3918–19, p. 113; Report on Victorian Land Regulations, South Australia, *Parliamentary Papers*, 1870–71, vol. 2, P.N. 23, p. 8.

5 Meinig, *op cit*, pp. 41–45, 52–53.

6 *ibid*, pp. 54–56; South Australia, *Parliamentary Debates*, 5 November 1874, cl. 2235.

7 Meinig, *op cit*, pp. 59–64.

8 Correspondence Concerning Annual Leases, South Australia, *Parliamentary Papers*, 1876, vol. 3, P.N. 145, p. 2.

9 Meinig, *op cit*, pp. 66–67.

10 *ibid*, pp. 76–77, 145–152.

11 John Ednie Brown, Annual Progress Report of the Forest Reserves, And Forest Conservancy Generally, South Australia, *Parliamentary Papers*, 1879, vol. 3, P.N. 83, p. 20; Meinig, *op cit*, p. 71; Michael Williams, 'George Woodroofe Goyder: A Practical Geographer', *Proceedings of the Royal Geographical Society of Australasia (SA Branch)*, vol. 79, 1978, p. 17.

12 Meinig, *op cit*, pp. 78–79.

13 *ibid*, pp. 82–83; South Australia, *Parliamentary Debates*, 22 June 1882, cl.163–165.

14 *Adelaide Observer*, 25 February, 4 March 1882.

15 *Meinig*, p. 90. A harvest of six bushels per acre as an average for the previous three seasons was established as the minimum profitable crop. Those who received less were allowed a remission of interest payments on a graduated basis. Farmers wishing to reselect a new holding could transfer the amount of their original purchase money and value of improvements as part payment on the cost of the new selection. *Adelaide Observer*, 4, 11 March 1882.

16 The dramatic fall in wheat yields is portrayed in an 1884 Parliamentary paper showing a map of South Australian wheat areas with yields by Hundreds set against the outline of Goyder's Line. The alignment of the Line with the poor yields in 1880–1882 is striking. South Australia, *Parliamentary Papers*, 1883–84, vol. 4, P.N. 76; Barry McGowan, 'Goyder's Line, Australia's first environmental debate? — An historical perspective', *Canberra Historical Journal*, no. 25, March 1990, p. 31; *Adelaide Observer*, 10 March 1883.

17 Meinig, *op cit*, pp. 91–92.

18 *ibid*, p. 170

19 Michael Williams, 'The northern areas: The last fifty years' change', *Proceedings of the Royal Geographical Society of*

Australasia (SA Branch), vol. 75, 1974, pp. 1–10.

20 Peter Bell, 'Heritage of the Upper North Region: Background history', unpublished paper.

21 Hans Mincham, *Hawker…Hub of the Flinders*, Hawker Centenary Committee, 1980, pp. 73, 81–83.

22 *ibid*, pp. 64, 115.

23 The Book Centenary Committee, *Quorn and District Centenary 1878–1978*, Lutheran Publishing House, 1978, pp. 145–146.

24 *ibid*, pp. 143–144.

25 Mincham, *op cit*, pp. 55, 59, 68, 71–75; information provided by David Frost, Cradock hotel, January 2002.

26 *ibid*, pp. 73–79, 116–117.

27 Williams, *op cit*, pp. 20–21.

28 The Book Centenary Committee, *op cit*, p. 131.

29 Lois Litchfield, *Marree and the Tracks Beyond in Black and White. Commemorating the Centenary of Marree 1883–1983*, Lois Litchfield, Adelaide, 1983, pp. 163–164; Helen Ferber, *Stagecoach to Birdsville*, Kangaroo Press, Kenthurst, 1995, pp. 21–24.

30 *Town and Country Journal*, 19 January 1884.

31 Litchfield, *op cit*, pp. 163–164; Ferber, *op cit*, p. 24.

A PLACE OF PUNISHMENT

1 David Burn, *An Excursion to Port Arthur in 1842*, J.W. Beattie, Hobart, 1998, p. 19.

2 Alex Graeme-Evans, *A Short History Guide to Port Arthur 1830–1877*, Regal Publications, Launceston, 2001, pp. 7–10.

3 Ian Brand, *Port Arthur. 1830–1877*, Jason Publications, Moonah, 1982, p. 21.

4 Brand, *op cit*, pp. 25–26; Graeme-Evans, *op cit*, p. 11; Margaret Weidenhofer, *Port Arthur. A Place of Misery*, B. & M. Reid in association with Port Arthur Historic Site Management Authority, Port Arthur, 1990, pp. 58, 62.

5 *ibid*, pp. 58–62.

6 Linus W. Miller, *Notes of an Exile to Van Dieman's Land*, SR Publishers Limited, Johnson Reprint Corporation, Toronto, 1968, p. 347.

7 Weidenhofer, *op cit* pp. 16–18, 67–73; Brand, *op cit*, p. 29.

8 *ibid*, pp. 63–65; Graeme-Evans, *op cit*, pp. 12–13.

9 *ibid*, pp. 12–13; Brand, *op cit*, pp. 29–30, 33; Weidenhofer, *op cit*, pp. 51–52.

10 Weidenhofer, *op cit*, pp. 34–35; Brand, *op cit*, pp. 42–46.

11 Graeme-Evans, *op cit*, pp. 18–19; Brand, *op cit*, pp. 32, 34; Weidenhofer, *op cit*, pp. 94–98; Miller, *op cit*, pp. 328–331.

12 Weidenhofer, *op cit*, pp. 98, 100, 103; Brand, *op cit*, pp. 32–34, Graeme-Evans, *op cit*, p. 20.

13 Ian Brand, *The Port Arthur Coal Mines 1833–1877*, Regal Publications, Launceston, undated, pp. 1–18.

14 Thomas Lempriere, *The Penal Settlements of Early Van Diemen's Land*, Royal Society of Tasmania (Northern Branch), Hobart, 1954, pp. 78–79.

15 Brand, *The Port Arthur Coal Mines*, *op cit*, pp. 59–79.

16 Graeme-Evans, *op cit*, p. 26; Brand, *Port Arthur*, *op cit*, pp. 71–74.

17 Burn, *op cit*, p. 18.

18 George Mundy, *A Record of Observations in Van Diemen's Land*, Adelaide, Sullivan's Cove, 1986, pp. 55–59.

19 Graeme-Evans, *op cit*, pp. 16–17.

20 *ibid*, pp. 16–17, 38; Brand, Port Arthur, *op cit*, pp. 52–54.

21 *ibid*, p. 70; Graeme-Evans, *op cit*, p. 46.

22 Brand, *Port Arthur*, *op cit*, pp. 66–69; Weidenhofer, *op cit*, pp. 75–85.

23 *Advertiser*, 22 August 1860, interpretation signs, Port Arthur; also Weidenhofer, *op cit*, p. 86. She commented that the men may have been located in C wing, which had been extended for the worst of the mentally ill.

24 Graeme-Evans, *op cit*, pp. 44–48.

25 Weidenhofer, *op cit*, pp. 124–125; *Tasmanian Mail*, 25 September, 30 October, 11 December 1886, 8 January 1887.

26 *ibid*, 27 February 1886.

27 *Hobart Mercury*, 31 January 1895.

28 *ibid*, 4, 5 January 1898.

29 Story told by a Port Arthur guide, March 2002.

PERDITION AND PARADISE

1 Alex Graeme-Evans, *A Short History Guide to Port Arthur, 1830–77*, Regal Publications, Launceston, 2001, pp. 6–7; Ian Brand, *Sarah Island Penal Settlements 1822–1833 and 1846–1847*, Regal Publications, Launceston, 1995, pp. 13, 18. Upon arrival in the colony the convicts were assigned to work for private persons, usually, but not always, in the country districts.

2 *ibid*, p. 15.

3 *ibid*, pp. 50–52.

4 Thomas Lempriere, *The Penal Settlements of Early Van Diemen's Land*, Royal Society of Tasmania (Northern Branch), Hobart, 1954, pp. 27–30; Brand, *op cit*, p. 20.

5 Hans Julen, *The Penal Settlement of Macquarie Harbour, 1822–1833*, Mary Fisher Bookshop, Launceston, 1976, pp. 55–59; Brand, *op cit*, pp. 56–57.

6 Brand, *op cit*, pp. 54–55, 65; Julen, *op cit*, pp. 73–75.

7 Brand, *op cit*, pp. 23, 42–43.

8 Lempriere, *op cit*, p. 37; Brand, *op cit*, pp. 23–28.

9 *ibid*, pp. 20, 42–43; Lempriere, *op cit*, p. 30.

10 Brand, pp. 16, 35–36; Lempriere, *op cit*, p. 39. According to Lempriere, the convicts from Gummet Island had to make do with a morning and evening meal only as they could not be trusted with provisions because of their many attempts to escape. Lempriere, *op cit*, p. 47.

11 The Round Earth Company, *Sarah Island. The People Ships & Shipwrights. A Guided Tour*, Australian Foundation for Culture & the Humanities, undated, p. 10.

12 *ibid*, pp. 4, 11, 13; Brand, *op cit*, pp. 51–53.

13 *ibid*, p. 67.

14 Margaret Weidenhofer, *Maria Island. A Tasmanian Eden*, Darlington Press, Richmond, 1977, pp. 18–20.

15 *ibid*, pp. 21–22; Lempriere, *op cit*, p. 58.

16 Weidenhofer, *op cit* , pp. 18–26. For an account of the establishment and operation of the probation system, see A.G.L. Shaw, *Convicts & the Colonies*, Melbourne University Press, Carlton, 1981, pp. 274–311.

17 G.C. Mundy, *A Record of Observations in Van Diemen's Land*, Sullivan's Cove, Adelaide, 1986, p. 11.

18 Parks and Wildlife Service Tasmania, *Parks and Places, Historic Darlington*, information brochure.

19 *ibid*; Weidenhofer, *op cit*, p. 26.

20 Mundy, *op cit*, p. 11.

21 Weidenhofer, *op cit*, pp. 30–32.

22 *Tasmanian Mail*, 23 October 1886, 1 January 1887.

23 Weidenhofer, *op cit*, pp. 36–38.

24 *Tasmanian Mail*, 7, 28 April 1888.

25 Weidenhofer, *op cit*, pp. 50–52.

WHEN COPPER WAS KING

1 *Sunday Tasmanian*, 10 March 2002.

2 Patsy Crawford, *King. The Story of a River*, Montpelier Press, Dynnyrne, 2000, p. 86.

3 Geoffrey Blainey, *The Peaks of Lyell*, St. David's Park Publishing, Hobart, 1993, pp. 24–32. In the following year Henry also acquired a one-tenth interest in the Iron Blow.

4 Gold and copper are associated minerals, and many copper mining fields began life as goldfields. In this instance the gold was also associated with iron.

5 *ibid*, pp. 32–68.

6 *ibid*, pp. 69–81. Pyritic smelting was introduced for the first time. It was dependent upon the heat generated by the combustion of the iron and sulphur in the pyritic ore as fuel for the furnace, thus reducing dramatically the amount of coke used in smelting.

7 *Zeehan & Dundas Herald*, 2 November 1894, quoted in Noeline Bradshaw, Gormanston, privately published and undated.

8 *Tasmanian Mail*, 27 June 1896, quoted in Noeline Bradshaw, *Goodnight Mt Lyell*, privately published and undated; *Town and Country Journal*, 9 May 1896.

9 Blainey, *op cit*, pp. 112–125. Crotty was angry at his inability to be a director of the Mount Lyell Company and at Kelly's adamant refusal to allow a trial survey of a railway between Mt Lyell and Kelly basin at the south east end of Macquarie Harbour. He had no difficulties in raising the capital for his own railway and smelters, for he had found a fabulously rich copper lode, which would yield more than three times as much copper as the Iron Blow.

10 David Bannear, *King River to Kelly Basin Archaeological Survey*, Occasional Paper no. 29, Department of Parks, Wildlife and Heritage and Forestry Commission, Tasmania, Hobart, 1991, pp. 60–68.

11 *ibid*, pp. 72–76. The Minister responsible was very dismissive of his critics, saying that the houses were mere huts or hovels, but obviously this was not the case in all instances.

12 *ibid*, pp. 79–81, 97.

13 Blainey, *op cit*, pp. 92–101.

14 *ibid*, pp. 125–129, 145–160.

15 *Hobart Mercury*, 2 June 1903; *Zeehan & Dundas Herald*, 26 May to 5 June 1903; Hans Julen, *A Brief History of the North Mount Lyell Copper Company 1897–1903*, H. Julen, Launceston, 1994, pp. 41–43; Blainey, *op cit*, p. 160.

16 Bannear, *op cit*, pp. 105–111.

17 *Zeehan & Dundas Herald*, 27 April, 1, 8, 15, 21–23, 27 May 1903; Blainey, *op cit*, pp. 184–186.

18 Edward John (Rocky) Wedd, *Linda, Ghost Town of Mt Lyell*, Strahan, 1987, pp. 2, 19; Blainey, *op cit*, pp. 184–186.

19 Wedd, *op cit*, pp. 1–2, 12–13, 17–18.

20 Blainey, *op cit*, pp. 214–230.

21 Wedd, *op cit*, p. 85; Blainey, *op cit*, pp. 233–235.

22 *ibid*, pp. 233–235; Wedd, *op cit*, pp. 86–90.

23 *Back to Gormanston*, 30 September 1922, courtesy of Noelene Bradshaw.

24 *Back to Linda Valley*, 17 March 1923, courtesy of Noelene Bradshaw.

25 Blainey, *op cit*, pp. 269–272, 293–294.

26 *ibid*, pp. 340–341.

27 Discussions with Noeline Bradshaw, April 2002.

FROM STEIGLITZ TO FRYERSTOWN

1 Ray Sumner, *Steiglitz. Memories of Gold*, National Parks Service, Victoria, Melbourne, 1982, pp. 10–17; Gold Centenary Memorial Committee, *History of Steiglitz 1835–1951*, publisher unknown, 1951, p. 3. The von Steiglitz family remained long enough to see the early gold rushes, but presumably they were discouraged by that experience, for they were pastoralists, not miners, and they returned to Ireland in 1853.

2 Sumner, *op cit*, pp. 23–36.

3 *ibid*, pp. 16–17; Gold Centenary Memorial Committee, *op cit*, pp. 4–6. The two main companies were the Steiglitz Quartz Crushing Co and Dr Otway's Crushing Co. The average yield was almost seven ounces a ton, which was extremely high. Despite the richness of many of these mines, most of the miners on the field in 1862 were engaged in alluvial mining.

4 Sumner, *op cit*, pp. 28–30; Gold Centenary Memorial Committee, *op cit*, pp. 6–7.

5 *ibid*, pp. 9–10; Sumner, *op cit*, pp. 20–21, 27.

6 Gold Centenary Memorial Committee, *op cit*, pp. 10–13; Sumner, *op cit*, p. 31.

7 Gold Centenary Memorial Committee, *op cit*, pp. 11–13.

8 Sumner, *op cit*, pp. 32–34.

9 *Geelong Advertiser*, 14 February, 4, 20 March, 19 June, 3 July 1895.

10 *ibid*, 3, 16 July 1895; Gold Centenary Memorial Committee, *op cit*, pp. 14–15. The newspaper became a one-sheet publication before it was sold in 1903 and incorporated into the *Meredith Sentinel*.

11 Discussion with Les Simmons, January, April 2002.

12 *Mount Alexander Mail*, 9 September 1854, 6 April 1855; G.O. Brown, *Reminiscences of Fryerstown*, G.O. Brown, Castlemaine, 1985, pp. 23–26.

13 *Mount Alexander Mail*, 3 August 1855; Brown, *op cit*, pp. 19–22.

14 *Mount Alexander Mail*, 16, 22, 1855, 26 June 1857; Brown, *op cit*, pp. 57, 71.

15 *Mount Alexander Mail*, 27 November 1857.

16 Brown, *op cit*, pp. 100–105; Ruth A. Rowe, *Fryerstown*, Constance Browning, 1982, pp. 5–6, 18. Ruth Rowe was born in Fryerstown in 1888. She remembered that the Chinese were

often teased by the boys, who sometimes stole their fruit and vegetables.

17 Lesley J. Morton, *The Duke of Cornwall Mine, Fryerstown*, Victoria, Lesley J. Morton, Melbourne, 1992, pp. 1–23.

18 Brown, *op cit*, pp. 178–189; Verne Hooper, *Mining My Past. A Life in Gold Mining*, Friends of Mount Alexander Diggings and Parks Victoria, Castlemaine, 2001, pp. 4–8; *Mount Alexander Mail*, 18 December 1857.

19 Brown, *op cit*, pp. 7, 82–86.

20 *ibid*, pp. 94–99.

21 *ibid*, pp. 106–110.

22 Rowe, *op cit*, pp. 8–10.

23 *ibid*, pp. 11, 16, 18–19.

24 Brown, *op cit*, pp. 131–132.

25 Rowe, *op cit*, pp. 4–5.

26 *Mount Alexander Mail*, 26 October 1855, provided by Jeannie Lister.

27 Mrs Bessie Tucker, *Original Firm of Ball & Welch*, private paper, provided by Jeannie Lister; Jeannie Lister, 'The old Vaughan burial ground', private paper, unpublished.

28 Alexander Land Protection Association, *Notes on the history of the Golden Point area, near Chewton*, 1989, pp. 26–48. Provided courtesy of the Castlemaine Historical Society.

TARNAGULLA AND BEYOND

1 Edna & Ken Arnold, *Tarnagulla & District. The Way It Was*, Crown Castleton Publishers, Golden Square, 1992, p. 94.

2 *Maryborough and Dunolly Advertiser*, 22, 29 July 1857; Lynne Douthat, *The Footsteps Echo. Impressions from Waanyarra*, Lynne Douthat, 1989, p. 7.

3 *Maryborough and Dunolly Advertiser*, 4, 8 December 1857.

4 *ibid*, 1, 19 January, 11, 25 May, 6 July 1858.

5 *Supplement to the Maryborough and Dunolly Advertiser*, 10 August 1858; *Maryborough and Dunolly Advertiser*, 3 September, 5 October 1858, 4 January 1859.

6 *ibid*, 10, 12, 19, 26 August, 2 September, 7, 10 October, 18 November 1859, 11 January 1860.

7 *Dunolly and Burnt Creek Express*, 14 June 1862.

8 *Maryborough and Dunolly Advertiser*, 15 August 1862.

9 *Dunolly and Burnt Creek Express*, 14 March, 11 April 1863.

10 *ibid*, 14 March 1863.

11 *ibid*, 16 May 1863.

12 *ibid*, 23 May 1863.

13 *ibid*, 26 October, 23 November 1863, 4, 21, 25 January, 25 April 1864.

14 *ibid*, 9, 23 May, 6, 23 June 1864; *Tarnagulla Courier*, 15 April, 19 August, 7 October 1865, 14 July 1866; Arnold, *op cit*, p. 36.

15 *Tarnagulla Courier*, 19 November 1864.

16 *ibid*, 30 November, 14 December 1867.

17 Committee of Management, Tarnagulla Recreation Parks, *Tarnagulla Recreation Reserve and Reservoir. A Brief History*, Tarnagulla, 1990, pp. 5–8.

18 *Town and Country Journal*, 26 November 1887; Arnold, *op cit*, p. 41.

19 *ibid*, pp. 15, 18–19.

20 *Maryborough and Dunolly Advertiser*, 10 August 1858; *Dunolly and Burnt Creek Express*, 17 January, 11 April 1863.

21 *ibid*, 11 April, 23, 30 May, 13 June, 8 August 1863; *Dunolly, Tarnagulla and St. Arnaud Express*, 29 October, 12 November, 31 December 1863.

22 *ibid*, 8 February, 7, 21, 28 March, 25 April 1864.

23 John Tully, *The Welcome Stranger Discovery Walk*, brochure, March 1990.

24 *Dunolly, Tarnagulla and St. Arnaud Express*, 26 October 1863, 24 November 1866, 30 November 1867.

25 Arnold, *op cit*, pp. 71–72.

26 Douthat, *op cit*, pp. 5, 9–11; *Maryborough and Dunolly Advertiser*, 10 August 1858.

27 Douthat, *op cit*, p. 57.

28 *ibid*, pp. 28–29; Arnold, *op cit*, pp. 9–13, 54–55.

29 Douthat, *op cit*, pp. 11–16.

A TALE TOO OFTEN TOLD

1 William C. Meldrum, *'Year By Year'. District Items of Interest*, Robert Luehman, Merino, 2001.

2 T.D. Clarke, *Some Early Memoirs of Merino*, 1937 Merino Back To Committee, republished 1995, pp. 3–12.

3 Meldrum, *op cit*, pp. 6–11; Margaret Kibble, *Men of Yesterday. A Social History of the Western Districts of Victoria 1834–1890*, Melbourne University Press, Carlton, pp. 434–435.

4 Meldrum, *op cit*, pp. 6–11, 15–16.

5 Discussions with Bob Luehman, January, March 2002.

6 Stockinbingal Public School Centenary Committee, *The Stockinbingal Story*, Stockinbingal, undated, pp. 7–15, 51.

7 *ibid*, pp. 17–18; *Cootamundra Herald*, 1 August 1911.

8 *ibid*, p. 19; *Cootamundra Herald*, 19 November 1913.

9 Stockinbingal Public School Centenary Committee, *op cit*, pp. 41–45.

10 *ibid*, pp. 46–49, 54–57.

11 Information provided by Gwen Smith, March 2002.

12 Information provided by Pat Shiels and Rae Webber, May 2002; *Canberra Times*, 17 March 1917.

13 Steven Guth, *The Galong School Centenary Book*, Galong, 1990, p. 8; Max Barrett, *King of Galong Castle: The Story of Ned Ryan: 1786–1871*, M. Barrett, Brighton, 1978, pp. 116–146.

14 Guth, *op cit*, pp. 10, 40.

15 *ibid*, p. 40; *The Harden Express*, 13 September 1917.

16 *ibid*, 28 February 1918.

17 Max Barrett, *Galong Cemetery*, Church Archivists' Press, Virginia, 1995, pp. 87–88.

18 Guth, *op cit*, p. 29, 33, 44; discussions with Greg and Athol Luke, April 2002.

19 *The Harden Express*, 19 July, 16, 30 August, 6 September, 18 October, 1, 8, 22 November 1917.

20 *ibid*, 11 April, 22 August, 12, 19 September, 3 October, 14 November 1929; 24 April, 21 October, 1930, 5 March, 9 April, 30 July, 10 September 1931, 21 April, 9 June 1932.

21 Discussions with Greg and Athol Luke, April 2002.

Index

Aboriginal Australians 53, 156, 158
  art 11, 87, 133–4
  heritage 11, 125, 156
  labourers 41, 47, 55
  legend 78, 86
  pearl divers 33–4
  prospectors and miners 11, 18, 46, 55
  race relations 33–4, 40–1, 55, 69, 73, 90–6
  stockmen 4
  women 33–4, 47, 55, 69, 95
Adelaide 54, 128, 135–8, 150–60
Afghan people 8, 18, 22–3, 55, 135, 141, 145, 168
Agnew 12
agriculture 160–8, 172–5, 222–8
Airly 108
Aitken, Thomas 60
Albert 143–4
alcohol 5, 16, 26, 41, 52–5, 60, 67–8, 71–3, 84, 89–94, 101, 114, 120, 126–9, 140–3, 149–52, 180–3, 194, 202–7, 227
Alice Springs 48, 50–5
Annean, Lake 4, 9
Anti-Chinese League 93
Arkaroola 157
Arltunga 48–56
Arthur, Lieutenant-Governor 180, 182
Ashburton goldfields 31
Austin, JB 151, 154, 157–8
Australian Council of Trade Unions 109
Australian Inland Mission (AIM) 41, 46–7, 155
Australian Labor Party 104, 228
Australian Natives' Association 6, 65, 195, 203–4, 223

Baker, William 136, 145
Ballarat 205
Barrier Ranges 126
Barron, Sir Harry 16
Barry, William 70
Barunga 46
Bathurst 109
Bayley's Island 4
Beltana 142, 152, 154–6
Belton 163, 165
Bernacchi family 186–9
Big Bell 3, 10–11
Binalong 227
Binnie, J 93–4
Birdsville 138
Black Elvire 39
Black Rock 159, 163
Blainey, Geoffrey 14, 191, 196
Blinman 151–3, 161
Blue Mountains 107, 112
Boer War 208
Bolla Bollana 158

Bookham 228
Boulder 20–2
Bowen River 82
Bowen 60
Bowly, Charles 92–3
Bowral 114
Boyd, Commandant James 178, 185
Bradshaw family 190, 198
Brady, Matthew 181
Broad Arrow 28
Brockmans Gully 39
Brocks Creek 42-4
Broken Hill 126, 130–6, 149
Broome 31, 37
Brown, HYL 52
Brown, John 163
Bruce 159, 163
Bulong 28
Burdett, Fred 40–1
Burn, David 171, 176
Burrundie 45
Burtville 25
Byerstown 84, 89
Byjerkerno Gorge 133–4

Cadnia see Sliding Rock
Cairns 68, 75, 83, 85
Calcifer 77
Calcutta 66
California 1
Cameron, Mary Jane 129–130
Canada 173
Canbelego 121, 123–4
cannibalism 96, 181
Capertee 108
Carnarvon (Tas.) 178–9
Carnegie, The Hon. David 41
Carrieton 163
Casterton 223
Castlemaine 204, 207–8
Castleton 70
cemeteries 3–4, 9, 12, 21(9, 38, 49–51, 72, 78, 81–8, 94–6, 134–6, 144, 181, 190, 209, 220
Charles Sturt's Central Australian Expedition (1844-45) 136–9, 141
Charleston 69–71
Charters Towers 61–4, 89
Chewton 205–8
Chile 183
Chillagoe 69, 75–8
China 15, 93, 181, 206
Chinese
  business owners 35, 43–4, 61–8, 85–8, 91–4, 166
  market gardeners 35, 43, 55, 62, 69–73, 85–6, 91–3, 119–126, 143, 166–8, 206, 224
  miners 43–4, 61–2, 68, 91–3, 205–6, 211–2
  race relations 44–6, 61, 68–9, 92–6, 121, 206, 211–2
  railway labourers 44–5, 168

scrub cutters 120, 125
temples 42, 45, 92
villages 42–5, 69, 88–9, 120, 168, 209, 211–12
churches and religion 5–11, 16, 20, 31, 36, 56, 59–67, 74–9, 83, 85, 98, 101, 108–111, 114, 117–35, 150–9, 166–8, 171–9, 181–9, 192–8, 201–8, 211–12, 215–20, 223–7
Claraville 54, 56
Clark, James 31–2
Cloncurry 64
Cobar 117–8, 122–5
Coleraine 223
Collinsville 83
Condon 37
convicts 171–186, 188
Cooktown 84–7, 91–5
Coolgardie 14, 22
Coolgarra 73
Cooper's Creek 138
Cootamundra 224–5
Corfield, W 68, 93–5
Cornish people 120, 205–9
Cossack 30–8
councils see shires
Country Women's Association 103, 109, 225
Courtenay, Commandant 174
Cracow 97–104
Cradock 159, 163, 165–6
Crossroads, The 49, 50, 54
Crotty 190, 194–5
Crotty, James, 191–2
Crowl Creek 121
Crush, Thomas 42
Cuddingwarra, 4
Cue 3–13, 21
Cue, Tom 4
Cumberland 69
Curr, Marmaduke 60

dairy industry 78, 120, 175, 220, 223–4, 228
Dalton see Black Rock
Dame Mary Gilmore see Cameron, Mary
Darling River 129, 137–8
Darlington 184–9
Darwin 39, 42
Davyhurst 28
Dawson River 101, 103
Dawson 159, 161–3, 167–8
Day Dawn 3–4 ,7–9
Day Dream 126–8, 131–2, 135
Day, Harriet 39
Deason, John 219
Delaney family 59, 66–7
Denmead family 99–101, 103
Depot Glen 136–8
Dickens, Charles and EBL 129
Digby 223
Dimbulah 78

disease see health
drought 85, 119, 123, 137–8, 142–5, 158-168
drunkenness see alcohol
Duke of Edinburgh 216, 220
Dunolly 212, 216, 219

Eaglehawk Neck 171–2
Eastern goldfields 13, 21, 28
Echotown 89, 92–3
economic depression
  1890s 52, 87, 145
  1930s 13, 46, 56, 65, 77, 82, 97, 112, 165–6, 204, 220–8
education 4, 15, 20–7, 31–8, 69, 70–9, 83–6, 92, 100, 104, 107–8, 114–124, 130–2, 143–5, 151–6, 166–8, 172–6, 182–9, 194–8, 202–3, 208, 211–12, 216–19
Edwardstown 91
Egan, John 222
Eidsvold 97
Eighty Mile Camp 39
Einasleigh 70
Elder, Thomas 154
Emuford 75
England 171–4, 180–8
Etheridge goldfield 61, 68–70, 77, 89, 95
Eurelia 159, 163
Euriowie 126, 132–5
Euro 28
Evelyn Creek 137–8

families 7, 18-9, 37, 46, 56, 61–5, 73, 81–3, 99, 112, 115, 120, 129–31, 151–6, 167, 172–4, 177, 182, 186, 188, 194–6, 215, 221, 226
Farina 151, 158, 162, 167–8
Farmers Mutual Association 163
Farmers and Settlers Association 225
farming see agriculture
Federation 8–9
Fitzgerald, Michael 4
Flinders Ranges 151, 158–9
Flying Doctor Service 41
Flynn, Rev. John 155
Forbes 224
Forrest, Sir John 25
Forsayth 69, 70
Fort Grey 138
Four Mile Diggings 140–1
France 186
Fremantle 41
Fryers Creek goldfield 205–9
Fryerstown 204–10

Galong 221, 226–8
Georgetown 69, 89
Geraldton 4
German Bar 89, 91, 94
ghosts 3, 38, 47, 66–7, 75, 81–6,

98, 109, 145, 179
Gilberton 68–9
Gilgunnia 119–24
Girilambone 122
Glen Davis 108–9, 112
Glen Luce 206
Goan Downs 120
Golden Gully 205
Golden Mile (WA) 20–1
Goongarrie 28
Gordon 159, 163–8
Gordon River 196
Gormanston 190–8
Government Gums *see* Farina
Goyder, George Woodroffe 160–3
Goyder's Line 160–5
Granite Creek 88
Grove Hill 43, 45
Grummet Island 182–3
Gwalia 12–20
Gympie 97, 103

Hales, Alfred 127
Half Way diggings 213
Halls Creek 39–42, 56
Hamilton 223
Hammond 159, 163–4
Hannan, Paddy 28
Hard Hills 214, 219
Harden 224, 226
Hartley Vale 107–8
Harts Range 50
Harvey family 125
Hatt, Captain David 211
Hawker 169
Hays, Fannie 42, 45
health
  diseases 4–10, 17, 21, 29, 46–7,
    65, 110–15, 121, 129, 138,
    141–3, 176–8, 193
  sanitation 4, 15, 21, 24, 53, 100-
    1, 110, 120, 129, 193
Heffernan, Ted 4, 7
Henrie, A 153
Herberton 73
Heron nugget 205
Heron, Thomas 205
Hill, WRO 93
Hillston 117
Hobart 171–5, 180–4
Hoche, Edward 168
Hodgkinson, W 60
Hodgkinson goldfield 61, 83–6
Homestead Protection League 193
Hong Kong 44
Hooper, Edward 14
Hoover, Herbert 3, 8, 13–15
Hope, George 5, 7
Horseshoe Bend 205
hotels 3–9, 11–19, 21–8, 30–6,
  41–9, 55–6, 61, 66–79, 83–7,
  91–9, 108–10, 117–36, 141–5,
  150–5, 159–68, 172, 178–9,
  187–198, 201–4, 207–8, 211–18,
  220–9
Hoy, David 182–3
Hutton, Dave 81

Ida 88
Idriess, Ion 41
Indonesia 35

Indonesian people 31
industrial disputes *see* mining,
  industrial relations
Inglewood 214
Ipswich 80
Ireland 29
Irvinebank 73–5, 78
Italy 19
  Italian people 8, 14, 18, 186

Jaowyn people 46
Japan 182
  Japanese people 8, 24, 31, 35–8,
    41
Jarman Island 37
Joadja 113–16
Johnburg 159, 163, 165
Johnson, J 141
Jones Creek 212
Jowalbinna 87

Kalgoorlie 18, 20–2, 28
Kanowna 27–9
Kanyaka 159, 160, 166
Karlson brothers 190–1
Katherine 46–7
Kelly Basin 184, 192–3
Kelly, Bowes 191–2
Kensington 22
Kidman Way 117, 119, 124
Kidman, Sydney 55, 129
Kidston 70–2, 75
Kimberley goldfield 37
Kingsborough 85–6
Kookynie 16, 23–5
Koorboora 73, 75, 77
Kunanulling 28
Kurnalpi 28

Lady Don 133
Lafarelle, Thomas 185
Lake Torrens 161
Lake's Camp *see* Day Dream
Lambert, Charlie 98, 100, 103
Lambing Flat 92
Lamond, Barney 40
Lapham, Samuel 184, 186
Lappa 73, 75
Laura (Qld) 87, 96
Laura (SA) 161
Laverton 21, 25–6
Lawlers 12–3
Leadville *see* Purnamoota
Leigh Creek 155
Lempriere, Thomas 181–2, 184
Leonora 12–6, 18–21, 26–7
Linda 190–8
Lithgow 109–110
Llanelly 218–220
Loddon River 206, 216
lodges 3, 6, 8, 16, 28, 65, 104, 114,
  128, 151–2, 195, 203, 207–8,
  215–16, 219, 223, 228
London 14, 65, 153
Loudon House 75
Long, Father 27, 29
Love, Andrew 201
Lovely Gully 151
Luchetti, Tony 110
Lucy, Bill and Margaret 45
Lukinville 89, 95

Macao 44
Mack, Charles 70
Macquarie brothers 95
Macquarie Harbour 180–4
Maiden Town *see* Llanelly
Malay people 31–2, 35
Malcolm 16, 26–7
Manna Hill 161
Maranboy 45–7
Mareeba 69, 83
Maria Island 171, 172, 184–9
Marree 160, 168
Marshall, Vanda 47
May, Sister 7
May, Vivienne 7, 21, 26–7
Maytown 87–89, 91, 94–6
McCormack, William 75, 77
McDonald, Sandy 55–6
McDonough, Mick and Bill 190–1
McMahon's Reef 228
McPhees Camp 39
McRae family 188
Mechanics' (miners') institutes
  5–12, 22–5, 27–8, 92, 130, 154,
  159, 203–5, 207–8, 216–19,
  223–4
Meekatharra 10
Melbourne 7, 188, 196, 208, 216-7,
  226
Melrose 160
Menzies 16, 21–5, 28
Meredith 203
Merino 221–4
migrant workers 8–10, 14, 18
Miller, Linus 173
Milparinka 136–8, 140–5
mining 163
  accidents and disasters 17, 19, 63,
    78–82, 196–7
  coal 78–83; 155, 173, 176, 180
  coke 79, 82, 110, 112, 121–2
  copper 69–70, 75–77, 82,
    117–122, 151–8, 168, 190–8
  gold 3–4, 7–29, 39–45, 59–65,
    69–72, 83–104, 117–125, 136,
    140–51, 191, 201–21
  industrial relations 63–5, 71, 75,
    82, 109, 111, 114, 122,
    129–130, 196–7
  limestone 135, 187–9
  oil shale 107–116
  rubies 50–1
  silver 59–62, 73, 85, 126–8,
    130–2, 134–5, 191
  tin 45–47, 73–4, 85, 132–5
mining companies
  Barrier Ranges Association 131
  Bewick, Moreing and Company 3,
    8, 12–15
  BHP 133–135
  Carpentaria Gold 65
  Chillagoe Company 69–70, 72, 76
  Commonwealth Oil Corporation
    110
  Golden Plateau 100, 102–4
  Great Cobar Mining Syndicate
    121
  Great Northern Copper Mining
    Company 153–154
  Hamersley Iron 37
  Homestake Gold 26

Milparinka Goldmining Company
  145
Mount Lyell Mining Company
  191–2
Mount Lyell Prospecting
  Association 191
National Oil Company 198, 102
New Ravenswood Limited 62–5
Newcrest 97
North Mount Lyell Copper Mining
  Company 190–4
Polymetal Mining Services 124
Premier Goldmining Company 10
Ravenswood Goldmining
  Company 62
Robe River Iron Associates 37
Sandy Creek Poverty Reef Mining,
  Quartz–crushing and Washing
  Company 213
Sons of Gwalia 12, 16–17
Tasmanian Copper Company 153
Woodside Petroleum 37
Mingela 65
Mitchell, Sir James 11
Mittagong 113–4
Moffat, John 73–6
Mohr, John 99, 100
Moliagul 217–9
Moss Vale 114
Mount Alexander diggings 204–210
Mount Allen 119
Mount Boppy goldfield 123
Mount Browne 136, 140–2, 144
Mount Drysdale 124–5
Mount Gambier 222
Mount Garnet 73, 75
Mount Gipps 127–8
Mount Hogan 72
Mount Hope 117–9
Mount Ida 27–9
Mount Jackson 72
Mount Kembla 107
Mount Lyell 190
Mount Margaret 26
Mount Molloy 73, 73–5
Mount Morgan (Qld) 104
Mount Morgans (WA) 26–7
Mount Mulligan 78–83, 86
Mount Pintapah 134
Mount Wells 45
Mountain, Thomas 34
Mueller, Warden 52, 54
Muldiva 77
Mulligan, James Venture 83–4, 89
Mulline 28
Mulwaree 28
Mundy, Colonel (Captain) George
  176, 185
Mungana 77
Muramatsu family 35, 37–8
Murchison goldfields 3, 9, 12, 21,
  40
Murdering Lagoons 95
Murphy, E 140, 142

Nannine 3, 9, 10
National Parks and Wildlife Service
  (NT) 56
Native police 73, 90, 95
New Charleston *see* Forsayth
New Chum *see* Llanelly

New Zealand 26, 183, 211
Newbridge 213
Newnes Junction 108, 110–1
Newnes 108, 110–3
Niagara 23
Norfolk Island 174, 184, 186
North Australia League 42
North Australia Observer Unit 41–2
North Coolgardie goldfields 22
North Lyell 191, 193, 196, 198
Northern Goldfields Loop 42, 45
Northern Land Council 45
NSW Parks and Wildlife Service 112–3
Nucculeena 153–5
Nymagee 119–123

O'Brien, William Smith 185–6, 189
O'Connor, Tassie 28
O'Grady, Manager 54
O'Reilly, Mick 46–7
Oaks, The see Kidston
Oates, Richard 219
O.K. 77
Onslow 30–4, 38
Oodnadatta 52, 54–5
Ora Banda 28
Orr, William 191
Orroroo 162–3
Overland Telegraph Line 154
Owen, W Lambden 22, 36

Paddy's Rock Hole 51, 54
Palmer goldfield 61, 69, 84, 87–97
Palmer River 87–9
Palmerville 89, 91–2
Parachilna 151, 154
pastoral stations 4, 41, 50, 69, 72, 129, 154, 155
pastoralism 30–4, 41, 52, 60, 93, 119, 125, 135, 138, 143, 155, 159-163, 168, 223–6
pearling industry 31–5, 8
Penghana 191
Pennyweight Hill 207
Penrose, John 126, 129
Percy River 68
Percyville 72
Perth 6, 22
Peterborough 159, 163, 165
Philippine people 31
Pierce, Alexander 181
Pilbara goldfield 37
Pillinger 190, 192–6
Pine Creek 44–5
Ping Que 43
police 9, 21, 28–31, 38, 41–7, 52, 68–9, 71–5, 83–5, 91–2, 104, 108, 114–17, 119–129, 132–6, 141–5, 151–9, 168, 179, 192, 197, 202, 219, 223–8
Political Labor League 195–6
pollution 63, 114, 196
Poolamacca see Euriowie
Poole, James 137–9
Port Arthur 171–180, 186

Port Augusta 55, 151, 157, 162
Port Phillip Bay 208
Port Pirie 135, 163
Poverty Reef 211–2, 217
Price, Julius 4
progress committees/associations 5, 11, 24–5, 41, 71–7, 85, 121–8, 135, 144, 167, 189, 193, 203, 212, 219, 228
prostitution 24, 36, 103
Purnamoota 126, 128, 132, 135

Queensland Mines Lifesaving Brigade 80
Queensland National Parks and Wildlife Service 96
Queenstown 190–8
Quorn 163, 165–6

race relations see Aboriginal Australians; Afghan, Chinese, Italian, Japanese, Malay and Philippine peoples
railways/tramways 9–10, 13–16, 20–8, 31–6, 42–5, 64–9, 70–9, 83–7, 92–6, 100–1, 108–15, 121–2, 130–5, 151–9, 160–8, 175–7, 187–96, 223–8
Ravenswood 59–67, 89
Red Cross 18, 223–228
Reid, John 133
Resch brothers 129
Returned Soldiers' League 102
Revolver Point 92
Robertson River 68
Rockhampton 100–1
Roebourne 32, 35–7
Roosevelt, Franklin 13
Roughsey, Dick 87
Rowe, Ruth 207
Ruby Creek 41
Russian Jack 40, 91
Ryan family 226
Ryan, George 99, 100
Rye see Walloway

Salvation Army 6, 18, 22, 28, 65, 127
San Diego (Tas) see Darlington
Sandy Creek (Palmer) 91–2
Sandy Creek (Ravenswood) 62
Sandy Creek (Vic.) 211–2
sanitation see health
Sarah Island 171–2, 180–4, 193, 196
sawmilling see timber industry
schools see education
Scotland 73
  Scottish people 74, 110, 114
Scullin Labor Government 77
Selheim, Warden 92
Shea, Robert 34
shipbuilding 175, 182–3
ships 32, 36, 90, 181, 183, 185, 179, 181
shire councils 3–9, 15–6, 21–6, 31, 37, 63, 110, 130–5, 197–8, 202

Shuttleton 121–2
Siberia (WA) 28
Silverton Tramway Company Act 130
Silverton 126–132, 134–5
Simmonston 159, 163, 166
Simpson Desert 138
Singapore 43
Sisters of the People 6–7
Slee, W 143
Sliding Rock 154–7, 161
Smith of Dunesk Mission 155
Soakage, The see Purnamoota
social and cultural life 5–28, 42–7, 59, 61–5, 71–9, 83–9, 92–4, 101–8, 111–16, 123–8, 130, 141–5, 151–4, 167–8, 173–8, 184–9, 193–7, 203–9, 212–28
South Australian Department of Mines and Energy 154
South Mount Hope 117–8
Split Rock 87
sporting life 3, 8–11, 16, 25, 42–4, 61–5, 72–7, 85, 101–4, 114–17, 121–8, 130–3, 144, 151, 159, 167–8, 173–8, 189, 193–6, 203–4, 208, 212, 219, 222–3, 228
Spring Creek (Vic.) 207
Spring Creek (NT) 45
Spring Gully 206
St Clement's Redemptorist College 227
St George, Howard 90
St Lawrence's College 226, 228
Stannary Hills 73
Steiglitz 201–4, 210
Steiglitz, Charles von 201
Stephenston 159, 163
Stockinbingal 221, 224–6
Stony Creek (Qld) 92
Strahan 184, 191–5
Strau family 95
Strzelecki Creek 138
Sturt's Stony Desert 138
Stutterd, Audrey 46–7
Sutherland family 111
Sydney 107, 113–15, 135, 180, 191, 226

Taam Sze Pui 96
Tarnagulla 211–20
Tarrawingee Flux and Tramway Company 135
Tarrawingee 126, 135
Tasman Peninsula 171, 174, 176, 178
Tasmania, Bishop of 186
Teetulpa 161
Temora 224–5
Thackaringa 126–7, 131
Theodore 98, 100
Theodore, Edward 75, 77
Thomsen, Hans 65
Thornborough 83, 85–6
Thorp, Sydney 59–62
Tibooburra 141–5
timber industry 7–9, 13–16, 75, 86,

100-1, 118–121, 123, 143, 175, 180–4, 193–6, 203, 208, 216–7
Top End, The 42, 56
Torbane 108
Townsville 59, 61, 64–5
Trezise, Percy 87
Triabunna 184
Twelve Mile (NT) 43–45
Twelve Mile (WA) 22

Uaroo 31
Uhrstown 89
unions 63–4, 108, 121, 130, 195, 203
United Irishmen's League 195

Valdivia 184
Vaughan 204, 208, 210

Waanyarra 212, 220
Walcott, Pemberton 34
Walga Rock 11
Walhalla 201
Walloway 159, 163
Warrata 144
Warrnambool 223
Watson, JT 80
Watsonville 73–4
Waukaringa 149–51
Weare, Father 65–7
Weitemeyer, Thorval 61
Welcome Stranger nugget 219
Welsh people 210
Welsh Village 204, 210
West Drysdale 125
Western District (Vic.) 221–2
Westrek Foundation 37
White Feather see Kanowna
White Range diggings 49, 52, 54–5
Wilcannia 129, 138, 140–3
Wilga Mia 11
Willochra Plain 163
Willochra 159, 163–4
Wilson 159, 163, 166–7
Wilson, Archibald 62–4, 67
Winnecke 48, 50, 52–4, 56
Wolfram Camp 73, 75
Wolgan Valley 110–12
women 5, 7, 46–7, 55, 74, 79, 81, 100, 102, 109, 133, 182, 220
Wonoka 159, 163
woodline see railways and tramways
World War I 10, 65, 118, 123, 145, 165–6, 197, 223, 228
World War II 11, 18, 37, 41–5, 72, 86, 92, 104, 165, 223
Wyndham 39, 41

Yam Creek 45
Yathong 120
Young Ireland Rebellion 185–6
Yudnamutana 157–8
Yunta 149

Zeehan 191, 194
Zillmanton 77

DARWIN

Brock's Creek
Grove Hill
Pine Creek
Burrundie

Katherine

Maranbo

Wyndham

Derby

Halls Creek

Broome

Old Halls Creek

Karratha
Cossack
Roebourne

Onslow

Old Onslow

Alice Springs

Nannine
Big Bell
Cue
Day Dawn
Agnew
Lawlers

Meekatharra

Laverton
Mt Morgans
Burtville
Leonora
Malcolm
Mt Ida
Gwalia
Menzies
Kookynie
Niagara
Broad Arrow
Ora Banda
Kanowna
Kununalling
KALGOORLIE–BOULDER

Wilson / Kanyaka / Gord

Quorn
Port Augusta
Ororoo
Port Pirie
Peterborough

PERTH